THIS IS ME! 2022

POETIC STARS

Edited By Sara Little

First published in Great Britain in 2022 by:

Young Writers
Remus House
Coltsfoot Drive
Peterborough
PE2 9BF
Telephone: 01733 890066
Website: www.youngwriters.co.uk

All Rights Reserved
Book Design by Ashley Janson
© Copyright Contributors 2022
Softback ISBN 978-1-80459-070-6

Printed and bound in the UK by BookPrintingUK
Website: www.bookprintinguk.com
YB0510T

FOREWORD

For Young Writers' latest competition This Is Me, we asked primary school pupils to look inside themselves, to think about what makes them unique, and then write a poem about it! They rose to the challenge magnificently and the result is this fantastic collection of poems in a variety of poetic styles.

Here at Young Writers our aim is to encourage creativity in children and to inspire a love of the written word, so it's great to get such an amazing response, with some absolutely fantastic poems. It's important for children to focus on and celebrate themselves and this competition allowed them to write freely and honestly, celebrating what makes them great, expressing their hopes and fears, or simply writing about their favourite things. This Is Me gave them the power of words. The result is a collection of inspirational and moving poems that also showcase their creativity and writing ability.

I'd like to congratulate all the young poets in this anthology, I hope this inspires them to continue with their creative writing.

CONTENTS

Towers Junior School, Hornchurch

Lily Barnes (11)	1
Ameya Drayan (10)	2
Phoebe H (11)	4
Lily Pashley (9)	6
Ivy Willkins (8)	8
Isabelle Bear (9)	9
Kayla Buchner (9)	10
Ivy Shanahan (9)	12
Florence Cross (8)	13
Phoebe Easom (10)	14
Ivy Smith (8)	16
Isla Sparks (11)	17
Hollie Milton-White (9)	18
Ellie Rossiter (11)	19
Oliver Trevor (8)	20
Eva Morgan (10)	21
Emily Meader (8)	22
Isla Ramirez (11)	23
Max Perry (9)	24
Joey Foss (8)	25
Scarla Barry (8)	26
Emma Crane (9)	27
Holly O'Leary (10)	28
Leah Elliott (7)	29
Humphrey Wild (8)	30
Emily Hargis (8)	31
James Halcro (11)	32
Skye Welham (9)	33
Amber Willings (9)	34
Seb Harris (9)	35
Jack Handley (8)	36
Maddie Mitchell (10)	37
Emily Thielemans (7)	38
Alfie Padalino (11)	39
Lila Taylor (9)	40
Harley Morgan (9)	41
George Rayner (9)	42
Jessica Short (7)	43
Isla Easom (8)	44
Adeel Islam (8)	45
Millie Spurdle (11)	46
Harry Lundgren (8)	47
Lacey Millard (7)	48
Ben Hudson (8)	49
Lexi Kyriacou (7)	50
Amira Malik (8)	51
Neryss Kaur (8)	52
Abbi Rose Hearn (9)	53
Jacob Funnell (10)	54
Jake Dwyer (7)	55
Rose Wall (8)	56
Adityaraj Rathore (8)	57
Lukas Ziutelis (10)	58
Billie-Leigh Cottage (7)	59
Michael Morrison (11)	60
Mason Robinson (8)	61
Avni Phull (8)	62
Jasmine Willings (9)	63
Lyla Mardon (9)	64
Mia Callender (8)	65
Nicola Ari (9)	66
Ersilda Hoxha (7)	67
Taylan Sheehan (7)	68
Matthew Ajose-Coker (8)	69
Maggie Tynan (10)	70
Robyn Regan (8)	71
Maisie Eary (10)	72
George Raymond (7)	73

Matthew Ley (7)	74
Momore Farri (10)	75
Abi Black (11)	76
Chloë Webb (8)	77
Louie Harris (10)	78
Joshua McNeill (8)	79
William Ford (8)	80
Rowan Cooper (8)	81
Lucy Tregidgo (9)	82
Albert Leigh (9)	83
Ella Rose (11)	84
Harry W (7)	85
Charlie Spurdle (9)	86
Rafe Stringer (8)	87
Charlotte O'Donovan (7)	88

Upton Priory School, Off Prestbury Road

Kieran Massey	89
Rose Sedgwick (9)	90
Sidney	92
Ela Rasool (8)	93
Thomas Carrington (8)	94
Annabelle Dale (9)	95
Natalie Shaw (8)	96
Charlotte Bradley (9)	97
Nevaeh Mason-Grant (8)	98
Ella Mae Wynter (9)	99
Lewis	100
Hugo Jones (9)	101
Lydia Neild (8)	102
Reuben Griffin (9)	103
Eric	104
Reggie Thomas (8)	105
Sienna Marshall (9)	106
Matthew	107
Izahak Thachil (9)	108
Corey Bennett (8)	109
Rory Liddle (9)	110
Dylan Atkin (9)	111
Bobby B	112
Sami Khan (9)	113
Zachary (9)	114

Evie Hext (9)	115
Charlie Ashton	116
Maisie Oliver (8)	117
Leia Jones (9)	118
Kaiden McCracken Houghton (9)	119

Wollaston Primary School, Wollaston

Riley Moore (10)	120
Amely Hills (10)	122
Riya Patel (10)	124
Louis Beard (10)	126
Annabel Richey (10)	127
Freddie Wagstaff (9)	128
Sophia W-A (10)	130
Samuel Rice (10)	132
Jake Cooper (10)	133
Luke Munns (9)	134
Jacob Watts (9)	135
Ciara Coleman Allen (10)	136
Patrick Peters (10)	138
Archie Batts (10)	139
Orla Kelly-Searing (10)	140
Sophie Regan (10)	142
Toby Donabie (9)	143
Logan Carter (10)	144
Eliana Peters (9)	145
Isabella O'connor (10)	146
Neo Higgins (10)	147
Archie Longdon (9)	148
Callan Glover (10)	149
Riley Coady (10)	150
Davis Gent (9)	152
Phoebe Schultz (9)	153
Ruby Mae Ricks (10)	154
Jude Sanders (9)	155
Ethan Sims (9)	156
Faith Clarke (10)	157
Harrison Richards (9)	158
Kai John Shelton Ryan (10)	159
Bella Marren (9)	160
Miles Jones (9)	161
Matthew Rose (10)	162

Aidan Forbes (9)	163
Tillie Scollins (9)	164

Worsbrough Common Primary School, Worsbrough Common

Brooke Wood-Kilgariff (9)	165
Ronnie Arnold (9)	166
Mia Pierre (8)	168
Gabriella Schofield (9)	169
Cacey Beevers (9)	170
Keigan Pemberton (8)	171
Vuyo Mkwananzi (8)	172
Lloydy Conway (9)	173
Madeleine Robinson (8)	174
Mckenzie Oldham (8)	175
Addison Connelly (9)	176
Lola Lloyd (8)	177
Breeanna Faulkner (8)	178
Faith Sullivan (9)	179
Xavier Aston (9)	180
Monika Bula (9)	181
Kara Chigwete (9)	182
Lexi Shirt (9)	183
Alannah Wilby-Dinsley (9)	184
Maddison Singleton (8)	185
Inês Tinsley (9)	186
Eben Parsons (8)	187
Seren Hawcroft (9)	188
Blake Allott (9)	189
Michael-Patrick (8)	190
Hary Mano (8)	191
Anah Imran (9)	192
Selma Hassan (9)	193
Lucy Johnson (9)	194
Alisha Wall (9)	195
River Lawton (8)	196
Helen Vasquez-Carpio (9)	197

Ysgol Gymraeg Bro Allta, Ystrad Mynach

Ffion Francis (11)	198
Olivia Morris-Brown (11)	200
Elektra Clarke (10)	202
Cariad Morgan (9)	204
William Chant (9)	205
Carys Rhianwen Mair Davies (11)	206
Lucas Owen Yeo (10)	208
Jac Davies (11)	209
Heulyn Webb Price (11)	210
Lexie Cox (10)	211
Isabelle Louise McBride (11)	212
Amelia Angel (10)	213
Abi-Mai (10)	214
Elena Bilenki (11)	215

THE POEMS

This Is Me

Hi, my name is Lily, I'm eleven years old,
I like to play football in the garden a lot,
I'm not a fan of Maths or English,
But I like TikTok and do funny videos with it,
I love WiFi and my phone,
But nothing is better than my bed, you know,
Sometimes I'm happy, sometimes I'm sad,
But when I see my friends, I get super happy,
I'm passionate about my dream job, as everyone should be,
I'm confident, I'm kind,
And other stuff combined,
I like to drink Fanta,
And a bit of funny banter,
I'm very tall,
But definitely not six-foot-four,
I like spaghetti,
And my friend is called Betty.

Lily Barnes (11)
Towers Junior School, Hornchurch

This Is Me

I like dogs,
But my friend likes frogs,
I love to write,
I really want a dog,
But it might bite.

This is me!

I am brave,
And I can go in a high cave,
I like the name Willow,
And the thing I sleep on is a pillow.

This is me!

I am tidy, I am clean,
And sometimes I have a bad dream,
I like Maths,
And my mum's friend's name is Cath.

This is me!

I am smart,
And I like the game Mario Kart,

I like the colour yellow,
And my favourite food is Jello.

This is me!

My cousin has a dog called Rolo,
And I like the food Polo,
My friend's mum's name is Linda,
And I come from India.

This is me!

I am funny,
And I really want a pet bunny,
This is who I am, this is me,
And someone in my school is called Mrs Lee.

This is me!

Ameya Drayan (10)
Towers Junior School, Hornchurch

This Is Who I Am, This Is Me

I'm as silly as a clown,
Laugh until I fall down,
I'm curious and kind,
A different person, you will find.

This is who I am, this is me!

I like riding my bike,
And eating things that I like,
I like to be free,
And I love PE.

This is who I am, this is me!

My friends are fun,
I only have some,
We play all the time,
And we love to rhyme.

This is who I am, this is me!

My dog's name is Coco,
He's a little bit *loco*,
He is a silly boy,
And he loves a new toy.

This is who I am, this is me!

I had fun doing this, what about you?
I hope you enjoy this as much as I do,
I liked writing this, it was fun,
But I have nothing else, so I am done!

Phoebe H (11)
Towers Junior School, Hornchurch

This Is Me!

I am hilarious and friendly,
Lucky Lily, I should say.

I love baking cookies,
Then eating them right away.

I live with my mum, step-dad,
And my sister Ruby.
Sometimes, I call her Rubs.
I have pairs of socks that live in twos.

When my mum does my hair,
Straight away it gets in a crazy mess,
But I don't like to play chess.

I like to play darts,
And I can get a bullseye,
Three times in a row.
I like to say no.

I like to stay positive,
Every single day.
And try to go the right way.

I am a cousin to more,
Than fifteen people.
So I have a big family, okay?
This is me.

Lily Pashley (9)
Towers Junior School, Hornchurch

All About Me

Head to toe is covered in me,
What do you want to be?
A fireman, doctor, or horse rider, you see,
What do I want to be?
You see you, I see me,
Be what you want to be.

Now let's talk about my tea,
I love pasta, but not a pea.
My favourite is a burger with ketchup,
Let's hope I don't mess it up.
Me and my sister both love fries,
Trust me, I never tell lies.

My little sister is called Bridget,
She mainly likes to fidget.
I get all my inspiration,
From a special occasion.
I like to be silly,
I'm also very tickly.

That's my family,
And personality!

Ivy Willkins (8)
Towers Junior School, Hornchurch

Spell Of Me!

Grab your spellbook and potions,
Because we'll make a person,
But make sure you're careful,
So the spell doesn't worsen!
First, pour a skull full of a bright smile,
Then add a bone's worth of a talkative child.
Load a cauldron with a cat-loving passion,
And some enthusiasm that makes the strife worthwhile.
Pull off your hats and search for a love of art.
Add a sprinkle of what makes you smart,
But most of all - a loving heart!
Now, mix it up with a strong broom.
Trust me, it will be worth it,
But there's no mistake,
Because no one is perfect!

Isabelle Bear (9)
Towers Junior School, Hornchurch

Me

I am perfect as I am,
On my toast, I like jam,
This is me,
This is me,
My favourite season is spring,
I do like the winter snow,
It's just too thick, so I don't know where to go,
This is me,
This is me,
One of my favourite foods is a Bakewell tart,
I am also very smart,
This is me,
This is me,
I'm Mrs Messy,
I can be very lovely though,
This is me,
This is me,
I'm very creative,
And super talkative,
This is me,
This is me,

A lot of the time, with things, I'm wrong,
I am very strong,
This is me,
This is me.

Kayla Buchner (9)
Towers Junior School, Hornchurch

All About Me

This is me, I am who I am.
I love space and I love penguins.
I am a cousin, daughter, and a sister.
I am also kind, tall, and sometimes weird.
I'm a bit chatty, but that's how I'm made.
I am a dancer and my second favourite animal is a giraffe.
I like to play video games, but not too much.
I am sometimes annoying but kind at the same time.
I like to be positive, which is a good thing.
I am a little bit messy, but not too much.
I am an incredible Ivy.
I am sometimes hungry, but not too much.
I am a bit funny because I make my family and friends laugh.

Ivy Shanahan (9)
Towers Junior School, Hornchurch

Everything I Love

I love the cold winter days,
And when I see my friends, I give them a "Hey!"
I like all animals, especially dogs,
But to be honest, I hate the frogs.
I don't like people who are sad,
Because that makes me mad.
A lot of the time I love to sleep,
But sadly, the secrets I can't keep.
I have to say, I love my birthday,
And hopefully, we have no hurt days.
Also, I have a little brother,
And we will be friends forever and ever.
Our friendship won't ever end,
And you'll always be my friend!

Florence Cross (8)
Towers Junior School, Hornchurch

This Is About Me

My name is Phoebe,
I am ten years old,
I love to dance,
And I hate being cold.

I love my family,
They think I am small,
I am really energetic,
I love to swim in the pool.

When I'm sad,
I love to doodle,
I hate big dogs,
Especially a poodle.

My least favourite colour is yellow,
My most favourite colour is blue,
I have a lucky number,
Which is number two.

I love my dad,
My mum works in a school,

I have two sisters,
They think they're really cool.

This is me!

Phoebe Easom (10)
Towers Junior School, Hornchurch

I Love My Teacher

I n school.

L earning things.
O n her chair.
V ery clever.
E veryone loves her, especially me.

M y favourite teacher.
Y ou are amazing.

T hey are happy.
E xcellent teacher for the class.
A very nice and kind teacher.
C heerful teacher jumping around the room.
H appy teachers I like.
E very teacher is cool but mine is cooler.
R ed clothes or yellow clothes I don't care, I still love her.

Ivy Smith (8)
Towers Junior School, Hornchurch

Life With Covid

Life with Covid is the worst.
Your parents shouting at you to do school work.
But I get it, they're just trying to help.
Your younger siblings jumping on you.
But I get it, they're just trying to cheer you up.
Your cats meowing ridiculously loud.
But I get it, they're animals.
Life with Covid may be the worst.
You have to isolate.
You can't do anything outside unless it's in your garden.
But I get it, you're protecting everyone
Now, that's life with Covid.
Stay safe.

Isla Sparks (11)
Towers Junior School, Hornchurch

I'm Amazing In Every Way!

H ollie is a happy hippo
O bviously sporty
L oves football
L et's make all the negative things go far away
I ndependent all the time
E verything about me is me and no one else.

I s a good friend
S uper writer.

H ollie is good-humoured and funny
A rsenal supporter in football
P arties are fun and food for me
P ractise football with my dad or friends
Y et my life is perfect, I wouldn't change it.

Hollie Milton-White (9)
Towers Junior School, Hornchurch

This Is Me

This is me,
The girl who plays football for Tigers.
This is me,
The animal lover with eight pets.
This is me,
The girl that's born on Christmas Eve.
This is me,
The girl who loves all sports.
This is me,
The girl who loves art and animation.
This is me,
The girl who goes to Scouts.
This is me,
The explorer who loves the outdoors.
This is me,
The girl who loves her family.
This is me,
The girl who isn't afraid to show who she is.
This is me.

Ellie Rossiter (11)
Towers Junior School, Hornchurch

Awesome Me!

I am a team player,
I scored a goal,
People think I'm a weigher,
And says my goal was very lol.

I'm with the ball,
But then I fall,
But then get up again confidently.

My favourite food is hot dogs.
Best food ever.
My body goes for a jog,
In any sort of weather.
I dream about sheep,
When I'm asleep.

Sheep are the greatest animal in the world,
They are really cute and fluffy,
In the wild as well,
And they always put on gel.

Oliver Trevor (8)
Towers Junior School, Hornchurch

These Are The Things I Love

I like ice cream,
It makes me want to scream.
Every time I eat it,
I feel like I am in a dream!

Dogs are so fluffy,
They make me feel like cotton candy.
When I pet them,
It's like I'm in doggy land-y!

I like making bracelets,
They calm me down when I am stressed,
When I'm not making them,
It makes me feel depressed!

Books are good to read,
Especially when I'm lying in bed,
Trying to fall asleep,
I get a sleepy-head.....

Eva Morgan (10)
Towers Junior School, Hornchurch

All About Me

E xcellent at writing stories
M agnificent at making my bed and my twin's bed sometimes
I ce cream is my favourite food
L ove of learning
Y oungest sibling in my house

M y favourite things at school are Science and English
E aster and Christmas are my favourite seasons
A mazing at Art
D ecember is my favourite month
E xcited about different things
R elaxing on my bed is my favourite thing.

Emily Meader (8)
Towers Junior School, Hornchurch

This Is Me

My name's Isla,
And McDonald's gives me fibre,
My favourite colour's blue,
In lockdown I danced on Zoom,
Now I dance in a dance school room,
I'm obsessed with highlighters,
I have a dog called Coco,
But luckily I don't have to pick up poo,
My best friends are Abi, Macey, and Maggie,
My name's Isla,
And McDonald's gives me fibre,
I'm half Spanish,
English too,
My name's Isla,
It's 2022!

Isla Ramirez (11)
Towers Junior School, Hornchurch

The Creative Me

M aking amazing art with paper maché.
A rt with everything you can think of.
X mas is a great time to do art.

P aper and pencils, drawing is fun.
E verything you love can be art.
R ight on time, let's get going, "It's looking great."
R ight and left, everywhere you look, art is there.
Y esterday was a great, art-filled day and now I can't wait to do it all again.

Max Perry (9)
Towers Junior School, Hornchurch

My Amazing Life

I want to be very fair,
Sometimes have really nice hair,
My mum won't let me do it,
So I just do it when she doesn't see me do it,
I'm really good at a game,
Joey is my name,
I'm very crazy,
And really lazy,
I want to stay up late,
But my mum said, "Go to sleep boy!"
So I did that night,
But I stayed up late the next night,
I like to play football,
But not basketball.

Joey Foss (8)
Towers Junior School, Hornchurch

This Is Me

Head to toe is covered in me,
This is who I want to be.

Look at my long golden hair,
As it sways in the fresh air,
Gymnastics is by far my favourite hobby,
My favourite flower is a bright red poppy.

Jumping out of a plane, I would never dare,
But I will always care,
I am friendly and kind,
And I've got a smart mind.

Head to toe is covered in me,
This is who I always want to be!

Scarla Barry (8)
Towers Junior School, Hornchurch

Emma Is My Name

H eroicness can show
A lthough
P eople can create
P eople can also put up a gate
I am bright and merry
N ew like a bursting berry
E mma is my name
S o, let's play a game
S o don't call me any other name

L ove I give
O n it goes
V ery loyal, you can trust me
E veryone knows our friendship will always be.

Emma Crane (9)
Towers Junior School, Hornchurch

My Favourite Emotion!

I make you jump up and down, I turn your frown upside down.
You don't want me to end, and joy I shall send.
I come without warning in the evening or the morning,
With me, the fun never ends.
I conquer all anger and bend all sadness in half.
From the tip of your toes to your brain,
This feeling is insane.
When you have me, you won't complain.
What is my emotion?

Answer: Happiness.

Holly O'Leary (10)
Towers Junior School, Hornchurch

Leah Elliott

L ike a cat.
E arly in the morning, I start school work.
A ll day, every day.
H elpful and caring.

E ach day as happy as a mouse with cheese.
L oving and caring every day.
L ove yourself.
I live my dreams.
O h no, what should we do?
T each your friends awesome stuff.
T eachers always love teaching.

Leah Elliott (7)
Towers Junior School, Hornchurch

This Is Me!

H umourous, hungry, and handsome, yeah, that's me,
U nique when it comes to thinking outside the box,
M illions of animals are my friend,
P ainless to cuddle and I'm a prehistoric beast,
H opeful all the time,
R elentless, I always try,
E ager and enthusiastic to finish my goals,
Y acking around constantly with Matthew, obviously.

Humphrey Wild (8)
Towers Junior School, Hornchurch

All About Me

E mily is my marvellous name
M ay is my birthday
I like treats and sweets
L ove my lovely, brown, luscious hair
Y ellow is not my favourite colour

H elpful and kind
A mazing at Maths
R espectful I always am
G ymnastics is my favourite hobby
I ntelligent is what I am
S tay positive all the time.

Emily Hargis (8)
Towers Junior School, Hornchurch

This Is Who I Am

I have many characteristics,
One of which is artistic,
At the back of the class doodling to my heart's content,
Although I usually don't ask for Miss Rehman's consent.
I'm imaginative, intelligent, and kind,
So let's quickly rewind.
I have many characteristics,
One of which is artistic.
My name is James,
And it rhymes with games.
This is who I am.

James Halcro (11)
Towers Junior School, Hornchurch

Marvellous Me

I'm as light as a feather,
And as pretty as a bird,
I'm as clever as a monkey,
And a little absurd.

I'm happy like a bee,
And I really like trees.
How do I make this poem,
All about me?

I'm enthusiastic and very
Fantastic, I like to rhyme,
A lot. I'm sweet and,
Friendly, and I like to
Tidy, and I'm not selfish anymore.

Skye Welham (9)
Towers Junior School, Hornchurch

All About Me!

I'm kind and funny
My favourite animal isn't a bunny.

My favourite food is pasta
I call my sister Jasta.

My hair is brown with a curl
It's what makes me a beautiful girl.

I live with my sister and brother
Dad, dog, and mother.

I'm a chatterbox I will have to say,
But I follow the right path every day.

This is me!

Amber Willings (9)
Towers Junior School, Hornchurch

Making Me!

1 cup of human
5 teaspoons of geography
1 handful of gaming
4 cups of friends
1 of every bike part
Place in school materials for nine years
1 spoon of books
Pour water in for two years
Place in microwave for eight days.
Then Seb will start to grow,
But it will be very low,
Then fry him in love,
Then your Seb will be ready to go,
High and above!

Seb Harris (9)
Towers Junior School, Hornchurch

Pokémon And Sonic

P okémon is short for pocket monsters
O ut of this world
K ing of card games
É xciting
M orkpeko
O utstanding
N ever want to stop playing it.

S onic is super fast and the fastest thing alive
O utstanding
N ever want to stop playing it
I ncredible
C ool.

Jack Handley (8)
Towers Junior School, Hornchurch

My Life

Hi, my name is Maddie,
I have one sister named Lauren,
She likes to torture me.

I like to write,
My dog is cute,
She hates kites.

I love space,
My favourite colour is purple,
I play guitar, which has its own case.

I know this isn't much,
As I could only write a touch,
My creativity is endless,
Unlike this poem.

Maddie Mitchell (10)
Towers Junior School, Hornchurch

Proud Brownies

B eing a Brownie is so much fun.
R unning in the hall and playing lots of games.
O wls help us make our crafts and earn badges, too.
W onderful friends I've made there.
N ever should I have been scared.
I really was made welcome.
E veryone is very kind.
S o that's why Friday is the best day of my week.

Emily Thielemans (7)
Towers Junior School, Hornchurch

Me!

I do parkour even though I'm very clumsy,
Fingerboarding is one of the things I do when I'm bored,
Wrenching on RC cars every hour,
Trying to give them more power.

Karate tournaments are very vital,
To achieve a title,
Sketching all over paper,
I'll do my homework later,
Running round with friends,
This life could never end!

Alfie Padalino (11)
Towers Junior School, Hornchurch

Inside Me

This is me.
Brave and bold.
I never tell secrets that I'm told.

But another me is quiet and shy.
So quiet that I want to cry.

Hiding deeper inside me,
Is the me that is usually nice,
She also loves playing in snow and ice!

Furthest down, screaming out loud,
Is the me that is always proud,

Of who she is.

Lila Taylor (9)
Towers Junior School, Hornchurch

Happy Harley

H arley is a happy kid
A sporty person
P ositive pupil
P rediction master
Y oghurt head

H onour to his parents
A nice kid
R eads Harry Potter books
L aughs a lot
E veryone likes me in my family
Y ells, "United!" when I see West Ham play.

Harley Morgan (9)
Towers Junior School, Hornchurch

The Lions And Me

I love, I love lions because they're like me,
They are hairy like me, they are lovely like me.
I love lions.
People think lions are scary, but they are not.
When I go to the zoo I see lions.
I get excited but sometimes their mane is messy,
It is funny, hahaha.
I laugh, but then I mess my hair up.
And that is lions and me.

George Rayner (9)
Towers Junior School, Hornchurch

All About Me

F riendly, kind, and awesome,
U seful, unique, ordinary, and intelligent.
N atural, normal, nice.
N oble, amazing, caring.
Y et brave, smart, and funny.

I'm as extreme as a rollerskater!
I'm a cheeky monkey!
My passion is to be a teacher.
I'm pleasant, stylish, and passionate.

Jessica Short (7)
Towers Junior School, Hornchurch

Nature And Animals

I walk outside,
I see some trees and they're all above me.
I love the ocean,
I just want a potion to make me into a mermaid.
I love dogs more than frogs,
And when I go to the forest I see some logs.
I could look at flowers for hours,
And I love fish in their dish.
I love the sun,
And now this poem is done.

Isla Easom (8)
Towers Junior School, Hornchurch

I Am Me

I love me,
People say I'm a happy lad.
But when I get stung by a bee,
I get a bit sad.

I love my little brother,
We always have fun.
But me and my mother,
Always go for a run.

I love cats,
They are nice.
They crawl on mats,
But I don't like the fact that they eat mice.

Adeel Islam (8)
Towers Junior School, Hornchurch

This Is Me!

Brown eyes, brown hair,
Tall and cool,
Dancing and prancing around a hall.
My hair is curly and wurly,
Twisty and turny,
Algebra makes my brain topsy-turvy,
Pastimes, I have many, like playing with my friends,
The fun never ends.
At school, art is the one for me,
Yes, this is me, mad and creative Millie!

Millie Spurdle (11)
Towers Junior School, Hornchurch

This Is Me

I like to drum
And collect Pokémon cards.
I am very smart.
I am silly.
I like games.

I am creative
And I like to act.
I am a lovely boy.
My favourite
Food is carrots.

My name is Harry.
I am funny like a dummy.

I really want to
Win this competition.

Harry Lundgren (8)
Towers Junior School, Hornchurch

I Am Like

I am a little girl,
My name is Lacey Lou,
I love to create,
And find things to do,
I am happy when I am making,
And shaking all my moves,
Jumping up and down,
Shouting, "Wahoo!"
I go to Towers Junior School,
Where everyone is lovely,
We all eat together and,
Make learning funny.

Lacey Millard (7)
Towers Junior School, Hornchurch

Ben Hudson

B rilliant at football.
E xcellent at maths.
N ice to other people.

H appy all the time.
U nity I show every day.
D etermination. I never give up.
S illy is what people call me.
O ften very cheeky.
N ot very good at rugby, though.

Ben Hudson (8)
Towers Junior School, Hornchurch

This Is Me

F lowers are lovely.
L ovely, colourful flowers.
O rdinary, familiar flowers fly in the wind.
W here the colourful flowers sit on the grass.
E ach day the glowing sun comes down.
R abbits jump on the colourful flowers and grass.
S tunning, colourful flowers.

Lexi Kyriacou (7)
Towers Junior School, Hornchurch

Smiley

S miley every day at school.
M y dream is to see people smile every day.
I n my mind, everyone is smiling.
L eah and my friends are smiling the biggest sunshine smiles.
E njoying all my lessons while smiling in my seat.
Y es, this is me, described as smiley every day.

Amira Malik (8)
Towers Junior School, Hornchurch

This Is Neryss Kaur

N ice is me,
E fficient and unique,
R esilient and flexible,
Y ippee!
S mart, of course caring,
S illy like a fantastic friend!

K ind forever,
A mazing and awesome,
U nity I show,
R eminds me of me!

Neryss Kaur (8)
Towers Junior School, Hornchurch

Abbi Rose's Life!

My name is Abbi Rose,
I'm a pinch of confidence,
I can be organised,
I am enthusiastic,
I love the environment,
It can be hard for me to be honest,
I have a brother called Alfie who is crafty,
And is aged two.
I had a dog who was lots of fun.
This is what people think of me.

Abbi Rose Hearn (9)
Towers Junior School, Hornchurch

About Me

My dog is called Duggie and he's a puggy.
I am happy when I play football and I do boxing too.
My birthday is the best like I never rest.
My favourite subject in school is computing, like computing at home.
My favourite thing to eat is a hot dog,
It gives me lots of energy before my jog!

Jacob Funnell (10)
Towers Junior School, Hornchurch

My Favourite Things

I love football and my FIFA game,
Also West Ham United, the park when it's sunny.
And my favourite colour is blue
My birthday when I get loads of presents,
Especially when all my friends come.
My Switch, my mum, and Christmas day
At night when it's dark and I watch films.

Jake Dwyer (7)
Towers Junior School, Hornchurch

This Is My Life

I'm as good as I am,
I'm sticky like jam,
I like staying partners with my friends,
For me, friendship never ends,
I like helping others and friends,
I try and shine like a star,
Everywhere people are,
I never want my life to change,
So I will never be the same.

Rose Wall (8)
Towers Junior School, Hornchurch

All About Me

- **A** smile of bright sunshine
- **D** etermined like a bird
- **I** ndependent at cleaning dishes
- **T** idying my toys in place
- **Y** oungest in the class
- **A** school parliament
- **R** espectful to each other
- **A** good friend
- **J** oyful Adityaraj.

Adityaraj Rathore (8)
Towers Junior School, Hornchurch

The Summer Masterpiece

It's something that is good in sunlight weather
It has multiple amounts of flavours
You like it in summer
Normally it's in local gas stations or a beach hut
Now wind and clouds blow away and let your sunglasses be used
And then you will find your lovely licking answer.

Lukas Ziutelis (10)
Towers Junior School, Hornchurch

My Favourite Things

My name is Billie-Leigh,
I am a little girl,
Creative as an artist,
I love to make scrumptious cakes,
I like nature like wild animals,
I like reading like an author,
Singer like Little Mix,
Food which puts me in a good mood,
Potter fan like Amber.

Billie-Leigh Cottage (7)
Towers Junior School, Hornchurch

Sport!

This is me, the goalie
Save after save
This is my life
And I'm not ashamed
I like to play footy
Day after day
Also basketball
It is quite the game
I like to play cricket
Bat after bat
Keep those balls coming
Bash after bash!

Michael Morrison (11)
Towers Junior School, Hornchurch

Football

- **F** ans go wild.
- **O** ver the goalkeeper.
- **O** h, what a goal.
- **T** hat was a great goal. That celebration means a lot to me.
- **B** ullseye goes in.
- **A** bsolutely.
- **L** ovely goal.
- **L** ovely, sweet goal goes in.

Mason Robinson (8)
Towers Junior School, Hornchurch

Harry Potter Is My Favourite

M agic Harry Potter and Hermione are my favourites
A n exciting adventure awaits them and me
G reat Lord Voldermort made his parents no more, he can't kill Harry
I s great news
C an McGonagall and Dumbledore save them?

Avni Phull (8)
Towers Junior School, Hornchurch

All About Me

J oyful when playing with Milo
A lways lies with me
S uper cuddly and sleepy
M ilo likes to bite my toes and fingers
I mpossible to keep still
N ervous at meeting new people
E asy to get to sleep.

Jasmine Willings (9)
Towers Junior School, Hornchurch

Lyla

I'm Lyla
I'm obsessed with dogs
I love yummy hotdogs
I don't like being sad
Because to me, that's bad
I like to sleep
Secrets I can definitely keep
I also have lots of friends
And that's the end.

Lyla Mardon (9)
Towers Junior School, Hornchurch

All About Me!

H istory is my favourite subject
E nthusiasm is my thing
A mazing at handwriting
T remendous at everything
H ilarious at jokes
E xcited about everything
R elaxing is my thing at home.

Mia Callender (8)
Towers Junior School, Hornchurch

All About Me

N ever going to give up
I ndependent
C aring
O n a learning track
L ove to learn
A lways kind.

A rty
R ight on time
I nterested in playing and learning.

Nicola Ari (9)
Towers Junior School, Hornchurch

This Is Me

E veryone loves me,
R eally good at listening,
S illy like my brother,
I ndependent like my dad,
L ovely as a flower,
D inner is my favourite ever,
A pple is my favourite fruit.

Ersilda Hoxha (7)
Towers Junior School, Hornchurch

This Is All About Me

T aylan is cool and the best.
A nxious like a fly.
Y ear Four is where I will be going.
L aughing is my favourite thing to do.
A nimals are furry like my hair.
N otebooks are my favourite.

Taylan Sheehan (7)
Towers Junior School, Hornchurch

Matthew

M agnificent at maths.
A mazing, academic reading.
T alented at rugby.
T errific at basketball.
H orrific at handwriting.
E xtraordinary at spelling.
W hat am I not good at?

Matthew Ajose-Coker (8)
Towers Junior School, Hornchurch

This Is Me

Netball is my life
I'm like a rolling dice
I love to skateboard
But I hate the car Ford
English comes in a jiffy
When maths is a bit tricky
I may be a prefect
But I'm not Miss Perfect
This is me.

Maggie Tynan (10)
Towers Junior School, Hornchurch

This Is Me

This is me
A person full of glee
I am bright
And positive all the time.

This is me
A girl full of creativity
Cuddly and exciting
Probably doing art things.

This is me
As you see.

Robyn Regan (8)
Towers Junior School, Hornchurch

Amazing Me!

M y smile is bright like the bulging sun,
A punch of confidence,
I 'm happy when I bake,
S illy but I'm sensible,
I love to sing and dance,
E legant but I am unique!

Maisie Eary (10)
Towers Junior School, Hornchurch

Me

G eorge has a giant heart.
E xtraordinary and out of this world at dancing.
O P at gaming.
R ight and wrong.
G eorge jams with his family.
E ggs are egg-cellent to me.

George Raymond (7)
Towers Junior School, Hornchurch

This Is Me!

M agnificent and magical,
A ffirm to win,
T errific and never teasing,
T aunting hero,
H acker at games,
E ager to reach my goals,
W anting to win!

Matthew Ley (7)
Towers Junior School, Hornchurch

How I Feel!

Feel like jumping up and down,
About to run around,
But I think I'll stay seated for a while longer,
A smile from ear to ear,
What emotion am I?

Answer: Happiness/excitement.

Momore Farri (10)
Towers Junior School, Hornchurch

This Is Me!

I eat cheese whilst I sneeze!
I like West Ham and that's who I am!
Gaming, rollerskating and football come next!
Family, friends, Isla, Macey, and Maggie,
Are always there. The love never ends!

Abi Black (11)
Towers Junior School, Hornchurch

Chloë

- **C** aring and funny,
- **H** appy always,
- **L** ovely and likeable,
- **O** h, my friends love me being myself,
- **Ë** nthusiastic, also always hungry, obviously this is me!

Chloë Webb (8)
Towers Junior School, Hornchurch

All About Myself

L oving to all family members,
O ptimistic to others,
U nbelievable football player,
I ncredible learner and listening,
E nthusiastic at everything.

Louie Harris (10)
Towers Junior School, Hornchurch

All About Me

J oyful and joyous
O h, so loud
S ports are my favourite
H eaps of friends
U se my manners all the time
A mazing at football.

Joshua McNeill (8)
Towers Junior School, Hornchurch

This Is Me

William is my name,
I can be as strong as I want,
I want to be as strong as I can,
It is me,
I like me,
And I want to help people,
And be a gym teacher.

William Ford (8)
Towers Junior School, Hornchurch

All About Me

R owan is dramatic
O ranges are my favourite fruit
W hen I play video games it makes me happy
A nd I like dogs
N ot cats, though.

Rowan Cooper (8)
Towers Junior School, Hornchurch

This Is Me

I'm a very lazy lion,
A deep sleeper,
I'm a McDonald's muncher,
A rapid runner,
A hugging monster,
I'm a pushy person,
This is me.

Lucy Tregidgo (9)
Towers Junior School, Hornchurch

All About Me

A ddicted to football
L oves sweets
B est at football
E xcellent at Maths
R eady to shine
T errible with talking.

Albert Leigh (9)
Towers Junior School, Hornchurch

This Is Me!

I love my family and my four pets.
My favourite colours are mint green
And light purple.
I love making bracelets,
It's one of my favourite things to do.

Ella Rose (11)
Towers Junior School, Hornchurch

This Is All About Me

H arry is hoppy,
A nimals are my favourite,
R abbits are my favourite animals.
R eally funny,
Y o-yo is my favourite toy.

Harry W (7)
Towers Junior School, Hornchurch

Me

Mischievous,
Energetic.
This is me and,
I'm glad because,
I have family and,
Friends and that's all
I need in the end.

Charlie Spurdle (9)
Towers Junior School, Hornchurch

All About Rafe

R eally like 3P
A wesome and caring
F un and cool
E xcellent and patient.

Rafe Stringer (8)
Towers Junior School, Hornchurch

This Is Me

F avourite animal is a cat
U nicorn is my favourite toy
N ice and kind.

Charlotte O'Donovan (7)
Towers Junior School, Hornchurch

This Is Me!

T echnology is my thing,
H ow does my XP go ping?
I am a fabulous gamer,
S ee, I am a great aimer.

I love the colour fiery red
S inging songs in my head.

W hen having a nice day and feeling good,
H appiness runs through my blood,
A t home, I have lots of fun,
T alking, walking until I'm done.

I wish I could be a pilot and fly a plane,
M aking my way around the world for my own gain.

A ddicted to karate,
B oy, I like a good party,
O ut and about, I like to explore,
U p and down, I climb more and more,
T ime for each other is what life is about. Be kind to each other.

Kieran Massey
Upton Priory School, Off Prestbury Road

This Is Me

To create me you will need:
A pinch of sugar,
A drop of paint,
A splash of hot chocolate,
A tablespoon of happiness, like how happy I am when I see my dog,
600g of sweetness,
A teaspoon of kindness,
A splash of friendliness,
A slash of scrumptious pizza,
A piece of paper,
7 markers,
A drop of water,
Half of a chocolate bar,
A quarter of a rainbow,
A plate full of my mum's spaghetti,
2 doughnuts,
A mystical, kind heart,
800g of honey,
A rare dream of being a singer,
A rare dream of being a dancer,

A delicious McDonald's Happy Meal,
A drop of sprinkles,
A sprinkle of fun,
A slice of the best cake and,
A tablespoon of smart.

And that's how you make me!

Rose Sedgwick (9)
Upton Priory School, Off Prestbury Road

This Is Me

S neaky like a ninja, scaring my friends because I have light feet like a cloud in the air,
I nside I am lazy, like a sloth, slow, so slow, that I can't get up,
D iddly, Squiddly, Sidney Diddly, I have so many names that I don't know them anymore,
N ow that I am nine, smart like a scientist in a lab making chemicals,
E verybody likes me, like a butterfly,
Y ou are great Sid, you know it.

Sidney
Upton Priory School, Off Prestbury Road

This Is Me

I am an acrobat and I don't like cats,
I love bowling but my knees keep crawling,
I love the fair and I like going on rocking chairs,
Next, my mum said, "Do your homework,"
Then I did it,
After that I checked it,
Then I went to the toilet,
When I went, the dog crept in
And wrecked it.
I love doing jujitsu,
And boxing
And looking after my horses.

   E la is my name
   L ollipops are my fave,
   A nd I love all my family.

Ela Rasool (8)
Upton Priory School, Off Prestbury Road

This Is Me

500 grams of cheekiness like a monkey,
200 grams of sadness like a wet weekend,
500 grams of sass like TikTok people,
700 grams of happiness like when I have chocolate,
10 grams of mean like a bully,
800 grams of generosity like light blue diamonds on Minecraft,
100 grams of strength like a star destroyer,
900 grams of smartness like a Star Wars droid ship,
1 gram of attitude like an angry Count Dooku.

Thomas Carrington (8)
Upton Priory School, Off Prestbury Road

This Is Me

My emotions can sometimes breach.
However I can always reach.
My name is Annabelle Dale.
I'm not a fan of ale.
But I am a fan of pizza.
As well as peas, ahh.
My soul has had a lot of injuries
And my feet have had equal upsy-daisies.
My pets are very cute.
Some have had injuries that are acute.
I'm good at sports.
And I always have support.
Feelings are always brave.
My uncle is called Dave.

Annabelle Dale (9)
Upton Priory School, Off Prestbury Road

This Is Me

N ow I'm talking about myself, I hope I'm not beat,
A s swift as a bird on my feet,
T o be me, you need some skill,
A nd I like to look at daffodils.
L ike the shining sun, my hair is when in the light,
I 'm almost always right.
E ducation is in my head and I love my toy Dalmatian.

Natalie Shaw (8)
Upton Priory School, Off Prestbury Road

This Is Me

My name is...

- **C** ute like a baby tiger,
- **H** appy as a free whale,
- **A** mazing at climbing, climbing like a monkey,
- **R** eally really loves the colour yellow,
- **L** ove to live in the jungle,
- **O** pen my own water park,
- **T** inkerer of magic,
- **T** ickly fingers to tickle my brother,
- **E** xcitable, little pot of joy.

Charlotte Bradley (9)
Upton Priory School, Off Prestbury Road

This Is Me

N ice helper whenever I can,
E asy to be happy wherever I go,
V ery sporty and can always fight for myself no matter what,
A lways become a friendly and hardworking friend,
E rupt with love and happiness,
H ow I am so strong and powerful, I could never get beaten, no matter what.

Nevaeh Mason-Grant (8)
Upton Priory School, Off Prestbury Road

This Is Me

To make me you need:
30 grams of craziness,
300 grams of happiness,
20 grams of honesty,
42 grams of helpfulness.

If you have this, then you can make me.

To keep me you need:
A comfy soft bed,
A room with books and electronics,
Food,
Things to do,
And very cute pets.

Ella Mae Wynter (9)
Upton Priory School, Off Prestbury Road

This Is Me

L ove in my heart makes me happy,
E veryone is kind in my eyes,
W hen I go on a rollercoaster I go crazy,
I am a superstar in maths,
S cience is very important in life because it is very scientific and you can learn new things.

Lewis
Upton Priory School, Off Prestbury Road

Rap About Hugo

My name is Hugo,
Hey, hey, mmmm, I like running and jumping,
Football, guns and cars,
Climbing, bombs, and food are my thing,
Sports and electronics.
Houses and money,
Hey, hey mmmm,
I am awesome at football and so is my friend,
Hey, hey, mmmm, Hugo!

Hugo Jones (9)
Upton Priory School, Off Prestbury Road

This Is Me

What will you will need to make me:
Sweetness,
Love,
Happiness,
Helpfulness,
Kindness.

How to make me:
A teaspoon of sweetness,
A sprinkle of love,
Two teaspoons of helpfulness,
A dash of happiness,
A splash of kindness.

And that is how you make me.

Lydia Neild (8)
Upton Priory School, Off Prestbury Road

This Is Me

An ounce of stress because sometimes I get a bit stressed at home,
A litre of fun,
A love of sharks and cats,
One million grams of sympathy because I'm so helpful,
Twenty grams of bravery and,
Two hundred and fifty litres of exploration.

Reuben Griffin (9)
Upton Priory School, Off Prestbury Road

This Is Me

I am young,
I am covered in black and red,
I am seven years old,
I have black shoes,
I am mischievous,
I am hilarious,
I have friends,
I love The Archers,
I love my dog,
I want to be a gamer,
I am an explorer,
I love the colour red.

Eric
Upton Priory School, Off Prestbury Road

This Is Me

Yeah, yeah, yeah, my family is great,
I love my mum, I love my dad, and especially my brother,
As well as my gran and of course my grandad,
He loves me so much, he's just so great.
Mum loves me so much yeah, yeah, yeah.

Reggie Thomas (8)
Upton Priory School, Off Prestbury Road

This Is Me

S pecial to my mum
I mpressed with my dancing
E xercise every day
N ever give up, ever
N ever regret knowing my special neighbours
A mazing to everyone and kind.

Sienna Marshall (9)
Upton Priory School, Off Prestbury Road

This Is Me

M y heart is colossal,
A happy soul I am,
T he curious kid,
T he big dreamer,
H elpful and jolly,
E very day is great,
W ith my attitude.

Matthew
Upton Priory School, Off Prestbury Road

This Is Me

How to make a Zak:
First, make the body with 5 grams of helpfulness,
Add 3.5 grams of happiness,
Then add 5 grams of kindness,
Finally put in the oven at 200 degrees C for 15 minutes,
And then you have a Zak.

Izahak Thachil (9)
Upton Priory School, Off Prestbury Road

This Is Me

I wake up in the morning,
I run down the stairs and grab my sword and shield
I sprint out the door and slay monsters,
And snap them to pieces,
I take out a katana for the final blow,
Shing!

Corey Bennett (8)
Upton Priory School, Off Prestbury Road

This Is Me

R iding my bike makes me happy
O liver is the best brother possible
R unning is my favourite sport
Y eeting into my bed makes me refreshed after a long day of work.

Rory Liddle (9)
Upton Priory School, Off Prestbury Road

Dylan

Dylan:

Ingredients:
A pinch of happiness,
A spoonful of love,
A splash of joy,
A bunch of fun.

Method:
Give it all a stir.
Bake at 150 degrees for two minutes.
You will have yourself a Dylan!

Dylan Atkin (9)
Upton Priory School, Off Prestbury Road

This Is Me!

A splash of joy,
A bunch of beauty,
A pinch of happiness,
A drop of appreciation,
A sprinkle of love,
A box of fun.

Stir for three minutes and you have yourself a Bobby!

Bobby B
Upton Priory School, Off Prestbury Road

This Is Me

My name is Sami,
I love my family,
As well as my granny,
My mum is an amazing cook,
My dad is an engineer.
My brothers are all nearly as cool as me.

Sami Khan (9)
Upton Priory School, Off Prestbury Road

This Is Me

Two thousand grams of happiness,
Two hundred grams of excitement,
Three thousand per cent of friends,
Googleplex amount of love,
I love my rabbit.

Zachary (9)
Upton Priory School, Off Prestbury Road

This Is Me

How to make me:
First, you need a big plate,
A dash of kindness,
Caring syrup,
A friendly hug,
A strong heart,
And an amazing family.

Evie Hext (9)
Upton Priory School, Off Prestbury Road

This Is Me

F ish and chips
A pples
M um
I am awesome
L icking ice cream
Y ouTube.

Charlie Ashton
Upton Priory School, Off Prestbury Road

This Is Me

What emotion am I?
I am always in joy,
I never hurt people,
I am really kind,
I make people grateful for who they are,
What am I?

Maisie Oliver (8)
Upton Priory School, Off Prestbury Road

This Is Me

L azy
E nglish is my favourite
I mpatient sometimes
A rt is my second favourite.

Leia Jones (9)
Upton Priory School, Off Prestbury Road

This Is Me

- **X** box
- **B** ugatti
- **O** n a football pitch
- **X** ander is the best brother.

Kaiden McCracken Houghton (9)
Upton Priory School, Off Prestbury Road

This Is Me!

This is me!
But it may not be you,
So take a deep breath,
And watch your world spin,
round and round with you.

My body's ingredients are quite complicated,
But I am certainly sure,
That they will make you elated.

So sit back in a relaxing chair,
Because they will almost certainly,
Make you spin through the air.

Salt, sugar, ginger, and bread,
It all describes,
What's in my head.

So this is me,
But it may not be you,
So sit back,
Relax,
And watch your world spin,

Round and round,
With you.

There are my ingredients,
But you don't know it all,
So here are my traits,
And I hope,
Very much,
That they don't make you drool.

Blissfulness, generosity and glee,
Those are the things that make me, me,
But that isn't the end, so don't forget,
Most importantly, me.

So you can stop reading now,
There's nothing to miss,
The rest is quite boring,
And trust me on this,

This is the end,
We will never speak again,
So I guess it's bye, now,

So go back to your pen!

Riley Moore (10)
Wollaston Primary School, Wollaston

This Is Me

To make me you will need:
20lb of brightness,
1 and a half bits of sadness,
6 and 5 bits of happy happiness,
1 and a half bits of independent work,
And finally, a cheese pizza,
5 cups of sleepiness,
8 packs of sprinkles,
7 packs of icing,
And last but not least, a big smile.

Now mix 20 pounds of busy brightness in a bowl,
Then get another bowl and put one and a half bits of sadness in a bowl then add it all together.
Next add 6 and 5 bits of happiness,
After that, add 1 and 3 batches of independent work,
Now add a cheesy pizza!
When you've done that add 5 cups of happiness,
Next add 8 packs of super sprinkles,
Now add 7 packs of icy icing,
Then add it to the oven and wait for 15 minutes (wait to cool down)

Now add some popping candy/pop rocks (beware
I'm a sour sweet and I'm a cringe child!)
Bake until you get baguette shape because it
makes me grin like a Cheshire cat.
This Is Me!

Amely Hills (10)
Wollaston Primary School, Wollaston

This Is Me!

How to make me:

To make me you will need...
1/2 cup of friendship,
1 pound of courage,
3 cups of uniqueness,
1g of nuisance,
50ml of smartness,
560g worth of books,
1 jug of love,
170g of curiosity,
A dash of sleepiness,
A sprinkle of mischief,
5 pounds of fashion.

Instructions:
(All ingredients can be found at Sainsbury's)
Firstly add in the 1/2 cup of friendship and the 1 pound of courage.
Next mix in the 3 cups of uniqueness and the 1g of nuisance.
Stir in the nuisance and smartness.

Drop in the 560g worth of books, the jug of love and the 170g of curiosity.
Slowly, sprinkle on the mischief and sleepiness.
Finally, plop in the 5 pounds of fashion.
Mix all ingredients thoroughly with a whisk until silky smooth.
If necessary, add more sleepiness
(I am sleepy like a sloth).
Put in the oven at 150°C and bake forever...

Riya Patel (10)
Wollaston Primary School, Wollaston

How To Make Me

Items:
1 Nintendo controller.
A pack of Pokémon cards.
A basketball.
A handful of my dog's hair.
A pinch of spice, happiness, rage and stupidity.
An iPad.
And finally a slice of pepperoni pizza.

The recipe:
Now, first you have to place the sprinkle of spice into a pot of boiling water.
Next, dip the basketball into the smouldering pot until it goes *pop* then drop the ball into the pot.
Now, sprinkle the happiness into the pot along with the dog hair.
Next, carefully open the pack of Pokémon cards and drop them in.
Then, smash the controller and drop the remains into the pot.
Finally, drop the rest of the items into the pot at the same time, and your very own Louis should pop out with a *splash!*

Louis Beard (10)
Wollaston Primary School, Wollaston

My Animals And Me

You might think rats are bad,
When you say that it makes me sad.
Well, they are really cool,
And I miss them when I'm at school.

I've talked a lot about rats,
Let's talk about cats.
You might think they are cute,
Oh, but they are fierce too.
My cat is as black as coal,
She always jumps into bowls.

I've talked a lot about animals,
Now I'll talk all about me.
I don't have a lot of words to say,
But I'll do what my heart desires.
I'm nice, smart, helpful too,
I'm kind, responsible, and a bit cute.
But most of all I'm intelligent,
So this is my house so let me be!

Annabel Richey (10)
Wollaston Primary School, Wollaston

This Is Me!

To make me you will need...
A very, very cheesy pizza,
Seven hours of Xbox,
Five cans of happiness,
Some pasta,
A pinch of cheekiness,
And some very cheesy Doritos,
Then some chocolate pudding.

First, you add seven hours of Xbox into a bowl.
Then you smash up the Doritos and mix it together.
Then add pasta to the very cheesy pizza and put it in the bowl.
Mix together until sticky then add five cans of happiness and mix together.
Then add a pinch of cheekiness into the sticky bowl and mix.
Then finally add the chocolate pudding to the bowl
Put it in the oven for 20 minutes.

Then take it out of the oven and let it rest for 10 minutes
Until you get a cheesy bubbly dinner.
That is me!

Freddie Wagstaff (9)
Wollaston Primary School, Wollaston

This Is Me!

I really like drawing.
It's my favourite thing to do.
I'm really good at it.
I do it every day.

I like stroking my cat.
She is really fluffy.
Her name is Tiger.
She's really playful.

I like all my friends.
They're really kind to me.
My BFFs are funny.
I like all my friends.

I love animals.
They are so cute.
I also love cats and dogs.
Even gerbils and hamsters too.
I love all animals.

When I grow up.
I will be a zookeeper.
Seeing all the animals.
I will never give up!

I do swimming.
I love doing it.
I love reading.
Diary of a Wimpy Kid.
And Tom Gates.

Sophia W-A (10)
Wollaston Primary School, Wollaston

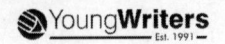

Samuel's Life

I love my guinea pigs of mine,
Laying their hay out line by line,
They are just so fluffy, cute and cool,
But really they are not very tall.

As well, I love playing football with my friends,
Because the fun never ends!
I have some good accuracy, sometimes...
So here's a paragraph about football that rhymes.

Doing fun activities here and there,
Making a campfire, sawing a chair,
Oh boy, do I like playing about,
And camping in a tent, and sleeping out.

I love my mum!
She is such fun!
But I love all my other family members too!
They're lovely people, and so are you!

Samuel Rice (10)
Wollaston Primary School, Wollaston

This Is Me!

I have two cats they are really fun to play with.
If they see birds they will meow in the window.
When the radiator is warm they will lie on it.

I like football I play with my friends and they play with me.
I support a good team with good players.
I have two really nice brothers that play with me and I play with them.
The reason I play football is because he got me into it.

I like to play on my Xbox with my friends and family.
I have lots of games on it which my friends play.
There are lots of games to play on a console.
When I play with my friends I have lots of fun with them.

Jake Cooper (10)
Wollaston Primary School, Wollaston

All Of My Hobbies

Roar, they go *zoom* past you,
As fast as light, faster than you,
Can't catch them even if you had ten seconds longer,
Even if you were sixty-nine thousand times faster.

Blues are the best they are third,
Of course they are better than Man United,
But I'm not sure they are very united.
Rubik's cubes are great for when you,
Are bored or when you're waiting,
For you're friends to finish Connect Four.

Winter is my favourite season mainly because of the snow,
But here in England,
We don't get much.

Luke Munns (9)
Wollaston Primary School, Wollaston

This Is A Poem About Me!

This is a poem about me!
I like apples and bananas you see.
I'm a bucket full of hope,
And I wash my hands with soap.
My mind's longer than a tree,
And wider than an open sea!

Now, here's something to know about me!
I like floppy fish and bees!
Bees because they're black and yellow,
And fish because they live in the sea!

I'm a silly, slow snail,
And I'm really pale.
But that's okay,
Because I will have a good day!
When I'm on a chair it's like a warm hug.
And sometimes I drink from a mug!

So that was a poem all about me!
Do you now know me?

Jacob Watts (9)
Wollaston Primary School, Wollaston

This Is Me!

I enjoy drawing,
I like playing with my pets
I adore dancing
Just like ballet!

I love sports,
Football and tennis
I fancy hockey,
Or maybe basketball!

I admire animals
Lions and leopards
Cats or dogs
Ducks and birds

I adore reading,
Dork Diaries and Diary of the Wimpy Kid.
They calm me down,
When I'm very stressed.

My friends are nice
They're very kind
They have a load of talent
And we all get along.

This is me!

Ciara Coleman Allen (10)
Wollaston Primary School, Wollaston

This Is Me!

To make me you need:
One bedroom of games,
One dog of fun,
10lb of Chinese food,
One slab of hot sausages,
One pinch of ice,
One pinch of Fortnite.

Now you need to:
Add a lot of Chinese food.
Mix in a games-filled bedroom.
Stir roughly while adding a slab of five hot sausages.
Next add a pinch of ice and a dash of fun.
Spread the mix neatly over a tray of baking paper and add a pinch of Fortnite.
Add one dog of fun.
Cook until glazed and fun-filled bubbles can be seen.
Sprinkle on happiness and leave to cool down for one hour.

This is me!

Patrick Peters (10)
Wollaston Primary School, Wollaston

This Is Me

I'm a sprinting cheetah going through trees.
I'm chatty like a chimpanzee.
I'm bouncy like a kangaroo.
I get bored when there's nothing to do.
My friend had a horse but it died from eating poo - trust me, it's true.
When I get in bed it shakes like a falling tree.
My brother's twelve and he thinks he's strong but I can get him on the floor.
Everything I buy makes me really poor.
I grab a remote and turn on the television.
Everything I do is inefficient.
But as happy as can be,
This is me!

Archie Batts (10)
Wollaston Primary School, Wollaston

This Is Me

I'm as pretty as a peacock,
I'm as sweet as a bee.
My name is Orla,
And this is me.

I'm as strong as a tiger,
I'm as wise as an owl.
When my little brother annoys me,
It makes me growl.

I'm as musical as an orchestra,
I like to roller skate.
I have two adorable hamsters,
And Hollie is my best mate.

I love Enid Blyton,
But J K Rowling is the best.
I play piano and guitar,
And my room is always a mess.

I'm as pretty as a peacock,
I'm as sweet as a bee.
My name is Orla,
And this is me!

Orla Kelly-Searing (10)
Wollaston Primary School, Wollaston

This Is Me

To make me you will need...
A lot of fun,
A lot of grey and blue,
A bit of yummy cheese and onion crisps,
A pinch of happiness,
A sprinkle of boredness,
A pinch of beauty.

Okay, now you will do this...
Alrighty, add the pinch of fun and then a bit of blue and grey.
Mix really well.
Then add a tad of cheese and onion crisps,
A pinch of happiness and a sprinkle of boredness,
Then again mix until you have a good syrupy consistency.

This is me!

Sophie Regan (10)
Wollaston Primary School, Wollaston

A Riddle

It's furry and cuddly
They are quite shy
It's cosy in any weather.

And they can jump really high
As quiet as a ninja
As stealthy as a spider.

They come out at the dead of night
You cant see them so
They're a big fright.

They could pounce
At any moment
Right when you think you're away
They will take you out any day.

What are they?

Answer: a cat.

Toby Donabie (9)
Wollaston Primary School, Wollaston

How To Make Me

To make me you need:
10 pounds of cheekiness
5 hours of Xbox time
5 cups full of fun
2 cups of mischief
Lots of sugar (this will make me bouncy like a balloon).

Instructions:
(All ingredients can be found at Tesco)
First, pour in the 5 cups of fun.
Then mix in the smoky pepperoni pizza.
Next, add 5 hours of Xbox time.
Stir in 2 cups of mischief.
Then drop in 10 pounds of cheekiness.
Then stir until bubbles of mischief are popping, then leave to cool down.

This is me!

Logan Carter (10)
Wollaston Primary School, Wollaston

My Favourite Animal

Its fur is white.
Freezing as night.
Not in a pack, just on its own.
It spends most times alone.
Its fur blends in with snow.
Just alone.

It eats seafood, mostly fish.
It loves it. Delish!
I know you're stuck,
So, I will give you a clue.
It lives in the North Pole.
Can't you guess at all?
It has lots of hair.

Right!
It is a polar bear.
That's my favourite animal.

Eliana Peters (9)
Wollaston Primary School, Wollaston

This Is Me!

Dancing is so fun,
Not in the sun,
You get all hot,
Which I am not.

My family are funny,
Very sunny,
We laugh together,
Making it forever.

My dog is very fast,
I can't last,
Cuddly and cosy,
Always dozy.

School is good,
Like I should,
Playing and laughing,
Forever lasting.

Isabella O'connor (10)
Wollaston Primary School, Wollaston

This Is Me!

I am active.
I am a kernel about to pop,
I am a seed who wants to sprout,
I am as kind as a doctor,
I am as soft as a hamster,
I am as strong as a hippo,
I am as lazy as a sloth,
I am as fast as a cheetah,
You would never know what hit you,
I am sneaky as a ghost,
I am as scared as a mouse,
I am as quiet as mice.
This is me!

Neo Higgins (10)
Wollaston Primary School, Wollaston

This Is Me!

I am good at cricket
But the other kids fidget
I like Man United
Because they are ignited.

I can only solve one side of a Rubik's
I learned it on YouTube
I have two cats
Who like my brother's puzzle mats.

I like Twenty One Pilots
I'm sure my birth flowers are violets
I like two cats
But hate bats.

Archie Longdon (9)
Wollaston Primary School, Wollaston

This Is Me

I have a dog I walk it every day,
Her name is Tallulah, she can bite,
So be warned, if she sees a dog, a squirrel or a bird she will run.

I love playing football,
I play in the summer,
But when it's hot we have a break, I play on the left wing.

I have an Xbox,
I go on it when I can,
Which is at night before I go sleep. I play FIFA 22.

Callan Glover (10)
Wollaston Primary School, Wollaston

This Is Me!

I'm a,
Quick feet master,
A super strike striker,
A footy GOAT

Tip, tip, tip, tap
Touch, bang!
Goal!

I'm capable,
Of any skill,
Maradona, flip-flap,
Cruyff turn and,
Anything you,
Can think of.

I'm a,
Quick feet master,
A super strike striker,
A footy GOAT!

My greatest goal,
Was a bicycle kick,
Hop, skip, jump,
Bang!

This is me!

Riley Coady (10)
Wollaston Primary School, Wollaston

This Is Me!

I am a Pokémon
I am a Fortnite God
I am McDonald's
I am a red Lego block
I am my birthday month of 11th of July
I am nine years old
I was born 2012
I have a good family
I have the best nan
I have a cheeky smile
I complete Nessy at School
I have the best mum
I am colour blind for red and green,
Yet these are my favourite colours
I have good BFF
This is me!

Davis Gent (9)
Wollaston Primary School, Wollaston

This Is Me

My dog and I, together we are happy.
I had a cat called Fanos, we played together and we were happy.
My sis and I, we play as good sisters.
My dog Reggie and I, we do everything together.
My grandad is in Heaven, I hope he is happy like me.
My dad is strong and he said I am as well.
I play Roblox really well.

Phoebe Schultz (9)
Wollaston Primary School, Wollaston

This Is Me

Long brown hair; soft, silky,
Like chocolate that's milky,
Smiley brown eyes,
Large in size!
I'm a paintbrush flicking along the page,
In April ten will be my age,
I love to swim like a fish,
When I blow dandelions I make a wish,
When I bike ride it almost seems,
That the tree at me all gleam.
Who is this: this is me.

Ruby Mae Ricks (10)
Wollaston Primary School, Wollaston

I Like Football

I like football
I support Manchester City
It is such a pity
How Man United
Are all ignited.

Manchester City are at the top
Did they drink too much pop?
How ecstatic they are
They should run a bar.

They have some of the best
There are a few pests.

Jude Sanders (9)
Wollaston Primary School, Wollaston

This Is Me!

I am a spicy crisp.
I am a rolling ball.
I am very small.
I love to eat chips,
The crunch on my lips.
I love gaming.
I love playing.
I have a chatty mouth.
I like to bake,
Especially chocolate cake.
I am a great gamer.
I am a dizzy Dorito.
When I go on a slide I say, "Whee!"
This is me!

Ethan Sims (9)
Wollaston Primary School, Wollaston

This Is Me!

I am as quiet as a mouse around people I don`t know,
I have a sheep called Domino,
I skate super speedy on the ice,
Just like a cat, I can be fierce but nice,
Aquarius is my star sign,
I have a rabbit and bearded dragon who are both mine,
I am a honey lover like a bee,
This is me!

Faith Clarke (10)
Wollaston Primary School, Wollaston

This Is Me!

To make me you need...
An Xbox, a PC and a lot of screen time,
You also need a big bag of fun and mischief,
Some pizza and sweets,
A picture of my family and sugar,
Happiness and sadness.

Then mix all together then you make this thing.
This is me!

Harrison Richards (9)
Wollaston Primary School, Wollaston

What Is My Hobby?

It has two wheels
It has a growling engine
It goes off-road like a thundering dune buggy
It's quite alarming
It has no doors
So always ride it with an adult on board.

Kai John Shelton Ryan (10)
Wollaston Primary School, Wollaston

This Is Me

I am useful,
I am confident,
I am careful,

I am caring,
I am loving,
I am hardworking,

I am fun,
I am different,
I am friendly,

But most importantly...
I am me!

Bella Marren (9)
Wollaston Primary School, Wollaston

This Is Me

This is how to make me.
I like the colour orange
And I love cats
Also helpful
And don't forget kindness
And last of all a loving heart.
This is me.

Miles Jones (9)
Wollaston Primary School, Wollaston

This Is Me

To make me you need...
Soft and scared
Some chocolate
Don't forget some water
A blue stone from space
And a red colour will come.

Matthew Rose (10)
Wollaston Primary School, Wollaston

This Is Me!

A kennings poem

I am a...
Car lover
Cold hater
Animal admire
Food devourer
Funny monkey
Rugby lover
Exited explorer
Enjoys outdoors
This is me!

Aidan Forbes (9)
Wollaston Primary School, Wollaston

This Is Me

As bright as the sun
As nice as the moon
Sleeps in the day and plays at night
What is it?

Tillie Scollins (9)
Wollaston Primary School, Wollaston

Brilliant Brooke

Brooke
My hair is as golden as Goldilocks' hair,
My eyes are blue like sapphires,
I am faster than a cheetah,
I am kind and funny,
My smile is a wave in the sea,
I am as lazy as a bear on a morning,
I am the daughter of Paige,
My climbing skills are like a ninja,
I feel relaxed when I am in the bath,
I like to play football,
My skin is as smooth as fabric,
My handwriting is as good as Miss Voyse's, I think,
I am crazy and pretty,
My eyelashes are as smooth as snow,
Wood-Kilgariff.

Brooke Wood-Kilgariff (9)
Worsbrough Common Primary School, Worsbrough Common

All About Ronnie
A kennings poem

Ronnie Arnold
Cool gamer
Quad biker
Coke drinker
Lazy sleeper
Roblox player
Motorbiker
Good footballer
Pizza eater
Snake lover
Fast boy
School lover
Chocolate hater
Karate lover
December birthday
Ronaldo fan
Book fan
Hard worker
Fortnite gamer

Boxing kid
Couple friends
Nerf fighter.

Ronnie Arnold (9)
Worsbrough Common Primary School, Worsbrough Common

Brilliant Facts About Me!

This is me...
My hair is as brown as chocolate milk.
My eyes are an endless void of brown.
I am clumsy as a blind sloth!
I am a cheetah when it comes to racing!
My ears despise loud noises.
My eyes are an ice cream.
My best skill is being sneaky as a ninja!
My hands are a small bunny.
My legs are as long as a giraffe's neck.

Mia Pierre (8)
Worsbrough Common Primary School, Worsbrough Common

All About Me!

Gabriella
I am helpful and kind
Cousin of Nevaeh-Rose
I enjoy going swimming and going for bike rides near Springs
I feel calm when drinking from spring water
I am calm and happy
Older sister of Esme
Enjoy playing a game of football also going to the park
Feels happy when doing experiments
Respectful and clumsy
Schofield.

Gabriella Schofield (9)

Worsbrough Common Primary School, Worsbrough Common

This Is Me
A kennings poem

Cacey Jane
Roblox lover
March 5th birthday
Bueno eater
Puppy lover
Bookworm
Tea drinker
Chatterbox
TTRS lover
Snow hater
School worker
Girl footballer
Summer lover
Loves pools
Coke drinker
Fab dancer
Loves friends
Cake lover
Coffee hater.

Cacey Beevers (9)
Worsbrough Common Primary School, Worsbrough Common

Cool Keigan

Keigan
My hair is blonde as tigers fur.
My eyes are as blue like the ocean.
My skin is white like snow.
I am wild as a tiger.
I am fast like a cheetah.
My skill is I am sneaky like a spy.
I like football.
I am as smart as a scientist.
My hair is as soft like cotton.
Pemberton.

Keigan Pemberton (8)
Worsbrough Common Primary School, Worsbrough Common

About Me!
A kennings poem

Fashion lover
Dog lover
Cat hater
Coffee hater
Tea drinker
Snow lover
Sun despiser
Chocolate eater
Sweet hater
Book reader
Love friends
Single singer
Dog Man bookworm
School worker
Chatterbox
Good footballer
Times tables superstar
Rich man.

Vuyo Mkwananzi (8)
Worsbrough Common Primary School, Worsbrough Common

This Is Me

I am Lloydy
I am as fast as a Lamborghini
I am strong as a bull
I amazing like a butterfly
I am smart as a humpback whale
I am kind as a snake
I am a snake-lover
My eyes are hazel as chocolate
My hair is ginger as a tiger's eyes
I am as good as a panda.

Lloydy Conway (9)
Worsbrough Common Primary School, Worsbrough Common

Magnificent Madeleine

My eyes are as blue as diamonds.
My hair is as silky as leather.
I am as sneaky as a fox sometimes.
I am as energetic as a kangaroo.
I am as quick as a motorbike.
I am a bundle of joy and fun.
I am as hard-working as a bee.
And I am as friendly as a baby animal.

Madeleine Robinson (8)
Worsbrough Common Primary School, Worsbrough Common

All About My Life
A kennings poem

Ronaldo lover
Loves caring
Amazing footballer
Friend William
Tea drinker
Jacket potato fan
April birthday
Funny person
Maths adorer
Mate Jay
Cuz Riley
Reading books
Playing Roblox
Eating chocolate
Cat lover
Coffee hater.

Mckenzie Oldham (8)
Worsbrough Common Primary School, Worsbrough Common

My Super Similes Poem

My eyes are as blue as ultramarine.
My hair is as golden as a gold block.
I am as smart as a scientist.
I am as fast as a cheetah.
I am as strong as a bull.
I am as happy as somebody could ever be.
I am as funny as a hyena.
My smile is as beautiful as the sun.

Addison Connelly (9)
Worsbrough Common Primary School, Worsbrough Common

All About Me

Lola
I am kind and pretty.
I am a bigger sister of Lilyanne.
Best friend is Alannah.
I enjoy playing with my friends.
I also enjoy going to see my mum.
I feel happy when I see my family.
Sometimes I inspire people, but sometimes I'm silly.
Lloyd.

Lola Lloyd (8)
Worsbrough Common Primary School, Worsbrough Common

My Kennings Poem

White-English
Bridlington lover
Cat hater
Beach lover
Coffee drinker
Snow hater
Dork Diary lover
Food gobbler
Dog lover (a lot!)
Rain worshipper
Sun hater
Sweets lover
Autumn lover
Chatterbox talker
Maths adorer.

Breeanna Faulkner (8)
Worsbrough Common Primary School, Worsbrough Common

All About Me!

My eyes are blue, shiny, sensitive sapphires.
My hair is as gold as a brick.
My smile can light up the world.
I am smart as a bookworm.
I am fast as a flash.
I am sweet as sugar.
I am pretty as a model.
I am kind as life.

Faith Sullivan (9)
Worsbrough Common Primary School, Worsbrough Common

Excellent Xavier

Xavier
I am smart and sweet
I am the friend of Libbie, Brooke and Alannah
I enjoy playing chess and playing with my friends
I feel like a nervous wreck when I don't know what to do
I am hilarious and confident
Aston.

Xavier Aston (9)
Worsbrough Common Primary School, Worsbrough Common

The Amazing Monika

This is me...

My eyes are as blue as the ocean
My lips are as red as a rose
My hair is as yellow as gold

I'm as slow as a sloth
I'm clumsy like a deer

My cheeks are like daisies.

Monika Bula (9)
Worsbrough Common Primary School, Worsbrough Common

KitKat Kara
A kennings poem

Black-African
Kind sassy
Funny cringer
Cat hater
Starbucks lover
Street dancer
Pop singer
KitKat gobbler
Coffee lover
Beautiful girl
Food eater
Cool girl
Loves sweets.

Kara Chigwete (9)
Worsbrough Common Primary School, Worsbrough Common

Amazing Lexi
A kennings poem

Dog lover
Coffee drinker
Chocolate eater
Snow adorer
School student
Sun worshiper
Loud speaker
Ronaldo adorer
Football lover
Roblox lover
School adorer
Bookworm.

Lexi Shirt (9)
Worsbrough Common Primary School, Worsbrough Common

The Amazing Alannah

Alannah
I am kind and loud
I am the best friend of Lola
I enjoy chilling and playing Roblox on my phone
I feel loved every day by friends and family
I am caring and crazy
Wilby-Dinsley.

Alannah Wilby-Dinsley (9)
Worsbrough Common Primary School, Worsbrough Common

Marvellous Maddison

Maddison
I am funny and kind
I am the big sister of Alex
I enjoy playing with Molly and drawing animals
I feel very cosy when I'm in bed
I am cool and a good friend
Singleton.

Maddison Singleton (8)
Worsbrough Common Primary School, Worsbrough Common

Me
A kennings poem

Fashion famous
Dog lover
Single singer
Chocolate devourer
Elephant smotherer
Love triplet BFFs
Dork Diaries bookworm
Sunny smiler
Art lover
Chatterbox.

Inês Tinsley (9)
Worsbrough Common Primary School, Worsbrough Common

This Is All About Me

Eben
I am young and fast
I am the big brother of Elias and Ezra
I like eating pizza and playing Roblox
I feel sad when I'm hurt
I am happy and curious
Parsons.

Eben Parsons (8)
Worsbrough Common Primary School, Worsbrough Common

The Super Seren!

Seren
I am kind and pretty
I am the younger sister of Ezri
I love Roblox and playing games
I'm happy when I'm with Ezri
I am playful and artistic
Hawcroft.

Seren Hawcroft (9)
Worsbrough Common Primary School, Worsbrough Common

Brilliant Blake!

Blake
I am kind and skilful
I am the brother of Marnie
I enjoy playing football and going on the Xbox
I feel confident in maths
I am helpful and caring
Allott.

Blake Allott (9)
Worsbrough Common Primary School, Worsbrough Common

The Amazing Michael Patrick

Michael-Patrick
Funny and happy
I am a middle child of four
I enjoy playing with my six dogs
I am happy when playing with Armando
Strong and fast
McDonagh.

Michael-Patrick (8)
Worsbrough Common Primary School, Worsbrough Common

My Kennings Poem

Hary Mano
Roblox gamer
Minecraft player
Tea hater
Dogman lover
Football fan
Juice drinker
Karate superstar
Unlimited energy
Maths genius.

Hary Mano (8)
Worsbrough Common Primary School, Worsbrough Common

The Amazing Anah!

Anah
Kind and bright
Middle sister of two
I love colouring pictures and playing Lego
I feel vibrant when I go outside
Helpful and thoughtful
Imran.

Anah Imran (9)
Worsbrough Common Primary School, Worsbrough Common

The Super Selma Story!

Selma
Quirky, bossy
Sister of Ouss and Ray
Art and craft lover
Feels happy when it's the weekend!
Kind, thoughtful
Hassan.

Selma Hassan (9)
Worsbrough Common Primary School, Worsbrough Common

Amazing Facts About Me!

Lucy
Helpful and kind
Big sister of Reece
I enjoy school and playing games
I am happy when I read books
Lazy and smart
Johnson

Lucy Johnson (9)
Worsbrough Common Primary School, Worsbrough Common

A Fact Poem About Alisha

Alisha
Funny, friendly
Friend of Breeanna
Loves maths and literacy
Dog-obsession, chocolate-eater
Independent, smart
Wall.

Alisha Wall (9)
Worsbrough Common Primary School, Worsbrough Common

About Me

River
Gamer, lucky
Loves playing games and reading
Feels happy when I'm nice
Important to me: family and friendship
Lawton

River Lawton (8)
Worsbrough Common Primary School, Worsbrough Common

All About Me!
A kennings poem

Helen is a...
Maths adorer
Dog hater
Tea drinker
Cat misser
Sun worshipper
Pizza fan
Drama queen.

Helen Vasquez-Carpio (9)
Worsbrough Common Primary School, Worsbrough Common

Me Is Me And You Is You

Hello, I'm me, I'm Ffion,
You are you - we're strangers
Perhaps we'll meet one day,
Recognise each other in a crowd.

I am going to introduce myself
To you: I am tallish, clumsy,
Bright, interesting, thoughtful
And above all, happy to chat.

I love to read - my favourite author
Is magical she takes me to Hogwarts
A one-way ticket to wonderland,
Maybe I'll stay there forever.

I love being a cook with my gramma
Learning to use all her recipes,
I love teasing my grampa
Turning all his jokes back on him.

If you meet me you'll meet my dog, Lili -
Just post me a smelly sock -

Don't worry, she won't eat it
She'll just know you when we pass in the street.

My sister Seren is more bouncy
Than a trampoline when she springs
High into sight, shouting and laughing
Catching a flying sausage for dinner.

Now that you've read all about me
It's your turn next to pack some surprises:
Reply straight away with a few clues -
And I bet I'll soon find out who you really are
Because me is me and you is you!

Ffion Francis (11)
Ysgol Gymraeg Bro Allta, Ystrad Mynach

This Is Me

I have big brown eyes
And straight blonde hair
I am shorter than most
But don't really care.

I have many features
I am more than you see
What is most important
Is what is in me.

I have many friends
Because I have a big heart
I am generous and kind
I am just cheeky when I fart.

I play computer games
And watch YouTube each day
But I know the importance
Of going out to play.

I enjoy dance
It can be tricky with socks

It's better with friends
Especially TikToks.

I like to read books
It's best in my room
It is peaceful and quiet
When I have nothing to do.

If I want a piece of cake
Or another kind of sweetie snack
I will sneak them to my bedroom
Holding them behind my back.

I am a typical girl
I explained myself as best as can be
Love me or hate me
This is me.

Olivia Morris-Brown (11)
Ysgol Gymraeg Bro Allta, Ystrad Mynach

My Life

This is my path
So please don't laugh.

I want to be a vet
To help people with their pet.

I'm going to learn to tattoo
It is something I've always wanted to do.

I love playing with my friends
We snuggle up and make great dens.

Chatting and giggling is so much fun
My mum calls up, "Elektra, tea!" but we're never done!

I have a tortoise called Shelley
I'd like to say he's not smelly
But that's why I clean his home
So he has a lovely place to roam.

My favourite food is jelly
It feels great in my belly

Raspberry, strawberry, I don't mind
As long as it's the wibbly-wobbly kind.

If there's something else you would like to know
Then please, give me more time to grow
I'm only ten years old so far
I haven't even got my own car!

Elektra Clarke (10)
Ysgol Gymraeg Bro Allta, Ystrad Mynach

About Me

Can I tell you a bit about me?
A nine-year-old girl, who loves her family
Reading Harry Potter books really makes my day
I love to imagine I'm in Hogwarts far, far away
Always talking and playing with friends
Dancing, singing or doing backbends.

A day at the beach when the sun's shining down
Look at me bodyboarding, you won't see me frown!
I do wish I wouldn't see so much litter,
Can't we care for the ocean and all of its critters?
I want to help the planet and also have fun
A lot's happened already but my life's just begun.

Maybe one day I'll be a big star
Or a fashion designer who can play guitar
Really there's no way of knowing this yet
Growing up will teach me a lot, I bet
At the minute I'm happy being me
Nothing can stop what I choose to be.

Cariad Morgan (9)
Ysgol Gymraeg Bro Allta, Ystrad Mynach

I Want To Be...

I want to be a journalist and write about the things I see.
I want to be a doctor to cure you and me.
I want to be an archaeologist and dig up lost treasure.
I want to be a teacher to help people to be clever.
I want to be an engineer and build fantastic machines.
I want to be an artist and capture my dreams.
I want to be a footballer and get paid lots of money.
I want to be a comedian and be very funny.
I want to be an astronaut so I can go to Mars.
I want to be an actor and work with all the stars.
I want to be everything because I am only nine.
But being me, for now, is absolutely fine.

William Chant (9)
Ysgol Gymraeg Bro Allta, Ystrad Mynach

I Am Who I Am

I might not be the most beautiful,
Or have the same style as others,
I might not be your first choice,
But I enjoy who I am on the outside!
So I am me,
But that's okay because I'm good at being me!
I don't care what you say about me,
Or if you make fun of me,
I'm happy with my life.

To everyone out there!
Everyone likes different things,
Like how my favourite colour is purple,
My favourite food is chilli con carne,
My favourite sports are football and gymnastics,
Even my favourite animals are giraffes, guinea pigs and dogs,
And how my favourite movie is Encanto!

So you see, everyone has different interests,
And those are mine,
So, I am me
And I am as special as can be!

Carys Rhianwen Mair Davies (11)
Ysgol Gymraeg Bro Allta, Ystrad Mynach

My Hero!

Some heroes wear capes,
Flying in the wind,
Some have magical powers,
And live in wonderful towers.

My hero has no cape,
Not even any superpowers!
Doesn't live in a tower,
But mine knows how to bake,
(Trust me she uses a lot of flour).

Some heroes save the day,
Even save other people,
My hero may not have powers
But she can still save us all.

My hero is my mother!
Who works for the NHS!
Without these amazing people
I don't think anyone else could help.

Thank you!

Lucas Owen Yeo (10)
Ysgol Gymraeg Bro Allta, Ystrad Mynach

About Me
Haiku poetry

I am Jac Davies
I am eleven years old
I live in Bargoed.

Dwi'n siarad Gymraeg
I'm in Ysgol Bro Allta
I am in Year Six.

My hobbies include
Rugby, karate, drawing,
And making comics,

I am creative
I am a very good friend
And I am caring.

I'm a good brother
My sister's name is Daisy
She is four months old.

I am different
And I'm proud to be myself
There's only one me.

Jac Davies (11)
Ysgol Gymraeg Bro Allta, Ystrad Mynach

Me, Myself And I

H air of gold.
E yes of blue.
U nique sense of humour.
L aughing out loud.
Y oung and happy.
N ever a dull day!

W hat of the future?
E ager to learn.
B usy with schoolwork.
B rain building daily.

P ractising always.
R esearching online.
I mproving my coding.
C omputing career.
E ncourage the dream.

Heulyn Webb Price (11)
Ysgol Gymraeg Bro Allta, Ystrad Mynach

My Dream

I dream of being a pilot,
Driving the roads above so high,
Through the clouds and the rain,
Flying high up in the sky.

I dream of being a pilot,
Plenty of beautiful sights to see,
Travelling from country to country,
What an amazing dream it will be.

I dream of being a pilot,
Looking down on the sea and fish,
But for now, I'll keep working hard,
So one day I can get my wish.

Lexie Cox (10)
Ysgol Gymraeg Bro Allta, Ystrad Mynach

This Is Me!

I love to draw and colour,
S ometimes I like to read,
A rt and creativity is a passion, and
B eing happy and laughing with my friends is the best feeling for me,
E nthusiastic and excited about everything Japanese,
L ively and loud is how my Mam would describe me,
L ucky to have such a great family,
E verything here is inspiring and important to me!

Isabelle Louise McBride (11)
Ysgol Gymraeg Bro Allta, Ystrad Mynach

This Is Me

A ngelic Angel, I'm caring and kind
M ature beyond my 10 years with sparkles in my eyes
E nthusiastic in everything I do, with a smile on my face I never go blue
L oving adventure at a crazy pace and my imagination running wild all over the place
I love to dance, I love to sing, I love to learn about everything
A melia Angel is my name, being the best is my aim.

Amelia Angel (10)
Ysgol Gymraeg Bro Allta, Ystrad Mynach

This Is Me

Always hungry some might say.
Brown hair, brown eyes, would sleep all day.
I'm tall and talkative with family and friends.
My hobbies are street dance, horse riding and following latest trends.
As life in lockdown has been quite strange for us all,
It has reminded me to always follow my goal.
My name is Abi-Mai and I am ten years old.
This poem is about me, to be told.

Abi-Mai (10)
Ysgol Gymraeg Bro Allta, Ystrad Mynach

Me

E veryone needs me by their side
L oving, caring, taking things in my stride
E ndless creativity and talent to show
N etball, piano, makeup, you all know!
A lways wanting perfection for all to see; but I'm happier when I say, "This is me!"

Elena Bilenki (11)
Ysgol Gymraeg Bro Allta, Ystrad Mynach

YoungWriters® Est. 1991

YOUNG WRITERS INFORMATION

We hope you have enjoyed reading this book – and that you will continue to in the coming years.

If you're the parent or family member of an enthusiastic poet or story writer, do visit our website **www.youngwriters.co.uk/subscribe** and sign up to receive news, competitions, writing challenges and tips, activities and much, much more! There's lots to keep budding writers motivated!

If you would like to order further copies of this book, or any of our other titles, then please give us a call or order via your online account.

Young Writers
Remus House
Coltsfoot Drive
Peterborough
PE2 9BF
(01733) 890066
info@youngwriters.co.uk

Join in the conversation!
Tips, news, giveaways and much more!

f YoungWritersUK **𝕏** YoungWritersCW **◉** youngwriterscw

Two Minutes to Midnight
(Matt Drake #33)

By
David Leadbeater

Copyright © 2023 by David Leadbeater
ISBN: 9798378545834

All rights reserved.
No part of this publication may be reproduced, distributed, or transmitted in any form or by any means, including photocopying, recording, or other electronic or mechanical methods, without the prior written permission of the publisher/author except in the case of brief quotations embodied in critical reviews and certain other non-commercial uses permitted by copyright law.

All characters in this book are fictitious, and any resemblance to actual persons living or dead is purely coincidental.

Classification: Thriller, adventure, action, mystery, suspense, archaeological, military, historical, assassination, terrorism, assassin, spy

Other Books by David Leadbeater:

The Matt Drake Series
A constantly evolving, action-packed romp based in the escapist action-adventure genre:

The Bones of Odin (Matt Drake #1)
The Blood King Conspiracy (Matt Drake #2)
The Gates of Hell (Matt Drake 3)
The Tomb of the Gods (Matt Drake #4)
Brothers in Arms (Matt Drake #5)
The Swords of Babylon (Matt Drake #6)
Blood Vengeance (Matt Drake #7)
Last Man Standing (Matt Drake #8)
The Plagues of Pandora (Matt Drake #9)
The Lost Kingdom (Matt Drake #10)
The Ghost Ships of Arizona (Matt Drake #11)
The Last Bazaar (Matt Drake #12)
The Edge of Armageddon (Matt Drake #13)
The Treasures of Saint Germain (Matt Drake #14)
Inca Kings (Matt Drake #15)
The Four Corners of the Earth (Matt Drake #16)
The Seven Seals of Egypt (Matt Drake #17)
Weapons of the Gods (Matt Drake #18)
The Blood King Legacy (Matt Drake #19)
Devil's Island (Matt Drake #20)
The Fabergé Heist (Matt Drake #21)
Four Sacred Treasures (Matt Drake #22)
The Sea Rats (Matt Drake #23)
Blood King Takedown (Matt Drake #24)
Devil's Junction (Matt Drake #25)
Voodoo soldiers (Matt Drake #26)
The Carnival of Curiosities (Matt Drake #27)
Theatre of War (Matt Drake #28)

Shattered Spear (Matt Drake #29)
Ghost Squadron (Matt Drake #30)
A Cold Day in Hell (Matt Drake #31)
The Winged Dagger (Matt Drake #32)

The Alicia Myles Series
Aztec Gold (Alicia Myles #1)
Crusader's Gold (Alicia Myles #2)
Caribbean Gold (Alicia Myles #3)
Chasing Gold (Alicia Myles #4)
Galleon's Gold (Alicia Myles #5)

The Torsten Dahl Thriller Series
Stand Your Ground (Dahl Thriller #1)

The Relic Hunters Series
The Relic Hunters (Relic Hunters #1)
The Atlantis Cipher (Relic Hunters #2)
The Amber Secret (Relic Hunters #3)
The Hostage Diamond (Relic Hunters #4)
The Rocks of Albion (Relic Hunters #5)
The Illuminati Sanctum (Relic Hunters #6)
The Illuminati Endgame (Relic Hunters #7)
The Atlantis Heist (Relic Hunters #8)
The City of a Thousand Ghosts (Relic Hunters #9)

The Joe Mason Series
The Vatican Secret (Joe Mason #1)
The Demon Code (Joe Mason #2)
The Midnight Conspiracy (Joe Mason #3)

The Rogue Series
Rogue (Book One)

The Disavowed Series:
The Razor's Edge (Disavowed #1)
In Harm's Way (Disavowed #2)
Threat Level: Red (Disavowed #3)

The Chosen Few Series
Chosen (The Chosen Trilogy #1)
Guardians (The Chosen Trilogy #2)
Heroes (The Chosen Trilogy #3)

Short Stories
Walking with Ghosts (A short story)
A Whispering of Ghosts (A short story)

All genuine comments are very welcome at:

davidleadbeater2011@hotmail.co.uk

Twitter: @dleadbeater2011

Visit David's website for the latest news and information: davidleadbeater.com

Two Minutes to Midnight

CHAPTER ONE

The General was not really a General. His name was Ivanov. He was an asshole. He made a point of telling everyone he was a General but, really, everyone knew he was an asshole.

He was a heavyset man, tall and broad, with a thick beard. His eyes were like tiny piss holes in the snow amid the ample fleshiness of his face. His double chins threatened to become triple any minute now. But his arms were brawny, his stomach flat, his voice a stentorian bellow that galvanised every last man under his command.

Ivanov hated his current situation. Kazakhstan was dreary and grim and cold, a barren, freezing landscape that would turn any man's dreams to mush. At the moment they faced frozen hail and wind and a vast, impenetrable darkness. They were bouncing along in three trucks, three large trucks, and Ivanov was sitting in the passenger seat of the leader. He had a seatbelt on, but even he was being jostled and thrown from side to side by the road's almost subterranean ruts. God only knew how the men in the rear were getting on. He half expected that, when they stopped, they'd find a pile of arms and legs and guns just resting and groaning in the middle of the back of the truck.

Ivanov tried to stay focused. The mission was as imperative as it was secret, as essential as it was deadly. Ivanov considered himself lucky to be on the payroll, even as he hung on to the grab handles and sped through darkness on this unfathomable Kazakhstan night. The driver didn't speak to him. There was no noise from the men in the back. The other two trucks were radio silent.

No talk until they arrived at the warehouse.

Ivanov was pleased with the progress so far. The job might be an uncomfortable one, but it was only a brief span of uncomfortableness amid the whole. Once the job was done, he could practically retire. Imagine that, he thought. Imagine being able to retire to some sunny beach, to lie back on a comfy deck chair with one of those umbrella-filled drinks, watching the world – and the women – go by without a care in the world, his days of murder and death and bloodshed behind him, only days filled with sunshine, sand and glittering seas stretching ahead.

Ivanov realised his mind was wandering. It was becoming more of a problem. Ivanov had an iron will; he could always focus as dead straight as a sniper shot on the job at hand. Until recently, that was. Recently, he found his mind straying, his thoughts flicking over a million different subjects, most of them involving him in a better place, a more amenable situation. Was he getting old? Soft? Past his prime?

Ivanov wouldn't believe it and doubled down on every moment. He doubled down on everything now, including how hard he pushed the men. It wouldn't endear him to them, but then he wasn't trying to be their class teacher. He was their leader in war.

War?

Yes, it is war. The thing they were doing – the thing they were here in Kazakhstan to do – was one of the worst acts of war. It could lead to obliteration.

Ivanov didn't care so long as he reached that sandy beach.

He concentrated now, tried to bring the mission parameters online in his mind. They were jouncing through the darkness, GPS sending out a good, clear signal, three trucks on a midnight road somewhere around the ass-end of the earth. There was nobody else around, the place being a wilderness. Of course, it hadn't always been that way, and that was the reason they were here.

Back in the 90's Kazakhstan had been a part of the Soviet Union. That was before a lot of states gained their independence. The Soviet Union had been a sprawling empire that stretched from the Baltic and Black seas to the Pacific Ocean. It had built and owned more property than it could ever remember, than it knew what to do with. There were abandoned factories, facilities, warehouses, tunnels, cold war shelters, sub pens, mountain retreats, workshops, manufacturing plants and industrial units stretching from one side of the old U.S.S.R to the other, many standing idle and collecting dust.

And many of these old facilities were far from empty.

Like the one Ivanov was headed towards, for example.

He checked his watch. 00.23. Bang on time. They'd planned the raid down to the last minute. They were approaching the facility now. Ivanov readied himself.

In old Kazakhstan, the boss had identified over one hundred so called 'dead' sites. These were places abandoned by the local governments, places they'd left to rot. Many had been forgotten through the years and were so far out of the loop that there was no one left to care. Some were so overgrown they didn't even appear to exist anymore. The dead sites stretched from north to south, from east to west, and that was just in one country. Ivanov could barely imagine how many there were across the length and breadth of the old Union. Thousands... and who knew what riches they'd stored in them?

Take the place they were at now, for example. Old codename: *Kurgan*. It was anything but pretty. A solid block rectangle, all angular shapes and concrete walls. Ivanov knew that because he'd seen the satellite photos when they were planning the mission. He knew that a deep forest and single track lanes surrounded the ugly block, and that a thick canopy of overgrowth mostly hid it. He was aware there'd been no human activity in years, that anything lurking there would not do so on two legs or necessarily draw breath. Ivanov watched now as the three trucks pulled up at their prearranged stopping points.

The sudden lack of motion made his head spin. Ivanov blinked, grabbed his weapon, and cracked open the door of the truck. The hot metal ticked in the dark, steamed slightly where droplets of rain hit it. All around was a deep pitch black.

Ivanov heard a loud commotion coming from the rear of the trucks, mercenaries climbing down onto the soggy, dark path. He slipped on his night vision goggles. Instantly, the surrounding scene lit up in luminous green. He took a moment to get used to it. Ivanov grinned as he noticed the time. They were bang on, still. The boss would be happy.

Which boss, Ivanov wasn't entirely sure. No way would their immediate superior be capable of utilising the thing they were about to obtain. That left an option Ivanov didn't really want to contemplate – that there were layers of command above him, several in fact. He didn't particularly like being the pawn at the bottom of the pile.

But his nose followed the money. And there was a pile of it on offer. He'd accept any humiliation if it resulted in a tonne of cash. His mind snapped back to the moment as the men ran from the side of the trucks to the ugly block building in front of them.

Ivanov fell in with them. Overhanging trees stood to both sides, their branches dripping water. The track was muddy. Ivanov's boots constantly slipped. He closed in on the front of the facility. It stood about forty feet high and had a corrugated metal roof. Foliage clung to those bits Ivanov could make out through the green glow. The men slowed as they approached the front door.

Ivanov pushed his way through them. They all carried AK-47M's, a light, reliable gun popular with the Russian military. It had low recoil, was compact, and had the standard issue folding buttstock. They also carried another staple of the Russian special forces. Glock 17's were holstered at their sides. The men stood around now, most of them holding their weapons at ease, whilst others formed a perimeter around the trucks. Everyone assumed they'd arrived under the radar, but it was better to be safe than sorry.

Ivanov nodded at the man standing right next to the door. He carried a pair of bolt cutters which he used now to slice through the thick rusty chain that, at some point in time, had been looped through the door handles to make them more secure. It might have been easier to wrench the door handles off. Ivanov didn't worry about that, though. The mercenary struggled with the cutter for a long minute before biting through and then letting the long chain rattle to the ground. It struck the paved floor with a thud. Ivanov watched the man attack the lock.

It didn't take long because of the lock's age and state of repair. The man grabbed hold of the black iron handles and pulled the door open. A heavy grinding sound split the night. Ivanov stood back as another man helpfully joined the first, struggling with the heavy, wedged door.

Ivanov waited. He surveyed the state of the men. Most were standing around, weapons now ready, just like him.

They had communications systems in their ears, but hadn't heard a whisper from the perimeter guard, which was a good sign.

Finally, the door stood wide open.

Ivanov waved some men inside. No way would he be going in first. The interior was currently a chunk of utter darkness. First, two men entered the warehouse and then two more. The darkness swallowed them up. Ivanov listened for a moment, heard nothing untoward, and followed them inside.

It was a vast space, stretching from front to back with no walls, no partitions. The mercs were shining their torches around. This was the unknown part of the mission, the one factor they couldn't plan down to the last detail.

Ivanov raised his gun, slightly nervous, slightly annoyed. They needed to get on with it. More men filed in behind him. That should help. The more workforce they got involved in this, the better it would be, the *faster* it would be. For all their planning, there remained several things that could still go wrong and sink them quickly.

The mercs fanned out through the warehouse. They knew what they were seeking.

And then Ivanov heard his name being spoken through the comms system.

'General Ivanov,' a voice said. 'Is this what we're looking for?'

Ivanov strode forward, passing through quite a crowd as he walked the length of the warehouse past old crates packed with grenades and rifles. Of course, it was typical that the item they sought was at the far end.

But once there, his feet stopped moving, and his jaw dropped in awe.

'That's it,' he said.

His heart pounded. He'd barely believed the intel,

barely believed this was possible. The reality of it hit him even harder now, drove into his brain like a twelve inch spike.

Several large stacks of crates in front of him comprised fourteen long-forgotten nuclear weapons.

'We only need one,' he said.

CHAPTER TWO

'General' Ivanov supervised the loading of the nuclear weapon onto a specially constructed heavy-duty dolly that they made up right there in front of the cache of weapons. The nuke itself wasn't huge. It stood about four feet high and was quite bulky. After the collapse of the U.S.S.R the former soviet republics were supposed to have returned all the soviet nuclear arms that were stationed in their countries.

But clearly not, Ivanov now thought.

Around the world, in every regime, many things happened that went under the radar. The collapse of the Soviet Union was a very volatile time. Could the government and its commanders have forgotten about fourteen nuclear bombs housed in Kazakhstan?

Very likely. In fact, it might well be the tip of the iceberg.

Ivanov knew there would probably be more, even single bombs out there, but the big boss, the end user, wanted just one from this cache of fourteen. So, one they would get. He watched half of the men lift and load the bomb onto the dolly as the other half planted the explosives.

The boss wanted no evidence left behind.

Ivanov hurried his men with curt comments and gestures. They went about their business competently. They started rolling the nuclear weapon towards the door, several men to each side of the dolly. Once outside, they would find it hard to load onto the truck, but the winch system should help. Elsewhere, men were planting explosives into the ground.

They had assured Ivanov that the explosives they were using wouldn't trigger a nuclear explosion. It didn't work that way. All they were trying to do was bury the warehouse under tonnes of rubble, leave it inaccessible for a long time.

They were ready now.

Ivanov moved out of the building. He didn't hurry, that wasn't his style. His men rushed around him, returning to their trucks. Ivanov walked back out into the drizzle and the stiff wind and watched them load the nuclear device onto the second truck. It went up with a hiss of machinery and then swung inside, where men would secure it to the deck with bolts. After that, they would fashion a crate around it.

Was it heavy? Ivanov had already seen four men lift it. The nuke was as mobile as it could get, considering its age. Ivanov swung his bulk back up into the passenger seat and waited for the driver to return. There was a buzz of conversation in his ears, men making ready for the exfil. Those in charge of the explosives reported they were ready.

Ivanov ordered the exfil.

The trucks fired up. Wipers screeched across the windscreen, clearing the water away. The driver turned the truck around, not a straightforward task on the single lane. A few minutes later, the three-vehicle convoy was trundling away from the forgotten building near the Russian border of Kazakhstan, heading south, and one man had his finger on the trigger.

Ivanov waited to give the order. Partly because he wanted to make sure they were clear, partly to remind the men who was in charge. They had a long way to go, and he wanted them under no illusions about who was the boss. The theft of the nuke was only the beginning.

Ivanov knew they were past the safe distance. He gave it another minute. Then, finally, he issued the order. Almost immediately, his passenger door mirror lit up with a bright glow. A dull thud echoed back as if travelling through the ground.

Ivanov watched as the warehouse exploded, collapsed, and disappeared under tonnes of rubble. A dark plume mushroomed into the air. He saw fire and heard small detonations for a while, and then nothing, not even the dull whumps of exploding bombs.

The convoy, with its immensely destructive cargo, vanished into the night.

CHAPTER THREE

Sabrina Quinn plucked the mobile phone off her desk and held it up to see who the caller might be. It was Ivanov, and he was right on time.

She held the phone to her right ear and jabbed the green button. 'Speak.'

'We have the cargo.'

'Any issues?' Sabrina was always clipped, abrupt, brusque with her audience.

'None. We secured the… cargo… and left a mess behind as instructed. We're on the first leg of our journey.'

'On time?'

'Yes, ma'am. The timescale is-'

'Don't call me ma'am, idiot.'

'Of course not. Sorry. We are ahead of schedule. The cargo is being wrapped as we speak, perfect for its next recipient. I understand that that is not you.'

Sabrina sighed to herself. These idiots were always fishing for information. For some, it would be the death of them.

'I could end you with one word, Ivanov.'

'Of course. Sorry, again. I know you will furnish me with all the information I need to know when you see fit.'

Sabrina shook her head. These assholes were condescending, as well as being stupid. She sat back in her plush leather chair and crossed her legs.

'Where are you now?'

'Still in Kazakhstan.'

'You have a long way to go. I suggest you call me when you're nearer to your destination, General.'

'Close to the warlord, do you mean? Yes, I will do that. But it feels to me like a terrible move to hand one of these things off to a mere warlord. I mean, what the hell's he going to do with it?'

Sabrina wondered how best to deal with the insubordination. She couldn't kill Ivanov just yet. She needed him. For now, she was forced to communicate further with a man she deemed unfit to slither through the grass at her feet.

Still, she stayed snappish. 'Not your concern.'

'The plan-'

'Is mine and mine alone, General. Now, do your job and stop talking to me. I will see that you get everything you deserve when the job is complete.'

It was a veiled threat. Of course, Ivanov was too bullish to see it that way. He let out a long laugh, thanked her, and then signed off. Sabrina thoughtfully ended the call, uncrossed her legs, and walked to the only door in the room. Inside here, she was never to be disturbed, a good rule but one that forced her to physically summon a manservant whenever she needed one.

Like now. She opened the door, saw John wearing his suit with the white shirt and gloves and shoes so highly polished they resembled a mirror. John looked expectantly at her, and Sabrina only nodded. He knew exactly what she needed.

It was early evening in London. Sabrina returned to her study. She crossed over to a floor-height window and looked out.

Dusk was settling over the city.

Sabrina had a good view of Knightsbridge, all the old buildings and the mews and the self-important shops. She was three floors up, so could look down on the people going about their daily business.

'Miss Quinn,' John said at her side.

It was her preferred form of address. She wouldn't hear of anything else. Lady this... Lady that... no, it was too much. She knew what she was. Her staff knew exactly what she was. And that was far more than most people knew.

She stood at the top of a shady organisation. Even she didn't know all its secretive branches and offshoots, but it had its hooks everywhere. Very little happened in the world that they didn't know of. Very little of importance, at least. Sabrina turned to the manservant at her side.

'Leave it,' she said neatly.

John placed a crystal tumbler full of bourbon beside her and backed away. He turned smartly on a heal and then left the room, closing the door behind him. He left Sabrina to her own thoughts once again, wondering if the plan that involved the nuke was really the right way to go.

People needed to be taught a lesson.

But... a nuclear one?

Sabrina hadn't come to the decision lightly, or alone. A committee had ultimately decided it. A committee that she didn't need to bend to, but one that she really should take notice of. She remembered the hoarse voices even now.

Hoarse after hours of arguing.

'They need to be taught a lesson.' One woman said.

'Need to be shown what happens when they don't do as they're told.' A man answered.

'Need to be brought into line.'

Sabrina had interjected. 'It's a high price to pay, civilian-wise, for a lesson learned,' she'd said.

'They mistake our good will for weakness.'

Sabrina had actually agreed with that one. 'But a nuclear lesson?'

'It will rewrite the map. Rewrite history. And the British government will never ignore us again.'

Sabrina had said, 'It's very final.'

'The fallout, the damage, can be contained by various means. We'll discuss that. But, as a statement, it is something that will reverberate in governments throughout the world. It will cement our global standing.'

Sabrina had listened to them, the nine-strong committee of men and women, all voting for the nuclear option with only her, the tenth, abstaining.

'I don't agree with you,' she had said finally. 'But I respect you as my board of advisors. I can admit when you are right and I am wrong. And if nine of you want the same thing, who am I to argue with that? Let the plans turn into action.'

And that had been mere weeks ago. Now they had a weapon, a route of delivery, and all the necessary checks in between. The weapon would travel a long way before it came to London along a circumvented route that allowed it to pass through several sets of hands that had nothing to do with Sabrina and her organisation, fully insulating them from any fallout. Of course, London's principal powers would be told that a lesson was forthcoming. Sabrina assumed they'd practically die of shock when they learned it.

And then they would fall into line.

Sabrina knocked back a third of the bourbon in one large gulp. It mellowed her, allowed her to see things from a different point of view. The committee's point of view.

Maybe they were right.

Maybe the nuke was the best option for London after all.

CHAPTER FOUR

It was Torsten Dahl's birthday. The team met in some large, busy, noisy eating establishment somewhere in the streets that surrounded the Capitol Building in Washington, DC. The evening was a balmy sixty-five degrees, the cloud-cover minimal, and stars littered the vast vault of the sky. It was one of those nights when the cares sloughed away, when the atmosphere of the surroundings and the contented civilians were infectious, when their world of action, death and last-minute chances seemed miles distant.

But they were still the Ghost Squadron. The public, the off-duty cops, the politicians, the bankers and the office workers... they had no clue who walked among them, no idea that those who really protected the infrastructure of the world at large graced them with their presence.

Drake and Alicia rolled up in a taxi around eight. They were both dressed nicely – though this being the Mad Swede's birthday, Drake hadn't exactly overdone it – wearing black jeans and jackets. Both had left their guns at home after some argument. It wasn't as though Drake felt naked without it – though he did – it was mostly that even just two weeks ago they were targeted right here in DC by a madman, an old enemy of Drake's who had tested them to their limits.

But, as Alicia said, 'I don't need my guns. I *am* a lethal weapon.'

It was true, true of them all. They'd seen action in most parts of the world, saved countless lives, survived crazy missions. Sometimes, Drake found it hard to keep track of them all.

Especially when long forgotten enemies came crawling out of the woodwork.

The last mission with the winged dagger had resurrected a few old, uncomfortable memories. Drake preferred to remain firmly in the present, always had. The ghosts of your past were dead and buried – they should remain that way.

He looked at Alicia as they approached the restaurant's main door. 'You should have done your hair, love.'

'I *did* do my hair.'

'Oh.'

Alicia slammed a palm into his solar plexus, doubling him over. 'I'm not cut out for this partying shit. Does it look ridiculous?'

'I've seen better coiffured sheep.'

Alicia narrowed her eyes, at last figuring out that he was joking. Drake was protecting his vulnerable areas, all of them, and getting an odd look from the doorman.

'Are you okay, sir?' the man asked.

'Aye, mate,' Drake said in his best Yorkshire accent. 'But watch this one. She's a real ballbuster.'

Alicia grinned as if to say, "you know it," and walked by him into the restaurant. Drake protected himself until she'd walked right past and then followed her. As they entered, a wall of noise hit them full in the face.

'Fuck me.' Alicia stopped in her tracks. 'It's like a fucking war zone.'

Drake, at home on the battlefield with bombs and bullets whizzing past his skull, stopped dead, too. There were people everywhere, seated at tables in their hundreds, sitting around the bar, standing on the peripheries and shouting into their mobile phones. Servers flitted between tables and around the room, carrying an unlikely number of plates one-handed in incredible balancing acts.

The loud din of conversation rolled over them in a wave.

Drake pushed Alicia further into the restaurant. Off to the right, he spotted Dahl's bulk, and then saw the others all seated around a table. Drake tapped Alicia on the shoulder and pointed them out.

'Want me to hold your hand until we get there?'

'Piss off, Drakey.'

The table was fully occupied by the time they sat down, and it was a big table. There were ten of them: Hayden and Kinimaka, Mai and Bryant, Dahl and Kenzie, Cam and Shaw. Drake said his hellos, clapped Dahl on the back as a special birthday present, and then took his seat. There was a moment of silence between them.

'How's the new apartment?' Drake asked Dahl.

During the last mission, some of them had lost their homes to Drake's nemesis and several fire bombs. It wasn't the brick and mortar they really cared about; it was the possessions they'd lost. They had few enough to start with.

'Good,' the Swede said. 'It has four walls and a floor above. Yours?'

Drake nodded. 'Same,' he turned to Bryant. 'You ever find the mole in your team?'

Their boss, the owner of Glacier Private Security and Mai's boyfriend, looked intensely uncomfortable. 'Still working on it.'

Also, in the last mission, someone had given their private addresses and other information to their enemies. That someone could only have worked for Connor Bryant.

'Can't be that hard,' Hayden said. 'Check their computer activity.'

'It's being done,' Bryant said. 'But, because of their sensitive nature, these investigations have to be conducted carefully and thoroughly.'

'I don't do careful,' Alicia said. 'And I only do thorough on Drakey's birthday. I would like to get my hands on our betrayer though.'

'The police will see to all that,' Bryant said.

'Let me at 'em,' Kinimaka grumbled. The big Hawaiian was sitting forward with his large hands clasped together so that they looked like meat hammers. 'I'll soon make them talk.'

Drake dropped the topic of conversation. They had come here for a lighter night, not a discussion based on something heavy they couldn't influence. They trusted Bryant by now. Not only was he their boss, he had been part of some of their missions.

Which was the only reason, despite being Mai's boyfriend, he'd been included in tonight's festivities.

'So what did you get for your birthday, Torsty?' Alicia asked.

Dahl had two daughters who lived with their mother in Stockholm. The Swede hadn't seen them in a while, but they zoomed regularly and had sent him a voucher. Dahl's face showed the strain of watching them grow up through technology whilst he and their mother went through an amicable divorce. Drake wondered if there was a safe topic of conversation anymore.

They ordered their food. The drinks came. They polished off several bottles of wine. The food, when it arrived, was delicious. Around them, the restaurant vibrated with friendly noise, rising and falling. They got used to the hubbub, the constant passers-by, the appearances of the overwrought servers. Drake enjoyed a medium cooked steak with chips and veg and peppercorn sauce, all washed down with a good amount of red wine. It wasn't often they pushed the boat out like this.

'So,' Alicia said partway through the night, leaning over the table. 'Are you two an item now?'

She was talking to Cam and Shaw, the two youngest members of their team. They had recently been away together, visiting Mai's ninja brethren in Japan, and had come back closer than ever. The ninja clan had wanted to include Cam's hardcore version of bare-knuckle boxing into their daily routines and had asked him to show them how.

Cam glanced at Shaw, who had slipped out of her ubiquitous black leather jacket for the night and wore a strapless dress. Shaw pursed her lips at him and didn't answer.

Cam turned to Alicia. 'I guess you could say that.'

'Sounds cagey to me.'

'We're a team,' Shaw said. 'But we don't need to share everything.'

Kenzie sat forward at that point. 'Don't worry,' she said. 'Alicia's a nosey bitch. Ask her about her past life as an exotic dancer.'

'That would be Mai,' Alicia said quickly.

'Thanks, Taz,' Mai said equally fast, and then turned to Bryant. 'Only as part of a mission for the Japanese police,' she told him.

'You'll have to tell me more,' Bryant said.

'Not likely,' Mai said.

Drake listened to the banter. He liked to hear them talk about inconsequential things, to basically shoot the shit. This team, this family, had been through so much together, from near-death experiences to the highs and lows of impossible missions, from kidnap and torture to fondness and affection. It was nice to hear them sounding normal, to act normal, to blend in with the everyday crowd.

As the evening drew to a close, Drake rose to his feet. 'To Dahl,' he raised his glass. 'He may be an old bastard, but he's *our* old bastard. He may get under our feet, but at least he's affectionate.'

The big Swede gave him the finger, but raised his glass and drank. They all drank. There was a moment of complete camaraderie between them, a quiet oasis amid the clamour where they were all connected by the family tie that they all felt. They drank and Drake sat down and they looked at each other.

Still connected.

'To us,' Drake drank again.

CHAPTER FIVE

The restaurant got busier and noisier the longer the night went on.

Drake had been hoping for some kind of comedown, a lessening of the uproar. But this was a busy place in the heart of DC and the clientele never stopped flowing. After the toast, Drake settled back with another glass of wine and tried not to think about all they'd recently lost in the house fires, how close they'd come to dying.

But they had got their enemy in the end. They had survived. They were here, now, in the moment, celebrating and alive. What better vindication was there of their skills, their adroitness as a team?

Drake narrowed his eyes but said nothing when Bryant's phone rang. He knew from experience that the man only fielded emergency calls on a celebratory night out. Bryant jammed a finger in one ear and spoke for a minute before rising to his feet and then walking out of the restaurant. Drake made a face at Mai.

'Is he okay?'

Mai looked non-committal, her long black hair framing her blank face. 'As far as I know. Nothing major's going on.'

Drake sat back, wondering. He guessed his mind and body had been conditioned by long years of similar phone calls, communications that instantly sent them to the more dangerous, far-flung areas of the world.

Ten minutes later, Bryant returned.

'Everything okay?' Drake asked quickly.

The man shook his head. 'Something big's happened,' he said, sitting down. 'And we're right in the middle of it.'

Drake frowned. 'Why?'

Bryant bit his lower lip. 'How do I say this?' he said, voice almost lost underneath the general restaurant clamour. 'As you know, when the government...' he made speech marks in the air as he spoke the last word. '... confronts a situation that's out of their control in a foreign land but still wants to be a part of it they call in groups like Glacier. Groups they've done business with before and they can trust. The government wants my help.'

'Important?' Dahl asked.

'Couldn't go any higher,' Bryant said. 'This comes from the very top.'

'The President's *wife?*' Alicia asked with a grin.

Bryant ignored her. 'I need you to act on this straight away.'

Drake, despite the man's words, despite the seriousness of his expression, blinked in surprise. It didn't feel right, not here, not now, not when they were relaxing in this hectic place with hundreds of civilians around enjoying the atmosphere.

'You're giving us a mission?' even Dahl sounded surprised. 'Here? Now?'

'I don't have a lot of choice. And there's nowhere we can go at short notice. So listen up.'

Drake placed his wineglass on the table next to his plate of eaten steak and braced himself. This was unusual. This was unheard of. Protocol demanded that this kind of thing didn't happen.

'A few days ago,' Bryant told them under his breath, speaking so softly they all had to lean forward. 'A crack team of mercenaries visited an abandoned warehouse in Kazakhstan. We think a man called Ivanov was involved. This all comes from satellite coverage and uncredited intel, you understand?'

'What was in the abandoned warehouse?' Kinimaka asked. 'I'm assuming it wasn't filled with dolls.'

'No, not really,' Bryant said. 'This warehouse, on the border of Kazakhstan and Russia, hasn't been used in over thirty years. It's one of those that first gets neglected, then gets forgotten. Inside... well, there's no easy way to say this. The building housed nuclear weapons.'

Drake felt his lower jaw drop. 'But isn't there... I mean, don't they keep track of these things?'

Bryant shrugged. 'We're talking about Russia here,' he said. 'A country that doesn't even care about its own people, its own population. A country that would send thousands of untrained civilians to a front-line war at the drop of a hat. During the cold war, they had over thirty thousand nuclear warheads. *Thirty thousand.* Think about that and then tell me if they might have mislaid a few.'

'If we're talking Russia, I can believe it,' Mai said.

'Even the U.S. loses fissionable material on a regular basis,' Hayden told them. 'That's a fact. It's been estimated at one theft every day.'

'That's actually quite scary to hear,' Kenzie said. 'Why'd you have to go and say that?'

Bryant held up a hand. 'This Ivanov character may have stolen a nuclear weapon, yes. We can't be entirely sure. He blew up the place afterwards to hide his tracks. The explosion put the entire event on our radar.'

'He must have known that would happen,' Hayden said logically.

'Maybe, but it's needs must,' Bryant shrugged. 'He had to hide his tracks, keep us guessing for another day.'

'But nobody even knew about the warehouse,' Kinimaka pointed out.

'That's not the point,' Bryant said. 'Ivanov had to assume the worst – that his theft would be spotted by at least one satellite pointing at the Russian borders. Blowing the place up gained him some time.'

'So where's Ivanov now?' Dahl asked.

'A great question. Ivanov loaded the nuke into one of three trucks and headed south. He drove through Uzbekistan and Turkmenistan. Guess where he ended up, and why.'

Drake thought about the regions involved. If Ivanov was heading south...

'Afghanistan?' he ventured.

'Exactly. Ivanov delivered the nuke to Afghanistan.'

'Shit,' Cam said.

'Right again. The satellites have tracked his journey, almost door to door.'

'If we have satellites on him, then surely we have drones.' Hayden said.

'I know what you're saying,' Bryant nodded. 'We track him and use drones to wipe him off the face of the earth, yeah? Well, as good an idea as that is, they did all the tracking *after the event*. We know only that he delivered the nuke to Afghanistan.'

'So Ivanov was a delivery boy? Not the chief recipient?' Shaw asked.

'Exactly. Ivanov delivered the nuke to an Afghan warlord.'

Drake shook his head. 'A what? Are you sure?'

Bryant nodded. 'As sure as we can be. Bizarre, eh? Afghan warlords, unlike other cells in that country, aren't exactly known for their penchant for nukes. What the hell would they do with one? Blow up their own country? They don't have too many ties outside their local jurisdiction. It's a bit of a mystery, I'm afraid.'

'And the powers that be want someone to check it out?' Kinimaka asked.

'No,' Bryant shook his head. 'They want the Ghost Squadron to check it out. Patrick Sutherland, the assistant director of the FBI, asked for you personally.'

Hayden nodded her head. 'Well, it's good to be recognised.'

'Sutherland certainly owes us some frigging favours,' Alicia murmured.

Drake tended to agree. He glanced around the restaurant, from the glass front doors to the sparkling bar built across the back wall. How different were their lives going to be in the next twenty-four hours?

'You're sending us to Afghanistan?' he asked.

'Reconnaissance mission. We need information.'

'This warlord,' Hayden said. 'Is he one of the friendly ones?' She knew the land comprised pro-American and anti-American tribal leaders.

Bryant sighed. 'I'm afraid not. But I can insert you with a friendly one, somewhere close to your destination.'

'You have that pull?'

'I have those contacts. There are a number of operatives already working in that part of the world.'

Drake could imagine why. He pushed his plate away and looked at the big Swede. 'So,' he said with a straight face. 'What do you think of your birthday present?'

Dahl only laughed. 'You know me,' he said. 'I'm easy. Besides, I was getting bored living in the same old place. All that shopping, watching TV, cooking dinners in the oven,' he shrugged. 'It's not me.'

'It's not any of us,' Alicia said. 'We move forward. That's what we do.'

Drake rose to his feet. 'How long do we have, Bryant?'

'An hour until wheels up suit you?'

Drake nodded. 'Can't wait,' he said with a touch of sarcasm.

'Don't worry,' Alicia said. 'I'll look after you.'

'Oh, that fills me with happiness,' Drake said.

'He means dread,' Mai told Alicia.

'Up yours, Sprite.'

The team rose to their feet, paid their bill and exited the restaurant. The weather had turned a little outside. A chill wind scoured the streets as if seeking them out, as if saying... welcome to the next part of your life.

They moved forward.

CHAPTER SIX

Drake knew exactly what to expect from the wilds of Afghanistan.

The chill night winds, the endless vault of the night watching over all. The mountains, the valleys, the blasted land with its scrubby brush. To him, it looked like a demolished wilderness, a place where nothing really lived in happiness, where nothing grew in contentment. The slopes of the cliffs were too harsh, the lay of the land too severe, the extremes too challenging.

He thought about all these things as their plane took them on the long journey. If all went well, they should land in the early hours of the morning. From there, they would venture out into the wider country to track down the friendly warlord. Bryant had arranged for transport to be waiting on the ground.

The plane shuddered as it cut through the skies. Drake leaned his head back, letting it all wash over him. The turbulence outside was strong today, jerking the plane back and forth. Alicia wasn't happy with it, and neither were Cam and Shaw. Drake could understand it with Cam – the young man hadn't taken many plane flights in his life – but he wondered if sometimes Alicia might be putting it on. Not that he'd ever tell her. That would be suicide.

The plane descended rapidly, swaying from left to right as it did so, and hit the runway with a squeal of tyres. It taxied to a stop and then they waited for the doors to be opened.

Drake wore army-issue fatigues and carried an MP5 with lots of spare ammunition. The others were similarly attired and equipped. They had backpacks and hats and wore tough boots. They exited the plane, stepped down to the tarmac, and looked around for their transport. It would have to be quick. Bryant had enough juice to get them into the country via a secret airstrip, but it was a dangerous exercise. Afghanistan was a big place, and the Taliban couldn't possibly hope to police the entire outer reaches, but Drake and the others couldn't just rely on luck.

As they watched, the plane prepared to take off again.

Two off-road vehicles pulled up, their headlights shining. They were old, and they were battered, and they blended well with everything else in the area. A turbaned local was driving each one, staring over the steering wheel at them with bright eyes as if willing them to get on with it. Drake understood the tension. The best thing would be to get as far away from here as possible in the next twenty minutes.

He checked his backpack as he climbed on board the first vehicle. The backpack held rations, water, a satellite phone for their exfil, and several other items. Essentially, it was a lifeline. Drake made sure it didn't stray too far as he climbed into the cab and took a long look around.

'Speak English?' he asked.

The driver waved at him and shook his head. 'Abdul Atta Kahn,' he said.

Drake knew that was the name of the friendly warlord they'd been tasked to find. These guys were the guides who would take them to him. Drake nodded, sat back, and buckled his seatbelt. He had no illusions that this would be a peaceful journey.

The road was pure dirt track, winding and rutted. It ran flat for a few miles and then wound up through the foothills of some jagged mountains. Drake could hear the engine labouring as it went, the wheels sometimes scrabbling for purchase. They saw no one, which was just as well. Drake assumed they'd been given the best guides in the business for that exact reason.

An hour passed. Then two. They wound through the foothills for a while, then cut through a pass between high mountains. The views on either side were stunning, distant peaks jagged and high and treacherous, all picked out by the stark light of a full moon. The little vehicles jounced and bounced their way along the dirt tracks, once hitting a road but not staying on it for too long. Drake held on as best he could, using the dashboard and the grab handle. The noise inside the cabin was all engine, making it difficult to speak.

Eventually, they came to a flat stretch of ground somewhere near the centre of a valley. It was a no-man's land. Their guide slowed and then stopped and then switched the engine off. He turned to Drake and pointed through the front window.

'Out,' he said.

'You want us to go out there? Where the hell too? Do I look that stupid?'

'Out,' the driver said, backing up the words with several chops of his hand.

Drake drew aside the canvas sheet that separated him from those in the back. Alicia's face was right there.

'Guide wants us to step out,' he said.

'Then I guess this is the end of the line,' Hayden said, rose and made for the rear of the truck.

Drake surveyed the terrain through the window. It was dark out there, the arid landscape just a black patch of indeterminate shapes. Of course, the guides couldn't help what time they'd touched down, and they'd had to leave the airfield in a hurry.

The team gathered in front of the first vehicle. Everyone had their guns up and most were eyeing the vehicles they'd just left.

'Where to?' Dahl asked in a voice that said, "I know already that you have no bloody idea."

'I guess we go this way,' Drake pointed vaguely north.

'Oh, listen to him speak. Let's all bow down to the tracking guru.'

Drake eyed their drivers through the windscreens. 'Maybe we should ask them.'

At that moment, there was a movement in the darkness, shadows melding out of shadows. Drake saw four men detach themselves from a black patch of landscape. As they came closer, he saw they wore the traditional long top and loose trousers and headwear that would differ according to ethnicity, tribe and region. Of course, there was a vast difference between what these men would wear and what the men in the towns would wear. That major difference being the guns and holsters, the bandoliers that were slung sash-style over their shoulders. The four men came forward and stopped in front of Drake.

The lead man, face grimy and sporting a thick beard, held out a hand.

'You follow,' he said.

Drake didn't like it. They were exposed down here in the valley, and they were being asked to follow strangers touting weapons into the utter darkness. Still, that was the mission.

'Abdul Atta Kahn,' he said, repeating the name of the friendly warlord they were supposed to rendezvous with.

The Afghan nodded and started leading the way. Drake

shook his head and fell in behind, eyes on the terrain. It was full of pitfalls, rocks and ditches and trenches, sharp drop-offs. It was all he could do to keep up with the four men.

Time was passing, and a false Afghan dawn was already greying up the darkness. He could still see very little except vague shapes and the backs of the men in front of him. He could smell the cold in the air, see his breath fogging. They kept the noise low and all he could hear were boots shuffling across the land. They passed between high boulders and shuffled once along the bottom of a deep gully. At one point, he could hear the rush of a stream.

'If they leave us...' Dahl whispered into his ear after about an hour.

Drake knew what he meant. They'd be stranded, lost, adrift in the Afghan desert. But the contents of their packs included a GPS, so Drake wasn't unduly worried.

During the second hour, Dahl tried to speak to the Afghanis.

'Abdul, he lives a long way, huh?'

Four blank faces stared at him. They stopped for a quick drink of water without responding. Drake nudged the Swede.

'Maybe they're stumped by your magnificent English accent.'

'Yeah, give 'em some Yorkshire, mate. That might be closer to Afghani.'

Drake drank water whilst he could and munched down an energy bar. Soon, they were on their way again, the only light cast by the silvery moon and stars. The wind started blowing briskly from east to west, scouring the hard ground.

Drake lost track of time. Eventually, though, the four men led them up into the foothills of a mountain. The trail went on and on, doubling back across itself and winding between high rocks. The going was tough and treacherous. Finally, they came around a tall, jagged rock and spied an open area in front of them, a wide space. Horses were tethered in a coral to the left. Many men stood about, some leaning against the mountain, others crouching or sitting or even sleeping under rough blankets. There was a cave entrance to the right.

But before Drake could even stop walking, a tall Afghani wearing the ceremonial dress of his tribe came up to them and held out a hand.

'I am Abdul Atta Kahn. I am pleased to meet you.'

Drake smiled, wondering at the man's form of address. Clearly, his team wasn't the first set of foreigners he'd met. But it was a good sign that he was making an effort.

'Drake, Matt Drake,' he said by habit, and quickly introduced the rest of his team.

They entered the camp, passed the horses and meandered through the middle open space until they came to a broad but dead campfire. Men soon got it going again, and Drake seated himself to one side of the Afghani tribal leader. Hayden was on the other. For a moment, everyone stared into the leaping flames.

Drake looked around. The skies were definitely growing lighter now. He could see men positioned on the mountain, lookouts all toting guns. He could see others going about their chores and still more tending the horses and cleaning weapons. It was a quiet camp. Everyone seemed to know what to do.

Abdul stared at Drake. 'You wear the dress of an American soldier,' he said. 'I was told to expect the English.'

'We're a mixed group but, yes, I am English working for America. Thank you for agreeing to help us.'

'It is nothing. I hate the bastard more than you do.'

Drake assumed he was talking about the other tribal warlord, the one who had taken delivery of the bomb. 'You can lead us to his camp?'

'With pleasure.'

Drake saw there was no love lost between warlords. He eyed Abdul's rifle, which was propped just a few feet away. The weapon looked well-used and well-maintained, as if this man knew exactly what he was doing. Drake guessed he'd been leading this tribe for many years.

'This man... this-'

'*Aazar,*' Abdul spat vehemently. 'He is a dog.'

Drake nodded. 'What can you tell me about him?'

'He pillages even his own people. Murders. Steals. He has no morality, no sense of right and wrong. If he decides he wants something, he just takes it. And his men – they are little more than mindless animals. No better than insects. They are a waste of... what do you say... life?'

'Breath,' Hayden said.

Abdul turned to her. 'Yes,' he said simply, and then turned back to Drake. 'Why are you here?'

Drake was a little surprised at the question, but sought to hide it. 'We believe Aazar has come into possession of something more deadly than most of us can imagine. We don't know what he wants to do with it. We're here to find out.'

'Then you need to move fast.'

Drake smiled. 'That we do.'

He watched as men handed out tin cups full of some hot brew. He accepted one and blew on it. When he tasted it, the beverage was sweet, like sugared tea. Not really his kind of thing, but it was hot, and it wasn't entirely unpleasant.

The team sat around, listening to Abdul Atta Kahn's

terrible stories of the warlord, Aazar. He came up with several accounts as the skies lightened and the campfire's flames were swept and flattened by the winds. Drake sat and listened and didn't complain. He was a guest in this man's home.

Eventually, Abdul ran out of things to say. He circled back around to the time constraints that beset the mission.

'I can show you the devil's camp tonight. Before then, it is suicide.'

'How far is it?' Dahl asked.

'From here? One hour. I will send scouts to explore a path to make it quicker. But tell me, are you going to kill the dog?'

Drake shook his head. 'How many men does he have?'

'A few hundred,' Abdul shrugged. 'I do not know.'

Drake found that hard to believe and suspected Abdul was guessing on the low side because he didn't want to admit that Aazar had quite an army to hand.

'Our focus is the weapon,' Drake said vaguely. 'That's what we have to concentrate on.'

Abdul nodded and threw more wood on the fire. 'Then settle in for the day. You leave at sunset.'

CHAPTER SEVEN

After a full day mooching around Abdul's camp, the Ghost Squadron was more than ready to take its leave. Drake, Alicia and Dahl spent the early hours retiring to the cave, trying to get some sleep. Later, Kenzie and Mai joined them. Cam and Shaw helped with the horses and then climbed the mountain along a few simple passes to gaze out upon a sprawling Afghan wilderness. Hayden and Kinimaka spent time around the campfire conversing with Abdul and then staring into the flames before finding blankets to curl up under. Sleeping on the mountain wasn't easy, but soldiers got their rest where and whenever they could. Drake, for one, could fall asleep anywhere, anytime.

They ate a tasty gruel and drank some more of the sweet beverage. They checked their weapons and made their plans. With the sun waning in the west, Abdul finally came to them and pointed out three of his men.

'They will lead you,' he said. 'Aazar has a large camp. We have been through it countless times. I can only wish you good luck.'

Drake shook the man's hand, the western gesture feeling quite odd in the Afghan wilderness but clearly what the warlord wanted. He hefted his backpack, checked his weapons, and followed the three men out of the camp and down the mountain. He settled in for a long slog and knew he should enjoy the half-light whilst it lasted. The sunset was only just starting to paint the western skies as they walked, a fiery conflagration that lit up the stark landscape with ardent hues and instilled a sense of beauty from one horizon to the next. They left Abdul's camp behind quickly and followed a twisting ravine for what felt like a solid half hour. After that, the guides slowed and turned with their fingers pressed to their lips.

'No talk,' one of them said.

Drake nodded. The team hadn't exactly been throwing a party back there, but they went absolutely quiet now. The group continued on, still following the ravine. Another ten minutes passed and then they were led up a narrow, rocky path that doubled back on itself countless times before bringing them onto level ground about a hundred feet above the ravine. The sky had gone fully black now. The moon was already casting a silvery glow over the earth. Drake watched his step as they clambered over a series of random boulders in search of a path.

Silently, they moved forward.

It was almost an hour after they'd left the camp when one guide quickly dropped to the floor. Drake didn't need to be told to do the same. Ahead, there were two men sitting atop a rock, staring off into the distance, their rough shapes silhouetted by the skies. They both smoked cigarettes and had the ubiquitous AK47's propped close by. The guides quickly backed out of there and sought another way.

Another twenty minutes passed.

They came through a twisting passage onto a cliff edge. The transformation was so quick, Drake drew a sharp breath. He swayed slightly. The ground fell away before him to a plateau below. He moved gingerly, although, as he stepped forward, he noted that there was actually a steep path that led downwards. The guides hadn't brought them here by mistake.

'Down, down,' one guide said.

They crouched, kneeled, and shuffled to the edge of the cliff. Below, the plateau, a wide chunk of flat rock, was occupied and, below it, the plain too. Drake could see countless tents arrayed across the landscape.

'There's an awful lot of activity down there,' Dahl said.

Drake had seen it, too. 'Hundreds and hundreds,' he said. 'You see the coral there?'

Dahl nodded. The coral, to the west, was twice the size of Abdul's. Many men were tending the horses. But that wasn't all. He saw a row of trucks too. And there were figures everywhere, stalking the plain below and wandering across the plateau.

'See the big tent?' Hayden said.

Drake looked at where she was pointing. The team stayed hugging the cliff, though he thought they were high enough to stay out of sight. The guides had moved away, making sure there were no nearby sentries.

'You think that's Aazar's tent?' he asked.

'Either that, or it's where the bomb's being held,' Kinimaka said. 'Just look at all the guards.'

Drake could already see them. The entire perimeter of the tent bristled with armed men, most holding their weapons at the ready as if they'd been told to remain alert. The tent was currently closed and nobody was walking in or out. Drake took his time to check and saw that it was by far the biggest tent down there.

'We can't be certain,' he said. 'But it's the likeliest candidate.'

Just then, the tent flap opened. A very tall man stepped out wearing the usual garb and sporting a long beard. The man looked to be in his forties but, from here, they could barely make his face out. Drake was thankful for the moon and stars, but wished for more light. He did see several men stand straighter as the newcomer stepped past and others bow their heads in deference.

'That could well be Aazar,' Alicia said.

'Let's monitor him.'

Aazar, if it was indeed him, walked to a nearby campfire and started talking to the men seated around it. The flames gave them a better view of his face and they saw it was wizened, creased, lived-in. If this was Aazar, he had had a hard life.

Drake noticed several scars across his cheeks before the man moved out of the direct light and back into the flickering shadows.

'This is impossible,' Hayden said. 'I count... over three hundred.'

They settled down. This was where they would observe the camp, see what happened through the night. Maybe Aazar would send half of his men away on a mission. Perhaps he would gather them all together. Maybe this... maybe that. They couldn't be sure until they'd performed a proper recce.

Drake grabbed water and ate another energy bar. He watched the camp, the various comings and goings. This far up, they couldn't hear anything, but could see that the men were vociferous, confident in their surroundings. They appeared to be working in shifts and, just like in Abdul's camp, knew exactly what was expected of them. The team crowded around Drake and took their time studying the comings and goings below.

By midnight, Drake was worried.

'There is no way we're gonna be able to infiltrate that camp,' he said. 'It's impossible.'

Dahl was beside him. 'I'm agreeing with the Yorkshire pudding on this one,' he said. 'Far too well manned. It's a twenty-four-hour concern.'

'I wish we could get another look in that tent,' Mai said. 'I could get close.'

They all looked at her. 'Not the way you're dressed,' Dahl said. 'Even you couldn't get inside that tent.'

It was true, Drake thought. The entire area around it was too well guarded. They watched for another few hours, hoping for something to change.

Nothing did. In the end, Drake and the others had to admit defeat and back away from the cliff. They did so slowly and carefully for several minutes before indicating to their guides that they wanted to be taken back to Abdul's camp.

'Do what next?' Kenzie asked.

'Plan B,' Drake said.

CHAPTER EIGHT

Back in Abdul's camp, the team were despondent, but Drake had had the entire journey back to put some thought into his Plan B. It wasn't pretty, it wasn't smooth, but it was all he could come up with.

They sat with Abdul around the campfire. It was early afternoon.

'Do you think you can do it?' Drake asked the bearded leader.

Abdul sat forward. 'I will do all I can to hurt that snake.'

'It's gonna be rough,' Hayden told him. 'You will lose men.'

'My men will stand against Aazar's tyranny without question.'

Drake reached out a hand and clasped Abdul's right hand, shaking on it. 'Thank you,' he said.

The warlord nodded. He rose to his feet and started calling his captains together. As Drake watched Abdul speak, he noticed several sets of eyes turned their way.

'Not everyone trusts us,' he mumbled.

'I'd be more worried if they did,' Kinimaka said. 'We're the outsiders, the infidels, and it looks like we're telling Abdul what to do.'

'He's up for it,' Alicia said.

'Yeah, but try telling the naysayers that.'

Drake saw Abdul reprimand a few of his own men and then looked away. They should work this out between themselves. The rest of the afternoon passed steadily, the wind rising and then falling, the arid lowlands empty of all life. Drake felt the tension of an approaching battle growing on him, felt the pressure deep in his gut. He used the hours of waiting to give Bryant a quick call on the sat phone.

'Nothing concrete yet,' he spoke over the crackly connection. 'But we think we know where the package is.'

'You've seen it?'

'No, but we have a good idea where it is.'

'What's the plan?'

'It's complicated. But we should have a sighting by tonight.'

'And then?'

'Well, Bryant, that's up to you and those you work for. What exactly do you want us to do with it?'

They'd already been briefed before they left, but Drake wanted no lingering doubts hanging in the thousands of miles of air between them.

'You disable it. If you have time, you remove the core.'

'We won't have time.'

'Then disabling it is the only option. I trust you remember how to do that?'

Drake assumed their boss was being sarcastic and didn't answer the question. Instead, he made sure Bryant knew how far Abdul was going to help them and mentioned compensation. It only seemed fair.

'I'll see what I can do. Contact me as soon as you finish.'

Drake ended the call. Bryant was nervous, he could tell. That the assistant director of the FBI himself had recommended the Ghost Squadron for this mission actually made Drake slightly uncomfortable. It put a lot of pressure and impetus on them.

'Are we ready?' Dahl asked as the sun crept steadily towards the west.

Drake lifted his weapon. 'Y'know, mate, this isn't gonna be easy.'

'If it's worth doing...'

'Yeah, I get that. But even with Abdul, the odds are stacked against us.'

'A situation we've been in countless times before.'

Alicia came up to them. 'Ready to go kick some Afghan ass?'

Drake winced, seeing the tribal soldiers standing all around. 'Even with Abdul causing the distraction, we've still got our work cut out.'

'Drake's not happy.' Dahl said.

'Well, don't ask me to make him happy,' Alicia replied. 'It's entirely too public here, even for me.'

Drake shook his head. 'I didn't think that was possible.'

'Well, I'm game if you are.'

'Game for what?' Mai came up from behind them.

'Alicia wants to make Drake happy,' Dahl said.

'Oh, wow. Has she tried breaking up with him?'

Alicia gave the Japanese woman a hard look. Mai only smiled. 'Just a suggestion.'

As they bantered, the sun continued to sink in the skies.

'How's Bryant?' Alicia asked Mai as she checked her weapons one last time. 'He still flirting with every hound he sees?'

'That's a front and you know it. Bryant isn't really a womaniser.'

'I guess we'll have to take his word for it. Whatever he said to get you, it worked.'

Alicia turned her back on Mai, leaving the Japanese woman fuming. By that time, Hayden and Kinimaka had arrived, followed by Cam and Shaw.

'Get your game faces on,' Drake told them all. 'This is gonna get rough.'

CHAPTER NINE

In the total darkness, Drake shifted. He was lying prone on the flat ground, several hundred yards from the perimeter of Aazar's settlement, hidden by boulders and bushes and scrub. The team crawled all around him, spread out, flat on their stomachs, having slithered their way for several hundred yards until they dared go no further, hidden from the many lights of Aazar's camp by the irregular landscape, any slight sounds they might make covered by the noise coming from the tents ahead. Drake had been right. Aazar's men were totally secure and confident in their environment. They trusted their guards and themselves implicitly. Drake had seen no sign of guards on the level ground close to the encampment and assumed they were all safely stationed up in the rocks.

But clearly they didn't have night vision goggles.

Drake donned his now, got a good look at the terrain ahead. He had no way of knowing when Abdul would start his attack, but assumed that it would be pretty obvious. For now, all they could do was wait.

The first sign he had was the sound of a distant explosion. It came from the far side of the camp and was followed by a flash of light. Looking ahead, Drake saw dozens of men turn towards it, at first incredulous. Then they started shouting, looked for their weapons, picked them up, and ran toward the sounds.

That was Drake's cue to rise to a crouch and then start forward. The others went with him, nine figures rushing through the dark, wearing camo fatigues and with their weapons ready, following a bee-line towards the largest tent.

Another explosion filled the night. Drake couldn't see what was going on, just the bright conflagrations that momentarily lit the dark sky. The camp was in uproar, people's attention drawn to the noise and the light and the violence that was happening there.

Drake stayed low, ran fast. He flew across the hard scrubland. The first tents he passed were small and coarse, just a place for people to lay their heads. He used them to hide behind, slipping between them after making sure the coast was clear.

The loud noises from the other side of the camp were coming more regularly now. It sounded like there was a fully fledged battle going on there. Drake felt a little guilty knowing Abdul was leading some of his men to certain death. But the mission was the mission, and a nuclear weapon was involved. Drake had dealt with nukes before and knew missions didn't come much more serious.

He crouched behind the latest tent. The material warped and bulged as a gust of wind swept the area, batting him in the face. He wiped his cheeks, glanced past the tent. There was a man dressed in desert garb and carrying a gun hurrying his way, not part of the battle. Maybe he was a guard.

Drake pulled back, crouched and signalled to the others. The man soon rounded the tent and hurried on by, so intent on where he went he didn't even notice the hidden Ghost Squadron. Drake breathed a long, deep breath. Maybe they were living up to their new name.

He didn't hang around, quickly rounding the tent and

creeping amongst half a dozen more, finding a winding route. It was difficult in the darkness, even with the night vision goggles. When the night sky lit up, Drake tried not to stare at it – the blasts caused his vision to flare brightly. Drake kept his eyes on the tents and the ground.

They also had a comms system nestled in their ears. Dahl used it now.

'Do you know where you're going, Drake?'

The Yorkshireman withheld a curse, concentrating instead on the way ahead. They reached another tent and crouched behind it. After a few seconds, Drake peered around the side.

The large tent was right in front of him.

'Boom,' he said into the comms.

'We were bound to stumble into it sometime,' Dahl said with a smile in his voice.

Drake continued to ignore the Swede, who thought he was funny. The truth was, the banter kept them all sane in the heat of battle. Drake watched the large tent for a while. Despite the ongoing conflict, there were four guards still standing around. Four that he could see. He had no way of knowing who or what was inside.

'Ready to engage,' he said. 'Four hostiles, minimum.'

He didn't wait for a reply, didn't want to force Abdul to engage in conflict longer than he had to. The camp looked pretty much emptied out from what he'd seen so far, which meant most of Aazar's men had headed for the fight.

Drake slipped out from behind the tent. He fired twice, sensing his team all round him. The guards spotted them the moment they appeared, surprise stretching across their faces. Surprise was soon replaced by pain, though, as the bullets struck them. Drake moved fast, knowing even the suppressed noise would bring anyone else in the area down on them.

The team ran towards the tent. Four guards fell. Hayden and Dahl were at Drake's side, the others just a few steps behind. They watched every direction. As Drake neared the tent, he saw several other figures entering the periphery of his vision.

More guards.

So they'd been stationed around the whole tent. The guards came running. Drake was too close to the first to use his weapon. He slammed it against the top of the man's head. The guy was shocked and staggered backwards, trying to bring his own weapon to bear.

Drake stepped in, grabbed the weapon arm, and broke it. The man's shout of agony was muffled by the headscarf around his mouth. Drake thrust an elbow to the throat, a palm strike to the nose, both blows designed to kill. The guard collapsed to his knees and then fell face first to the floor.

Around him, there had been three more gunshots. Three more guards fell to the floor. Dahl was standing over one of them.

The team fanned out, did a perimeter check of the tent. They were clear. Drake approached the tent's main flap. He reached out and threw it back, stepping in, ready to shoot. Once inside, his eyes widened.

It was a large area, and it was jam-packed. There was a large bed in one corner, a proper four-poster with netting and carved legs. Drake had to take a moment to wonder how the hell it had got here. Maybe Ikea delivered it flat-packed. One to ask Dahl about later. His eyes swept eagerly across the other items that stood before him.

An oblong table that would seat six. Several piles of packing crates, none of them larger than a wine box. Some of them were open, displaying packing material and rows of bullets and a few handguns. There were chairs too, kitchen chairs, dotted around the place. Drake saw clothes scattered here and there and old rifles propped up. He saw a half-eaten plate of food.

There was no space for a nuclear weapon.

No telltale box, no open crate with a metal fin sticking out. Drake studied the place with growing consternation.

'We're in the wrong tent.'

'Oh, great,' Alicia said. 'That only leaves a couple of hundred to check.'

Drake span on his heel. 'Then we'd best get checking.'

CHAPTER TEN

Drake ran from the tent, back out into the sultry night. The sound of gunfire got quickly louder. Abdul was still attacking from the east and Drake had to make the most of it whilst the battle continued.

'Split up,' Hayden said. 'Every tent.'

It was an arduous, thankless task. They got straight on with it. They separated and ran from tent to tent, sweeping aside the flap with their guns ready, scanning the inside before moving on. Drake saw empty dwelling after empty dwelling, at least empty of nukes. He saw only sleeping bags and low tables and a bunch of items he didn't recognise. He moved as swiftly as he dared whilst staying highly vigilant both inside and outside the tents.

The team worked west to east, checking every tent they could find. They drew closer to the battle. The noise of conflict increased in volume. Alicia entered a tent only to find a man hidden in there, clutching his gun and resting on his knees. She assumed he feared the fighting and didn't want to get involved. But she didn't ask him. Instead, she leapt across the tent and smashed his skull in.

Cam came across another. This man was praying. Cam hooked him around the neck and squeezed until he passed out. The team found no sign of the nuke.

Drake used the comms to gather them together just a few hundred feet west of the firefight. He crouched in the deeper shadows cast by a large tent.

'No nuke,' Alicia said quickly.

'You think the intel was wrong?' Hayden asked.

Drake didn't want to think that might be true. If it was, that nuke could be anywhere by now. 'We have to work on the assumption that the intel was strong,' he said. 'That nuke has to be around here somewhere.'

'Well, there's only one person who will know for certain.' Kinimaka said.

Drake looked at him. 'Aazar,' he said. 'The warlord.'

Dahl shifted slightly. 'Who is currently otherwise engaged.'

'But we know what he looks like,' Mai said. They'd got a description from Abdul's men and had spotted him the day before.

Drake looked at her. 'Interesting,' he said.

'Wait, are you suggesting what I think you're suggesting?' Cam frowned. 'You wanna kidnap an Afghan warlord in the middle of his own battle and interrogate him?'

Drake smiled. 'I think that covers it.'

They removed their night vision goggles. The area they were heading to was very well lit up. Drake led them to the end of the row of tents and took a good look at the battle. Abdul's forces had swept in from the low hills, caught their enemy by surprise, and engaged them on the flatter lands. Drake had seen some sights in his life, but this one took his breath away. Abdul's forces had assaulted their enemies on horseback, firing from their steeds, striking downward with their weapons. A few of them even carried RPG's. Abdul's forces galloped and trotted and whipped this way and that among Aazar's men, who tried to pick them off from the ground.

It was a wild battle. The skill shown by Abdul's men, firing from horseback, was incredible and made Drake blink in shock. Their steeds leapt over crates and galloped between gun positions, running back and forth, easily manoeuvrable. The constant sound of gunfire overrode everything. Aazar's men littered the ground and there were several riderless horses.

Drake took in the battle for a while, the ebb and flow of it. It was kind of a melee. There didn't seem to be a lot of structure to the attack and the defence. Aazar's men were still in shock, reacting, whilst Abdul's men remained proactive, striking at their defensive positions.

Thankfully, though, one man stood out from it all.

It had to be Aazar. He was a tall, spare man wearing the usual desert garb and toting a machine gun. He could only use his weapon sparingly, for fear of hitting his own scattered fighters, but he concentrated on hitting the horses and then their riders. There was a grin stretched across his mouth.

And he threw orders everywhere.

As Drake watched, Aazar ordered men to attack a phalanx of horses. Some were picked off by Abdul's warriors, others just dived aside at the right moment as the thundering hooves came by. Either way, Abdul's men were winning.

Aazar screamed out orders. He pointed to the left where, through a series of tents, in the light provided by gunfire and explosion, Drake could just make out a row of trucks.

Aazar was resorting to four wheels and far more horsepower than Abdul could muster.

His men leapt up, Aazar with them. They started racing away from the heart of the battle towards the trucks.

'Come on,' Drake said.

The team leapt up too, stayed within their own line of tents and ran in a circumvented way towards Aazar's destination. Their route was longer, but they ran as fast as they dared. The battle continued to flare off to their right.

Drake flew along, but with care. They needed to talk to Aazar, even if it *was* amid a battle. And he didn't want to run smack-bang into an enemy fighter as they raced for the trucks.

They all ran in a long line, arcing towards Aazar. Drake counted eight men with him. If they all reached a truck each, with firepower, they might well rout Abdul's men from the field.

Drake was a couple of hundred feet behind Aazar when the man reached his row of trucks. His eight-man team jumped for the nearest vehicles. The Ghost Squadron was closing in on them. First, one truck fired up and then another. Drake could see Aazar in the passenger seat of his own vehicle, yelling at a man to get the thing going, holding his gun upright between his legs. The engine roared.

Drake arrived at that moment. He leapt up to the step, grasped the handle, and pulled. The driver's face locked onto his with a shocked expression. He had no recourse; he'd flung his rifle down to drive the vehicle. Drake grabbed hold of his top and dragged him out of the vehicle, depositing him on the ground where Shaw was ready to take care of him.

Drake stared at Aazar.

'I need to talk to you, pal.'

Aazar's own door was being wrenched open by Kinimaka. Aazar didn't know which way to turn. His machine gun was bulky in the small interior. Kinimaka grabbed his shoulder and yanked him out the other side of the truck.

Drake jumped down and ran around the front. He could see the other trucks, saw the rest of his team assaulting them. Dahl and Kenzie were hitting the second in line, Hayden and Mai the third. Engines were running but none of the trucks had moved. Besides catching Aazar, Drake thought, they were helping Abdul out, too. He saw men being thrown out of the trucks, left and right.

Aazar scrambled to his feet. Kinimaka, twice as wide, knocked him back down to his knees. Drake grabbed Aazar's gun and threw it away. Drake got in the man's face.

'We need to talk.'

Aazar grunted and spat in the dirt. His features twisted. The man had blue eyes that were currently wide and filled with hatred.

'Fuck. You.' The warlord said in a thick accent.

Drake wasn't quite ready to deal with him yet. He wanted to make sure his team had neutralised the other men. Glancing back along the row of trucks, he saw Kenzie and Dahl, Cam and Shaw, Hayden and Mai and Alicia with their own captives, all dragging them along the floor. Alicia and Mai were still tussling with their opponents, but Drake was in no doubt who would win.

'So,' he said, turning to his captive. 'Aazar. That's your name, isn't it?'

Around them, the battle continued, gunfire and bombs discharging every second.

Drake crouched behind the truck, using it for protection, and grabbed Aazar by the front of his shirt. He hauled the man upwards until they were face to face.

'Where is the nuclear weapon?'

Aazar snarled at him.

Drake dropped the man and slapped him around the face. Then he punched him in the right ear. Aazar yelped and put a hand up, features twisted in agony.

'You understand me?' Drake threw another punch, this time to Aazar's left ear.

'I speak your shit language,' the warlord muttered. 'You will regret this.'

'I already regret it. I already regret sneaking into your shit tent. Fighting your useless men. I regret it all. But you know why I'm here. Where's the nuke? Tell me where it is now, or I'll beat the truth out of you.'

Aazar, on the ground, threw a kick at Drake's shins. Pain slammed through his brain, but Drake only reached down, grabbed Aazar by the throat, and hauled him upright. Aazar gasped and fought for breath.

Face to face, Drake smashed a fist into Aazar's midriff, holding him upright, then another. He wouldn't let the man collapse. He targeted the solar plexus next and then the man's groin. Still, he kept him on his feet with a hand around the neck.

Aazar couldn't speak, but his face clearly revealed the agony he was in.

'Nuclear weapon,' Drake said evenly. 'That's all we want. Tell me where it is.'

'I... don't have... a... nucl-'

Drake hit him again. 'We know you have it. We saw you take possession. Lie to me again, Aazar, I dare you.'

The warlord's eyes were frantic, flicking left and right as if seeking a way out, or as if looking for his men, anyone who could help him. But his men were being subdued. Further away, on the battlefield, Abdul's fighters were being driven back by a force of warriors who had now collected together and were using their guns. An RPG flew from horseback. Bodies and crates erupted from the point of the explosion, flung wildly into the air, their bodies silhouetted against the flames.

Drake punched Aazar in the right eye. 'The truth or I'm gonna start breaking bones.'

'It's gone! Listen to me, asshole, it has gone!'

Drake frowned and shook his head slightly. *Gone?*
'What the hell are you talking about?'
'I guarded it. I handled it only. It was never meant for me. I am part of a chain.'
Drake couldn't believe what he was hearing.
Part of a chain?
'What the hell are you talking about?'
'The militia leader has it now. He took possession as agreed. The deal was settled and paid for weeks ago. It has gone to the Pakistani militia leader, Gujjar.'
Drake stared. 'You've sold it on.'
'Yes, as agreed. I had the weapon for a few days only.'
Drake glared at Aazar, at the dormant trucks, at the battle, and at the flares of gunfire to the east. *The nuke was gone.*
What the hell were they supposed to do next?
'Do you know where this Gujjar hangs out?'
Aazar looked confused. 'Hangs out?'
'Where he lives. Where he operates. His place of business.'
Aazar shook his head. 'Pakistan,' he said.
Drake couldn't believe the nuke was already in Pakistan, transported there days ago. The trail was already cold.
Kinimaka bent down to lay a huge hand on Aazar's head. 'Are you telling us the truth? I think he needs a bit more persuasion, Drake.'
'No, no, no,' Aazar squirmed and looked suitably cowed. 'I have no reason to lie. The weapon has gone to Gujjar.'
'Why?' Drake couldn't understand it. 'I mean, why give it to you in the first place if you were only going to keep it a day or two?'
'It is the *chain,* as I told you. No one man knows what the other is doing or is a full part of the plan. It keeps the end user... secure.'

End user, Drake thought. Shit, that was one way of putting it.

He spoke into the comms. 'Secure your captives. We're gonna have to get the hell out of here. Contact Bryant.'

'Why?' Alicia asked him. 'What about the nuke?'

Drake eyed Aazar as he answered. 'It's gone,' he said.

CHAPTER ELEVEN

Drake and his friends pulled out of the battle. They wished they could have contacted Abdul, told him that the fight was over, that they no longer needed his efforts, but they had no way of doing so. Instead, they secured Aazar and his men, left them tucked in by the line of trucks, and made their way back through the tents to the edge of the camp.

It devastated Drake. Somehow, they had missed the nuke. But it hadn't been here for long. Aazar had passed it along almost immediately after taking the delivery. Drake led the team through the tents, away from a skirmish, and then toward the guides that they'd arrived with. From there, it was over an hour's journey back to Abdul's camp.

Giving Drake plenty of time to think.

'This Gujjar,' he said. 'You think he's the final recipient?'

'If he is, he's gonna regret it,' Dahl said angrily. 'Tonight was a waste of time.'

'Not a total waste,' Hayden said. 'We got Gujjar's name.'

Drake knew Dahl was speaking from a place of frustration, which wasn't exactly where Drake was dwelling. That was with Abdul and the men he would have lost. He stayed mostly quiet all the way back to Abdul's camp.

'From another point of view,' Kinimaka said. 'This is the first actual proof we have that the nuke is being bought and sold, changing hands,' he said. 'It's a big step forward.'

Drake waited until they reached Abdul's camp and then called Bryant on the sat phone. Quickly, he explained the situation.

'Liaise with Sutherland, with the FBI, the CIA, whatever,' he said. 'We need to know quickly how to proceed and we need some info on this man, Gujjar.'

'You say he's Pakistani?'

'That's what the warlord told us. I wouldn't trust anything the bastard says, but it's all we have.'

'He come clean with this, or did you beat it out of him?'

'What do you think?'

Drake ended the call and walked right up to Abdul. 'You have broken off the attack?'

Abdul nodded, his long beard wagging. 'As soon as that snake pulled out his heavy artillery, just after you left, I believe.'

'Did you cause a lot of damage?'

'We killed many of his dogs,' Abdul sat on a rock, facing a low-sputtering campfire, his eyes full of fire. 'Unfortunately, we took losses. More than we expected.'

Drake felt it deep down. He wanted to apologise, but knew he couldn't. It wasn't his place, wasn't what Abdul would want to hear.

'We were successful,' he knew this line of conversation would be more up Abdul's street. 'We found out where the nuke's been taken.'

'It was not there?' Abdul looked pained. 'Your weapon?'

Drake shook his head and sat down. 'I crossed paths with Aazar. I beat him up a bit for you.'

'You should have killed the dog.'

Drake understood, but he wouldn't kill a captive in cold blood. He didn't explain that to Abdul. The man had a long list of grievances against Aazar and wouldn't understand. Instead, he went on.

'We believe the nuke's in Pakistan now. Transported there by Aazar or maybe collected by a man named Gujjar. Have you ever heard of him?'

Abdul shook his head. 'Another snake,' he spat. 'They stick together, destroying our land, our way of life, as they go. They do not care that their actions have consequences on our lives, our way of living. This is the way for hundreds of centuries. This is *our* way. Why should we change?'

Drake admired the man and his followers. They lived with the land, off the land, and they steadfastly refused to change. He stared into the heart of the fire.

'How many men did you lose?'

Abdul shook his head, not speaking. As Drake waited, the men who'd been in the battle arrived back atop their horses. Some were bleeding, others had wounds that needed swift attention. Some rode as though they were warriors returning in victory. Others carried the bodies of the dead across their saddles.

Drake and his team leapt up to help the wounded. They spent the rest of the night tending to them, closing wounds, applying pressure, strapping up broken bones. It was the least they could do, and Abdul looked grateful for their help.

'Thank you,' he said more than once.

But it was Drake's way of thanking Abdul. It turned out he had lost over twenty men in the attack.

The morning dawned with a subdued air, something akin to the drab, washed-out sunrise that bled over the horizon. Drake and the others were still waiting for Bryant's call, unsure what they would be called on to do next. Pakistan wasn't exactly that far away, but Drake assumed the U.S. would have other teams in the area. They washed as best they could and ate a tasteless breakfast, drank hot beverages, and made sure their patients were as healthy as they could make them. One man, his thigh shredded, was still bleeding, losing too much blood, so Drake helped one of the Afghans stem it using a good, old-fashioned mix of gunpowder and fire. It wasn't pretty, but it did the job. The procedure sent the man into oblivion for a few hours, which also gave him some rest.

Drake joined the others around a campfire. There was a slight mist on the ground, something the day would soon burn off, but ethereal. It drifted around them as they sat facing the flames. After last night's action, their bodies were pent up, wanting more. They had to rein themselves in.

Drake jumped when their sat phone rang. The noise was incongruous inside the camp. Hayden reached out to answer it.

'Yes?'

They could all hear Bryant's voice through the speaker.

'The job's still ours,' he said.

Hayden frowned. 'What the hell does that mean?'

'It means you're still on the mission. You're still chasing the package. They want you to continue.'

'Surely they have people closer,' Drake said.

'I can get you into Pakistan very quickly. I-'

Now Dahl leaned forward and interrupted. 'You realise this threat is very real now, don't you? Before... it was unknown.'

Bryant sounded angry. 'Of course we realise it's real. You're the best team in the area. There're choppers on route to you right now.'

'That's frigging dangerous,' Alicia said.

'So is the package you're chasing. We're pulling out all the stops here.'

'So that'd be you and...' Hayden pressed him.

'You know who. You're friend, Mr Sutherland.'

Drake didn't push it any further. If the assistant director of the FBI wanted them on the case, then they were on the case. He got to his feet and stretched, then proceeded to field strip his weapon and make sure it was clean.

Soon, the helicopters would be here.

CHAPTER TWELVE

The transport wasn't exactly quiet, but it was fast and reliable, and it cut through the Afghan mountains without incident. Two choppers, one following the other closer than Drake was comfortable with, but twisting and turning so much that it forced him to hold on tightly. The pilots knew the terrain; they knew where the hostiles gathered, and they knew how to avoid any trouble.

Morning turned into afternoon. The choppers reached Pakistan and refuelled. They went on. Hours passed. The chase continued, though Drake was very aware of lost time.

'Is this where we're gonna get shot down?' Dahl asked quietly.

Drake knew what he meant. 'Somehow, using back channels, Sutherland has got us passage into and through Pakistan,' he said. 'Otherwise, the air force would be on us by now.'

The others nodded quietly. If anyone could do it, Sutherland could. The man was well connected, well liked. It didn't come as any surprise that Drake and his team flew from Afghanistan into Pakistan unchallenged.

'You have any intel for this militia leader?' Kenzie asked.

Hayden nodded, checking her phone. 'We have GPS coordinates for a known camp, but it's well into the mountains. Hard terrain. We can't land on the spot for obvious reasons, so we're gonna have to find a path that leads us to it. And these mountains...'

Hayden left the sentence hanging. It was clear that she was worried. Drake checked her phone and then handed it to Dahl. Both men now understood. Drake saw that the militia leader's camp sat in a maze of passes and gorges, probably well-defended. The entire area was a warren.

'We're going to need someone with intimate knowledge of the region,' Dahl said aloud. 'If we're going to stand any chance of getting in and out of there. One wrong move, and we'll never find our way out.'

Drake nodded his agreement. For now, though, the helicopters were landing. They deposited the team on a flat plateau, bade them farewell, and then lifted off again. Night was falling. Drake could practically taste the cold in the air.

'Where the hell are we?' he asked.

'I'll check the GPS,' Kinimaka said. 'But somewhere in the mountains of western Pakistan.'

'Civilisation?' Alicia asked pointedly.

'Somewhere not too far away,' Kinimaka said. 'I think I spotted lights on the way down here.'

Drake walked to the edge of the plateau, looking down. They were halfway up a mountain, black rocks and ledges and gorges everywhere. The failing light was casting shadows across the landscape. At the foot of the mountain, Drake saw scrubland and brown fields stretching away as far as a distant, verdant forest. That was about as far as he could see.

At his back, Cam, Shaw, and Kenzie were getting on with building a camp. They weren't about to go traipsing down the mountain as the darkness closed in, GPS or not. Kinimaka pinpointed a town not too far from where they were as Cam and Shaw started up a small fire and pitched several tents. Drake unrolled his sleeping bag and climbed into the closest one.

'Wake me in three hours,' he said.

He was asleep almost before his head hit his backpack, then wide awake again just before Dahl kicked him. The Swede was grinning. 'Nothing to report,' he said.

Drake took his turn on watch. He sat on the edge of a cliff and watched the landscape below, listening for any noises around them. The night was clear; it smelled fresh and clean. Sounds travelled up here, and twice he heard the sound of an animal that could be hundreds of yards off. He had his gun ready, his senses sharpened, but didn't see any need to wake the others. It was a short three hours, to be fair; he shared the watch with Mai, who was stationed above. Soon, he was swopping shifts with Alicia and climbing back into his tent to get a bit more shut-eye.

Morning came with a fiery dawn that lit the skies and the mountain peaks. They shared a quick breakfast of rations, coffee and water and then crowded around Kinimaka's GPS.

'Nearest town, three miles that way,' the Hawaiian pointed west. 'Roughly.'

Drake glanced in that direction. 'We're gonna stand out like Dahl's ego,' he said.

The Swede frowned at him. 'I'm sure they'll be used to foreigners in town,' he said.

'Maybe, but we're gonna have to be careful. This militia leader-'

'Gujjar,' Mai said.

'Yes, this Gujjar. He might have spies in the town.'

Dahl shrugged. 'We'll be as cautious as we possibly can.'

They moved off shortly afterward, taking a circuitous route down the mountain. The going was steady, the paths winding but always leading steadily down. Soon, the team had reached the foothills and were finding the way much easier. They kept an eye open for unwanted company, but saw no one else during their journey.

Drake reached the scrubland first and started across it. It was still cold, a rising sun not yet having burned off a low morning fog. His breath plumed from his mouth. He kept walking, kept his circulation going, step after step, until they reached the edge of the scrubland and started across a patchwork of green fields. After an hour or so, they entered the forest.

'Town's a half hour away,' Kinimaka told them, still holding the GPS. 'We got a plan?'

They kept walking, everyone trying to come up with something different. The trees were densely packed, giving them a headache as they tried to thread a path through. As they walked, with Kenzie, Cam and Shaw acting as outlying guards, they talked quietly.

'Who speaks the language?' Drake asked.

Hayden held up a hand. 'I can get by.'

Kinimaka wasn't far behind her. 'I'm worse, but I can make it work.'

Mai also spoke up. 'I understand it,' she said. 'But I'm not fluent by any means.'

'All right,' Drake said. 'I'm ruled out, because I haven't got a clue. Alicia's ruled out, Kenzie and-'

'Hey, why are you ruling me out?' the blonde spoke up.

'Because you're as dumb as a row of doorknobs,' Mai said. 'Embrace it.'

Alicia turned on her. 'I'm not the one shagging Connor Bryant.'

Mai sighed. 'And what makes you say that I am?'

''cos you're easy, bitch. You're a first date cert. And how many times have you been out with that womaniser?'

'I keep telling you. It's all a-'

'Yeah, yeah, it's all a front. He's not really like that. It's just for show so he can stay on the right side of his chauvinistic pals. Do you really buy that?'

'You don't know him like I do.'

'Naked, you mean?' Alicia grimaced. 'Crap, don't put that vision in my head.'

'To be fair,' Drake spoke up as they cut through a thick stand of trees. 'He's helped us out more than a few times. He's almost part of the team.'

'I can accept that,' Alicia said. 'He's useful. He comes through in a push. But that doesn't mean he's anything but a philanderer.'

Mai looked at her with a new expression on her face. 'Are you worried about me, Taz?'

Alicia's lips curled up at the mention of the old nickname. 'I just don't wanna see your mopey face after he does the dirty on you.'

'If he does, he'll regret it.'

Alicia waggled a hand. 'Really? What would you do to him?'

'Well, he'd be walking funny for the rest of his life. Let's leave it at that.'

Alicia grinned. 'Does he know?'

Mai shook her head. 'It's not the kind of thing couples go around discussing. Though you clearly do.'

'Drake's well aware of where his balls will end up if he strays.'

'And *you*,' Mai said softly. 'What if *you* cheat, Alicia?'

The Englishwoman looked surprised. 'Me? Why? Are you saying you're available, Mai?'

The Japanese woman shook her head and turned away. Alicia laughed. They continued on through the dense forest. Kinimaka kept them apprised of their progress on the GPS. Early morning passed, then turned into a rest stop and a bite to eat and a drink. After that, around late morning, Kinimaka urged them to a stop.

'The town's twenty minutes away,' he said. 'Time to split up.'

They slowed, hunkering down in the woods, then picked Hayden and Mai to continue into the town. Kinimaka was considered too intimidating. Hayden would have to lead the conversation.

'It's not gonna be easy,' Drake told them. 'Take it steady.'

'Don't get ripped off,' Alicia gave them a final pep talk. 'Or murdered.'

The last Drake saw of Hayden and Mai that morning was their backs disappearing through the trees.

CHAPTER THIRTEEN

Hayden and Mai noted the time, just after noon, as they entered the town from the east. The outskirts bristled with ramshackle huts, rutted dirt roads and the low stumps of many trees, as though someone had carved the community out of the forest at some point in the past. Which seemed a fair description to Hayden. The forest surrounded the town as far as she could see.

They moved down a dirt road. They'd left their backpacks and primary weapons back at the camp, thinking a handgun, spare ammo and a military knife would be enough to protect them at the same time as presenting a relatively harmless exterior. They walked with caution, watching in every direction.

They passed men and women standing in doorways, low hanging timbered roofs just above their heads. Four kids were kicking a dirty old football in the street as they passed by. Further in, there was more industry. A few low-slung buildings that might be small factories; a small lot with four cars for sale; a row of shops and a restaurant. The streets were narrow, the ground replete with ruts and gravel and boulders. Hayden kept hoping she'd come to a major thoroughfare where maybe they'd find a proper road, but it never happened.

From doorways, street corners and dingy alleys, countless pairs of hooded eyes watched them. Nobody spoke. Hayden and Mai saw no reason to start any conversation until they reached a place of opportunity.

Which came soon enough.

They found three shacks with signs hanging outside that looked like drinking establishments. Hayden entered the first, looked around the dingy interior, and walked straight back out. There was only one man inside, and he was propping up the bar, a row of shot glasses at his side. Mai led the way into the second, where Hayden ordered drinks at the bar and then asked the bartender about the prospects of hiring a guide.

'To where?' he asked.

'The mountains,' Hayden said, keeping it simple.

'Dangerous,' he said. 'You should not go there.'

Hayden didn't mention that they'd just come from there. 'But what if we wanted to? Is there anyone?' her limited grasp of the language forced her to speak as directly as possible.

The barman picked up a pint glass and started cleaning it. 'You be careful,' he reiterated. 'This is a dry country, you know.'

Hayden had known it, but out here, in the sticks, didn't think anyone really minded. They were probably drinking home grown brews, anyway. She looked around the ramshackle hut. 'Is there anyone?' she asked again.

'You wait,' the man said. 'You buy, and you wait.'

Hayden nodded, ordered more of the rot-gut clear liquid everyone else seemed to be drinking, and did as the man said. They both stayed on high alert, watching the doorway and the back, their hands never straying far from their weapons. The bartender disappeared for a while and then reappeared, but didn't say a word to them. Twenty minutes passed. Finally, the door opened, and a man pushed through and looked straight at them.

'Baashir,' he said.

Hayden rose to her feet. 'Are you a guide?'

The man called Baashir held up a hand and came over to them. He ordered a drink at the bar. Baashir was a short, squat, bearded man with broad shoulders and scruffy black hair. He wore baggy clothes that might conceal anything from a packet of cigarettes to a bazooka and walked with a slight limp. He seated himself on a bar stool and stared at them through hooded eyes.

'You want a guide? I am the best there is. At least, here in Chitor,' he laughed. 'Which isn't saying a lot.'

'You speak English,' Mai said.

'I was educated in Islamabad. I am here by choice.'

Hayden didn't ask why, didn't want to perhaps insult their new friend. Instead, she gave him a vague idea of the journey they wanted to make through the mountains.

'Why do you want to go there?' he asked. 'It is very dangerous.' Hayden thought there was a look of knowing in his eyes, as if he'd figured out exactly what they were doing.

'It's our mission,' she said. 'It's where we need to go next.'

'Just the two of you?'

Hayden shook her head. 'There are others. All we need is someone to show us a way through those mountains.'

'And the way back.'

'Yeah, that too. Can you do it?'

'Why should I? That's Gujjar's territory. He isn't a nice man.'

'We'll pay you,' Hayden said, ignoring the name drop. 'If you can get us through.'

'You'll die up there.'

'You'll find we're more death resistant than you might imagine.'

Baashir eyed the two women. 'Why do you want to go?'

Hayden saw the question as slight progress. 'No reason you would want to know. It'd be better for you if you just concentrated on the route. Leave the rest to us.'

Baashir nodded, accepting that. 'When?'

Hayden held out two open palms. 'Whenever you're ready.'

'Ten thousand.'

'What? Dollars? Are you crazy?' Mai burst out.

'Keep your voice down,' Baashir said. 'I don't want these people knowing about my business. Eight thousand.'

'Four,' Hayden said.

Baashir looked surprised. 'Really? Okay, that'll do. Show me the money.'

'In here? After what you just said?'

Baashir grinned. 'Good, just making sure you were listening. I can take you up into those mountains for that. But I can't promise you won't die when you get there, so it's gonna have to be money first.'

He jumped down from the barstool and headed for the door. Hayden and Mai followed him. They joined him outside in the street.

'Do you have the money on you?' he asked.

Hayden looked left and right. She looked a long way up the street in both directions and into the shadows that formed near alleyways, investigated shop doorways and the windows of overlooking homes. She couldn't see anyone lying in wait for them. She took a moment, noticing Mai doing the same.

'We good?' she asked.

'I can't see anything dubious,' Mai said.

Hayden drew Baashir into the nearest alley. It was ripe, stinking of refuse and garbage. Debris littered the floor. She dug a hand into her pocket and came out with a wad of cash, counted off four thousand American dollars. Then she put a hand on Baashir's shoulder.

'You take this,' she said. 'But we don't split up now. We don't leave you alone. Understand?'

'What if I want to take a piss?'

'Then Mai holds it. That's how it has to be, Baashir.'

The Pakistani nodded, accepted the money and told them he would have to make a pit-stop back home before starting the journey. He asked them if they had provisions, weapons, cold and wet weather gear. The questions he asked calmed Hayden's racing brain, showing that Baashir actually might know what he was doing.

Mai tested him before they took it any further. 'You say you know where we're going? You say you know the region. How do you plan to get close with no... scouts... seeing us?'

'I can get you in and out,' Baashir said. 'I told you that already.'

'You're gonna have to do better than that, Baashir.'

The squat man pursed his lips. 'There is a route,' he said. 'Known to very few. It leads through a series of caves. That's how I can get you close, and it's how we will make our escape.'

'So you know exactly where we're going?'

'To visit Gujjar. I don't want to know your business with that man. He is... the worst.'

'We aren't here to make nice with him,' Mai said.

'I gathered that, otherwise I would not have helped you.'

Hayden led them out of the alley and towards Baashir's home, which turned out to be a block hut in the middle of a narrow, dirt-strewn street about three blocks from the pub. The people standing around here were heavy-lidded and listless, their children sitting in the street in dirty clothes. Hayden and Mai watched Baashir as he led them into his home, constantly on the lookout for an ambush.

'Don't cross us, Baashir,' Mai said.

'I would not do that. I know the dangers and I am ready to face them.' He started loosening a block above his small fireplace, shoved the money behind it, and then headed for the bedroom. Mai followed him inside.

'I will change clothes for the journey now.'

'I won't watch too closely.'

Ten minutes later, they were back on the street. Hayden still didn't trust Baashir as far as she could throw him, but the man led them unerringly to the edge of the town limits.

'Where are your people?' he said.

Hayden nodded. 'Follow me.'

CHAPTER FOURTEEN

A strong wind howled through the mountain peaks, growing in strength the higher they got. At first, the going was easy. Baashir led them through a series of foothills, following bare trails through the rocks, making his way easily among the bigger boulders. The man stayed in front, guiding them, looking back often to make sure they all followed.

At first, they didn't need to keep a lookout. Baashir told them they were hours from Gujjar's camp and the GPS confirmed it. Drake walked along in the man's wake, hoping he was as good as he seemed to think he was.

Baashir had taken the time to tell them a bit more about the caves that led upward from the base of one mountain and let out somewhere to the east of Gujjar's stronghold. They might be guarded, he thought, but not heavily. The greatest ally they had was the enemy's complacency, their arrogance too. Why would anyone want to infiltrate Gujjar's camp? Who would be stupid enough?

Drake pushed the pace, aware that the nuke had been with the militia leader for some time now. What would he be doing with it? What was his endgame? That the nuke had gone from a tribal warlord to a militia leader was nothing short of strange. It was an odd network to use, but he guessed, highly anonymous. It kept the limelight away from the man who really wanted to own the nuke.

Or woman, Drake thought.

Baashir led the way through the rocky passes, winding up the mountain. Still, they were several hours from Gujjar's camp. Drake followed closely in the man's footsteps, monitoring his friends strung out below him and the higher ground that they were aiming for. It turned into a long slog.

'You seem to know your way,' he said at one point to Baashir.

'I could find my way blindfolded,' came the answer. 'I used to live in these mountains.'

'Part of Gujjar's crew?' Drake grew more wary.

'No. These militia leaders come and go. It has not always been Gujjar. And the lifestyle was not for me.'

'What do you do, Baashir?'

'Me? I take foreigners into the mountains.' Baashir said with a wide grin and continued on, head down.

Drake followed him even more closely.

Behind them, Hayden kept an eye on the GPS, not entirely trusting their guide. She kept nodding, though, signalling that all was well.

After some hours, Baashir showed them a cave entrance, nothing more than a crease in the rock face. Ordinarily, Drake would have eyed it dubiously and moved on, but Baashir led them right inside.

The entrance to the cave was narrow and curved. It led for some way into the mountain. At first, the space above their head was enormous, which suited them fine, but then the ceiling grew lower and the walls came closer. Soon, they were squeezing through a claustrophobic hell.

'What makes me wonder,' Hayden breathed at one point. 'Is who the hell explored all these caves in the first place? I mean, why would you want to do this?'

'It was a needs must situation,' Baashir told her. 'Some

men were being pursued by Pakistani special forces who chased them into the cave system, forcing them to use it. They did, and they escaped.'

Drake took his time, squeezing through the narrow passages. After a while, the ceiling disappeared again and then the channels became wider. It was always an uphill trudge. His face dripped with sweat, his calves ached. The pack on his back felt heavier than before, but he was used to dragging the extra weight. They all were, with the exceptions maybe of Cam and Shaw.

'I'm spotting quite a few offshoots,' Dahl said. 'How do you know which way to go?'

'Again, it is from memory, my large friend. It is all up here,' Baashir tapped his head. 'So you would be wise not to let me die today.'

'Do you know what this Gujjar looks like?' Mai asked out of the blue. 'I know we're here for him, but we do not know.'

Baashir shrugged his shoulders as he walked. 'Gujjar is a tall man and well-known for having a scar that stretches from his eyebrow here,' he touched his face, though he was looking away from them. 'To his chin, here.'

Drake lost count of the minutes, the hours. They practically climbed a mountain from the inside. It was only when Baashir slowed down that his training kicked back in.

'What is it?' he whispered.

'We're getting close. There may be sentries ahead, at the entrance to the tunnel.'

'We're close to Gujjar's camp?'

'A few hundred feet ahead.'

Drake laid a hand on Baashir's shoulder, stopping him. Everyone moved in front of him. Drake hugged the curve of the cave wall, started inching forward. His gun was ready.

More importantly, so was his knife. He didn't want to make any excess noise just yet.

He came around a bend and, there in front of him, was the wide cave entrance. It was a jagged semi-circle and, from his vantage point below, revealed nothing but the night sky. That, and the two figures that sat in the entrance.

Two men, with their backs to the caves, staring out, presumably, over Gujjar's camp. Both men held guns between their legs and were smoking. They were chatting quietly.

Drake turned back to the others. 'Sentries,' he whispered. 'Two.' He drew his knife.

Dahl joined him up front. Together, they crept forward, approaching the backs of the two guards. The first thing the guards knew of an enemy's presence was the cold, thin steel slicing through their windpipes, and by then it was far too late.

Drake laid his man down gently on the ground and then dragged his dying body back into the cave system. Baashir averted his eyes, gagging. Drake left his man bundled in a corner. Dahl threw his on top.

As a team, they carefully approached the cave entrance.

Drake stayed low, crawling. The camp came into view a few inches at a time. It was a mishmash of block buildings and wooden structures, of campfires and braziers burning solid fuel, of groups of men, of parked-up trucks and shelters that might hold arms or food supplies or horses. It sprawled for a few acres across the rocky plateau below.

Drake took out a pair of binoculars and studied it closer. Beside him, Dahl and Hayden did the same. They scanned the camp for several minutes.

'It's badly lit, which is a plus,' the Swede said. 'Other than that, I see nothing that will help us.'

Drake agreed. There were no obvious structures that may house the bomb, nothing that told them where Gujjar slept or worked out of. They didn't even know what the militia leader looked like other than a few observations. But speaking of faces, there were many ethnicities below; some men were clearly European mercenaries.

He glanced back at the dead guards. 'We can wear their clothes, blend in,' he said. 'Move among them. Then we can bring some more back for the others.'

Dahl nodded. Soon, the men were ready to go, properly attired. They first sat in the cave entrance exactly as the dead men had done, praying that there wouldn't be a shift change anytime soon, and then slowly started making their way down the mountain. They carried their own guns. Less than a minute later, they came to the floor of the plateau.

Drake found the first unfortunate individual, a man taking a leak behind a truck. He used his knife once again, stripped the body of its outer clothing, and then rolled it completely under the truck. Dahl did the same with another man. Soon, they'd carried three more sets of clothing back up to the cave.

Dahl wiped the sweat from his face. 'The rest of you should be okay,' he said. 'I've spotted a few mercs around wearing European clothing.'

Two by two, they made their way to the plateau floor, leaving Baashir behind to hide among the rocks.

They gathered around the back of a truck.

'It's a thankless task, yes,' Drake said quickly. 'Every shelter, every hut, every building. We're looking for that nuke. If you see it, jump on the comms. That's it.'

He was aware of the long hours that had passed since Gujjar took delivery of the weapon. He knew they were behind in the race. But what more could they do? The U.S. couldn't just go blundering into Pakistan, all weapons blazing. Equally, though, they couldn't just let the theft of a nuclear weapon go unchallenged.

The team split up without another word. Drake checked the back of the truck they were hiding behind, then the next and the next in line. He worked quickly and smoothly, jumping up into the back of one vehicle to check out a suspicious-looking crate. It turned out to be an unopened box of HK MP5's. Drake continued his search of the rows of trucks. After that, he moved on to the huddle of nearby buildings.

Somewhere, within this huddle of militiamen, there lurked one of the worst nightmares of the modern world. Drake just hoped he could find it before Gujjar decided what the hell he wanted to do with it.

CHAPTER FIFTEEN

Alicia ducked between buildings, flitting from shadow to shadow. She wore one of the stolen items of clothing simply because they'd spotted no other women here. The garb hid her identity well. She tried the handle on the first building, found it unlocked, and took a quick glance inside. It was storage, full of building and digging equipment, everything from a shovel to a jackhammer, a bag of cement to a grungy mixer.

Alicia moved quickly, only too aware that they'd already dropped more than a few bodies in their wake. A bit of bad luck, and someone would raise the alarm quickly. And bad luck really was Alicia's middle name. More than the others, she drew it constantly.

Of course, lately things had taken a bit of an upturn. She and Drake were making their relationship work; she was ribbing Mai consistently, almost every day, and they were no longer stuck mooching around Washington, DC. A stolen nuke might not be good for the world, but it sure kept Alicia Myles on the move.

She cleared a second building and then a third. They were all storage sheds. Alicia walked steadily between buildings, keeping her head down as she passed a man going the other way. He didn't even look at her, intent on his job. She approached a fourth building and paused at the entrance.

Inside, she could hear laughter. Alicia put a hand on the door handle. A quick glimpse wouldn't hurt; a quick look around and then a hasty retreat.

She opened the door, stuck her head in. Three pairs of eyes swivelled towards her. The men were lounging on ratty sofas, their feet up, boots off. They held bottles of beer in their hands and were all staring at a television screen that was showing a football match. The picture was jumpy, erratic, but the men seemed to enjoy it.

Alicia made her recce in just a few seconds. She put up a hand, started backing out of the room, when one man said, 'Hey, that's a fucking woman.' Another said, 'Grab her.' And then the men were moving. They dropped their beer bottles and scrambled off their chairs; their bare feet slapping the floor. Alicia didn't want the fight to spread outside, so stepped back into the room and closed the door behind her.

The men pulled up short.

'What the-'

She didn't wait for them to finish. These men, these animals, had chased her because she was a woman. If a man had entered, they'd have taken no notice. Now, they were going to wish they hadn't.

She kicked out at the first, broke his knee and saw him face plant the floor. She whipped her knife out, danced around the second man's swipe and buried her blade between his third and fourth rib, whipping it quickly back out. By the time the third man swung a fist at her, Alicia was dancing aside, three times as fast, ducking to the left and then stepping in, jamming her knife in his stomach and lifting him by the neck, carrying him back across the floor.

The guy she'd sent to the floor first was whining.

Alicia, not wanting to attract more than her fair share of

attention, dropped the third man in a heap and leapt back for the first man. She jumped onto his back, reached down, and slit his throat from ear to ear. The sound of his blood spattering the ground told her he was dead, or soon would be.

She rose. The three men had learned the error of their ways, not that they'd be able to tell anyone about it. And now there were three more bodies to contend with.

Alicia found the key, left the building and broke the key off in the lock. She hoped that would keep people out for a short time, at least. Maybe they wouldn't notice and assume someone had simply locked the door from the inside. It was hope, and the more bodies they dropped, the harder it was going to be.

Alicia slipped quietly towards the next building.

Mai drifted through the shadows, using her skills to blend with the pools of darkness. This had once been her life, her sole existence. She had come a long way since then, embarked on a great journey, and she still had no clue where she was going.

Or who she really was.

The ninja? The policewoman? One of the founding members of the Ghost Squadron, or team *Spear*, as it had then been known? That had been a long time ago. Many missions had passed since the *Spear* days. Mai remembered when she and Drake had been an item, when they had searched through the gates of hell, when a nuclear weapon had devastated Devil's Island.

Speaking of nukes...

She focused on the moment. A group of men passed her by, not noticing her in the shadows. They were laughing and joking, smoking and holding their guns in neutral positions. They seemed happy, and Mai wondered what calibre of man would be happy doing a job like this. She shrugged, turned her head, and looked for a building to investigate.

The first, a low-slung shed, contained heaps of canned food. There were also several containers of water in there. A back-up storeroom. She moved on to the next. Constructed of blocks, this building looked far more sturdy than the first. She could hear noises coming from within. A little peek wouldn't hurt.

The door was ajar. She pushed it a little further and then glanced inside. A man sat facing her. His MP5 was laid out on the table in front of him and he was using an oily cloth to clean it. The guy looked focused. He didn't even glance up as Mai looked around.

And saw the large tarpaulin-covered crate in the corner behind the man.

She cursed silently, but didn't back away. She walked boldly into the room. The guy still didn't look up. Instead, he inspected his weapon and spoke with his head down.

'What do you want?'

Mai closed the gap between them, a shade slinking through the air.

Finally, he looked up as Mai sat on top of the table next to him. His eyes went wide, registering shock. His mouth hung open. Mai put him to sleep in just a few seconds, using a palm and then her fist. She debated sliding her knife across his throat, but then decided she could just as easily tie and gag him. She took a few moments to do that and then slid his frame off the chair and into a corner, where she covered it over with tarpaulin sheets and then made them look messy, as if they were just a piled-up heap of tatty rags.

Mai stepped over to the covered crate and looked inside.

It was just an oblong wooden box, and it contained six RPG's along with a few grenades. She debated disabling the weapons, but then decided she didn't have the time. Every moment they lingered and searched boxes for the wrong item was a moment they risked discovery and capture.

She moved on. Left the building and moved to the next one. The shadows seemed to cling to her, just a dark figure that blended with her surroundings, flitting from one door to the next, a silhouette in the night. The trick was to move fluidly, lithely, not sharply.

And Mai knew all the tricks.

CHAPTER SIXTEEN

Between them, the Ghost Squadron ticked off building after building, stayed mostly out of trouble, and dealt with it where they had to.

Drake's ear crackled with a sudden communication.

'I've got Gujjar,' Dahl's voice said. 'Big hut next to the building that looks like a coral. Black metal door.'

Steadily, the Ghost Squadron made their way through the darkened camp, stepping gracefully from corner to corner, using the darkness and the obscurity, sometimes walking with their heads down past several armed men, sometimes creeping in the shadows of the surrounding mountains.

They converged on Gujjar's hut.

One by one, they entered. It was quite a crowd that ended up standing beside Dahl as he sat beside Gujjar, his knife to the man's throat.

'Say hello to all my little friends,' the Swede said.

Gujjar was tall, unkempt, and gangly. As Baashir had assured them, there was an old scar that ran almost the length of his face. His beard was straggly, his hands filthy. His eyes were wild, staring from face to face as if trying to take them all in.

'What do you want with me?' he asked in English.

Drake bent down so that he was face to face with the militia leader.

'Nuclear weapon,' he said. 'Where is it?'

Gujjar's face instantly transformed into a grin. 'Oh, that. I knew taking that in would cause trouble, but I just couldn't turn down the money.'

'Taking it in?' Mai said. 'You make it sound like a stray.'

'In effect, that's exactly what it is. But I'm sure someone will take it in, eventually.'

Dahl let the man feel the blade of the knife against his skin. 'Talk to us.'

'I am talking. I don't think you will kill me. You need me. You need to know about the nuke, right?'

Alicia, as expected, stepped up. 'We don't fuck around, asshole.'

And she rammed her knife into his thigh. Dahl quickly clamped the man's mouth as his eyes bulged and he tried to let out a piercing scream. The only sound that emerged was a muffled squawk.

'I'd talk to us,' Hayden said.

Alicia wiggled her knife. 'Quickly,' she said.

Dahl kept his hand over the man's mouth until his screams appeared to have subsided. Then he carefully removed it, a finger at a time. Drake still stared into Gujjar's eyes.

'We're special forces,' he said evenly. 'Luckily for you, we're not here to kill you or your men. But we are here to collect that nuke. Now, tell me where it is.'

Gujjar spat on the floor. He glanced down at his bleeding thigh. 'It is nothing,' he said. 'I am paid to keep my mouth shut.'

Dahl clamped him again. Alicia didn't hesitate. She stabbed the other thigh, and this time kept her knife in the wound. Gujjar writhed and let out muffled screams and tried to throw Dahl off. The attempt was laughable.

'You're making this really hard on yourself,' Drake whispered.

At that moment, there was a knock at the door.

'Gujjar?' a voice shouted. 'You in there? I need to talk with you.'

The team stiffened and then moved away from the door. Dahl kept his hand around Gujjar's mouth. Cam stepped to the door and opened it slowly towards him, taking cover behind it.

A figure stepped in from out of the darkness.

The figure blinked, eyes adjusting to the light. By the time he could see, Shaw had delivered two blows to the solar plexus that stunned him, and Kenzie had fixed her own hand over his mouth to stop him from crying out. She forced him to his knees.

The newcomer now faced Gujjar, their faces a few feet apart. The man's eyes were wide and scared.

'Nuclear weapon,' Drake went through the same spiel. 'The first of you to tell us where it is lives.'

The men stared at each other. Gujjar tried to snarl, fighting against Dahl's grip. Alicia's blade was still stuck in his thigh. The newcomer was staring at it with terrified eyes.

Drake levelled his Glock at Gujjar's head. Shaw aimed her own handgun at the new guy's. Slowly, their mouths were released.

'I ask again,' Drake said. 'And I want to hear just a whisper in reply. Where's the nuke right now?'

The new guy opened his mouth to speak, but Gujjar jumped right over him. 'It's gone,' he said. 'We moved it on.'

Drake felt a sinking feeling. 'What are you talking about?'

'We took the nuke in almost a week ago. It didn't stay long.'

'You're just a part of a network,' Hayden said.

'Yes.'

'Who's the end user?'

'I don't know that. That's the whole point of the network. Nobody knows who's beyond the next man on the list. It could be reams of paper long for all I know.'

'Who did you sell it to?' Dahl asked.

At this point, the newcomer jumped in, clearly not wanting to die. 'Colonel Mitrovic,' he said.

'Who is Colonel Mitrovic?'

'He commands an army of rebels in Serbia,' the man said. 'He's one of the worst men on the planet.'

Drake looked at Gujjar, the militia leader. 'How so?'

'Mitrovic takes great pleasure in murdering his own people. Genocide is a way of life for him. Some say he practically runs Serbia and that the government fear him. Mitrovic is… an unpleasant character.'

Drake shook his head. 'You knobs need talk. You're all as bad as each other.'

'I am not on that terrible scale-' Gujjar began, his voice slightly raised, but then Alicia wiggled her knife in his thigh. Gujjar clammed up. Dahl grabbed his mouth and closed it just in case.

'And where does this Colonel Mitrovic operate exactly?' Kinimaka asked.

The two men shook their heads and tried to offer a few suggestions. Drake guessed they were wild guesses, something to placate the enemy.

'We missed it again,' Dahl was saying almost to himself. 'And we're just under a week behind the damn thing.'

'Mitrovic is next.' Drake said.

'The weapon went on a long journey,' Gujjar offered. 'It is a clumsy, big weapon, and it will have taken them a lot of resources to get it moved to their camp. It would have taken time. If you get to Mitrovic fast, you may find that he still has it.'

'It's who's behind all this that worries me,' Dahl said. 'Because they clearly want this nuke for a purpose.'

'And they're obviously well connected,' Hayden said. 'Huge players. All we can do is try to keep track.'

'Speaking of that, hadn't we better get out of here?' Cam asked.

Just then, there was a commotion outside the door.

CHAPTER SEVENTEEN

Drake held up a hand, silencing everyone.

It was a loud noise, the scuffle of several pairs of boots, the grunts of more than one man. Nobody was trying to be quiet. Drake saw a look of hope cross Gujjar's face, and then the man's mouth opened wide to yell out a warning.

Drake filled it with the butt of his rifle. Teeth flew. Blood fountained over the man's face. He fell back with a gurgle. Drake turned to Cam, who was closest to the door.

'Ready?' he said. 'Open it.'

The young man crouched, grabbed the handle, and pulled the door in as fast as he was able. Drake got a glimpse of several bodies outside, probably three men. They were laughing, their voices raised, and they didn't stand a chance.

First Cam stepped out, then Shaw, employing their newly learned skills with the old methods of attack. Then Mai was among the enemy, slipping from body to body, punching and kicking and debilitating. Kenzie followed them, a knife in each hand. Where the others stunned and broke their foes, Kenzie finished them with a few telling slices and slashes of her weapons. From Drake's vantage point, it was a mess, just writhing shadows in the night, but from closer up it was a bone-cracking, bloody rout.

But it wasn't noiseless. The men yelled out as they died. They shouted as their arms and legs cracked, as the sharp blade entered their bodies. In the end, though, they all collapsed in a heap.

The entire team rushed out to help. They dragged the dead men inside quickly and shut the door. Gujjar had a haunted look on his face. The other man just looked terrified and put his hands in the air. Drake nodded at them both.

'Tie them up very tightly.'

Alicia, Hayden and Kinimaka jumped to it. Gujjar was bleeding profusely from the mouth, but they had no choice but to gag him, hogtie him, and leave him on the floor of the hut. They quickly did the same with the second man.

'Move,' Dahl said. 'We're dead if we hang around here.'

Cam had the door open. They all stepped out into the night. Already, they could hear a commotion running through the camp, see figures dashing through the darkness. They decided it was best to join them and hurried off in the direction of the caves, sticking together because it looked, at this moment, like the camp's men were gathering in groups. Maybe they saw strength in numbers.

Drake ran past three men, trying to look purposeful. One of them cried out to him, a question in a language he didn't understand, but he waved it away and kept running. The others were all around him. The caves grew nearer, the rocky edifice towering over them.

A face flashed out of the darkness, a European face. It was wide and fleshy and bushy and its little piggy eyes latched straight on to Drake.

'Hey,' the man grumbled. 'I fucking know you.'

Drake couldn't believe what he was seeing. He recognised the face too. He'd worked with it before he joined the Spear team long ago. The sight of the man brought back unpleasant memories.

'You still a goody two shoes, Drake?'

The Yorkshireman barely slowed down. He let loose a haymaker, smashed the fleshy guy in one of his plump cheeks and watched the spark go out of his eyes. The guy collapsed in an ample heap, lights out.

'Not exactly,' Drake replied.

They jogged nearer to their target. Ahead, another knot of men was rushing towards them, shouting. Above, the glowing constellation of stars lit up the vault of the night. The women moved to the centre of the pack, keeping their heads down. The men nodded at their supposed brethren as the two groups passed in the semi-darkness.

'Fight's this way, bro,' one man called out.

'No fight,' Dahl called back. 'We've been sent to the perimeter.'

That caused a few moments of confusion, but both groups kept going. Drake came across another straggler who challenged them. Before he could do anything, Alicia had laid him out and then proceeded to drag him under the nearest truck. Drake wasn't sure if the man's biggest shock had come from Alicia's fist or from recognising she was a woman.

'It's been a long time since they saw any females,' she said, as she lugged the body about. 'I feel sorry for the mountain goats around here.'

Finally, they reached the foothills. Drake took a moment to scan their backs. He slowed, turned around, took in Gujjar's camp. It was noisy, but not excessively so. They hadn't found Gujjar and the bodies yet. That scenario wouldn't last forever, though.

They hurried up the mountain, following the same passes they'd used to descend it not so long ago. The rocky heights stretched above them. Drake ran sure-footedly, glancing back as they rose above the camp. They stayed low, hugging the darkness. It took them just over ten minutes to reach the cave entrance and, by then, they were all panting a little.

Baashir was waiting for them, sitting unmoving and cross-legged on a rock. The initial sight of him made Drake jump.

'Crap,' he said. 'Mate, I thought you were fucking Gollum.'

Baashir looked aggrieved. He jumped down from the rock, looked over the camp with a sniff and assessed them.

'Did you get what you came for?'

'Not exactly. But we aren't out of the race yet.' Dahl said.

Baashir turned away and led them back into the caves. From the heights, Drake took a last look over the camp below. There was a rising noise, more running figures. They had probably found Gujjar by now. Shadows flitted back and forth, most of them brandishing weapons, none of them looking particularly wary, which would have been the right thing to do. Men were running to the arms stores, clambering with bleary eyes out of huts and tents, flinging open the doors of other buildings. A search was underway.

It wouldn't be long before they thought about the caves.

Drake hurried inside and followed the others back down the narrow passages. The going was easier this time, always downhill, and the claustrophobic parts didn't feel so bad because they knew they were headed out, rather than in. He ran easily at the rear of the pack, listening out for any signs of pursuit.

There were none.

A while later, Baashir led them out of the foot of the caves. The night was still dark, the stars still illuminating part of the sky. The moon hung over a lofty peak, its surface apparently dissected by the jagged mountain. The team didn't slow; they hurried all the way back to town.

Along the way, Hayden asked Baashir if there was a hotel in town. Anywhere they could get their heads down and make a plan.

'There is one place. I'd call it a guesthouse. It won't be cheap, though.'

Hayden sighed. 'Is anything cheap where you're concerned, Baashir?'

'Hey, I do not make up the rules, nor the prices. It is commerce, right?'

'Commerce?' Alicia repeated. 'I'll commerce your ass if you lead us to a fleapit.'

'That actually sounds kind of nice.'

With Baashir and Alicia trading ever more dubious insults, the team made their way back to town.

Drake did manage to get his head down for a while. The bed was scratchy and lumpy, but he'd slept in far worse conditions. The team was housed in three rooms, using mattresses that were laid out on the floor. They left two sentries on guard, one watching the rooms, one watching the house from afar just in case Gujjar visited the town during the night. Not that they thought that would happen. The assault on his camp could have come from any direction, from any militia. He wouldn't know where to turn and would eventually put it down to an unpleasant experience. But the Ghost Squadron was nothing if it wasn't a cautious animal.

Six hours later, the team met up outside, seated around plastic tables and in plastic chairs. They had some kind of breakfast laid out before them and many mugs of tea and coffee. There was also fresh bottled water. It was a bedraggled group that met up that morning.

'No shower,' Alicia complained, and then looked at Kenzie. 'You stink.'

'Only of roses, my darling.'

'I noticed Dahl has kept his distance this morning.'

Kenzie looked at the Swede, who held up a hand. 'Don't get me involved.'

'We're not the cuddling kind.'

Alicia ate her breakfast and then sipped her coffee. She sat back, waiting for someone to start the conversation.

Hayden could always be relied upon to speak up. 'We need to discuss everything Gujjar told us before we make a call,' she said.

'Which wasn't a whole lot,' Kinimaka said.

'Maybe not. But we did learn new information. We learned that this Colonel Mitrovic from Serbia has the bomb now and that he's a bad dude. He could easily be the end user.' Hayden sat back.

'If so, what's his angle?' Drake asked. 'Who's he gonna nuke? His own people?'

'Gujjar said the man commits genocide on a daily basis.'

'But still... that would make him the king of a charred land. Who wants to be the king of a charred land?' Mai asked the question.

'I think the answer to that question would surprise you,' Drake said. 'More than one man, more than a dozen, I would think.'

'They all have ways of justifying it,' Dahl said. 'Warped ways.'

'Call Bryant,' Kinimaka said. 'Every second we sit around is a second wasted.'

Alicia fixed Mai with a grin. 'Yeah, call Bryant,' she said. 'Don't forget to tell him how much you love him.'

The Japanese woman flipped her off.

It was Hayden who called Bryant. She told him about Gujjar, about everything the militia leader had said. She told him about the well-travelled nuke and their fears that Colonel Mitrovic might be the end user.

'I've heard of Mitrovic,' Bryant told them. 'In fact, I have several men inserted into his regime. But we need to be careful. They're deeply embedded. I'll get the transport organised for you.'

'You're sending us to Serbia now?' Dahl asked.

'I think you should stay on the trail of the nuke.'

Drake leaned forward. 'Before it vanishes altogether.'

The deeper meaning of his words, the terror they instilled, quieted all those around the table and also Bryant far away in his office.

What was Mitrovic really going to do with that bomb?

CHAPTER EIGHTEEN

The big military transport rumbled through the night towards Serbia. On board, Drake and his team managed to resupply their weapons, their rations, and the rest of their packs. They sat back in the webbed seats, their heads against the shuddering sides of the plane, and tried to catch a little shut-eye.

Drake snoozed. Always best to catch some sleep when you could. For a long while, no one spoke in the massive cargo hold aboard the big plane as everyone slept or dozed or just sat back with their eyes closed.

As they neared Serbia, the phone brought them all to full wakefulness.

Hayden answered it. 'Yeah?'

'It's Bryant. I have some good news for you.' The man's voice rattled through the speakerphone.

'Did they find the nuke?'

'No, no, not that good. I told you I had men embedded in Mitrovic's organisation, didn't I?'

'You did.' Hayden said.

'On the quiet, through back channels, they have managed to arrange a meeting for you, a meeting with Colonel Mitrovic.'

Drake blinked rapidly. 'Are you fucking kidding me?'

'Isn't he supposed to be some kind of madman?' Mai asked.

'Madman? Well, mad is a relative term. Mitrovic isn't a good man, but I wouldn't say he's *mad.*'

'I would,' Alicia said quietly. 'And I don't understand why we would try to meet him.'

'He runs Serbia behind the scenes. And admits he's taken delivery of the nuke. At least, he does to me. You guys are the closest team we have.'

'Shouldn't we be going in there with all guns blazing?' Dahl asked.

'Too many men. Mitrovic has an army.'

'So we're gonna *chat?*' Alicia blurted out

'That's the idea.'

Drake didn't like it. 'What does Sutherland say about this?'

'The FBI like the idea. They see it as a de-escalation. He did mention that he'd only allow certain people to do the talking, though.' Bryant cleared his throat as though embarrassed.

Kenzie was already looking at Alicia. 'That rules you out.'

The Englishwoman nodded. 'Actually, I can understand that.'

'Drake, Hayden, Dahl, Kinimaka. You four are the nominated speakers.'

'Me?' Mano said, surprised. 'I can put my foot in my mouth just as easily as I can walk into a table.'

Bryant pretended not to hear the comment. 'You're landing in half an hour. An entourage will meet you and take you straight to see Mitrovic.'

Drake couldn't believe what he was hearing. 'Bryant,' he said. 'This is a trap.'

'The higher-ups are keen to explore every possibility,' Bryant said. 'It's out of my control.'

Drake looked irritable. 'It appears to be out of our control, too.'

Nobody liked it. The plane roared on, carrying them to their inexorable fate. Was Mitrovic playing a clever game? Was he genuine? Or was this his way of neutralising a threat?

All these questions were on Drake's mind as the plane came in to land.

The engines powered down. The plane finally stopped juddering. They shrugged into their backpacks and made their way to the door. One of the co-pilots was already there, operating the mechanism that opened it. Drake reached the opening first.

He got a look outside. Sunshine bathed the tarmac and glinted off the bodies of the cars that waited down there. Drake could see black limousines with tinted windows. He ducked his head so that he could exit the plane and start down the steps, kept hold of his backpack and kept his hand near his gun.

Once on the tarmac, a man wearing wraparound sunglasses came forward to meet them. He held out a hand, but only Hayden shook it. When he spoke, it was with a thick European accent.

'I am Zoran. The Colonel is waiting,' he said. 'I will take you to him. He is looking forward to your talk. But there can be no weapons, I'm afraid.'

'You should be afraid, mate,' Alicia said quickly. 'I could-'

Hayden held up a hand to silence her. 'Please,' she said, and then addressed Zoran. 'You are armed. You are an army. Cover us, yes, but I won't let you take our weapons away.'

'The colonel will not like it.'

'The colonel can go suck a-' again Alicia couldn't help herself.

Again, Hayden cut her off. 'The colonel wanted to talk to us. He arranged this. We bear him no animosity.'

Thankfully, Alicia stayed silent.

Zoran licked his lips nervously. 'We will cover you every step of the way. The Colonel is expecting a private meeting, but that will have to change. Get in the car.'

Drake didn't like it. Every bone in his body rebelled. If the directive hadn't come down from the assistant director of the FBI, he'd have refused it. But they owed Sutherland – they owed him almost as much as he owed them.

The team gathered around, hands close to their guns. Drake saw a dozen armed men clustered around the cars, most of them wearing sunglasses and suits and some even holding their guns ready. There was no doubt that the enemy outnumbered them.

'A dozen?' Dahl whispered in his ear. 'Clearly, Mitrovic doesn't know my reputation.'

Drake cleared his throat. 'I think you mean *our* reputation.'

'No,' Dahl replied. 'Honestly, I meant mine.'

They climbed into the cars, taking the back seats only. The engines were already running, the air con welcome after the heat outside. It was awkward in there with guns and backpacks, but they made it work. Zoran climbed into the front of Drake's car and spoke an order in Serbian. Immediately, the vehicle set off.

They left the plane behind, along with the airfield. Zoran immediately started to talk.

'The Colonel wants no quarrel with your country. That is why he wishes to discuss the, ah, package.'

'It's made him a marked man,' Hayden pressed the point.

'The Colonel understands that. But he thinks you will understand.'

Drake could think of a dozen things to say in response, none of them pleasant. But, somehow, he managed to hold his tongue. 'Our country will be quite interested to hear the colonel's excuses.'

Zoran frowned. 'The Colonel does not believe in excuses, I'm afraid. He does what he wants, takes what he wants. That is how he has become such an outstanding leader.'

Drake again struggled with several replies. In the end, he didn't have to because Hayden spoke up far more diplomatically than he would have.

'It surprised us to hear he wanted to talk.'

Zoran laughed. 'Your country is enormous and has many weapons. Serbia, not so much.'

Drake didn't laugh. It was all he could do not to mention war crimes.

The car wound its way through the verdant countryside, cutting through hedgerows and flat fields. The road was smooth and wide and soon they were approaching a compound, fenced off with chain-link mesh topped with rolls of razor wire. Drake hadn't been fully aware that the colonel lived in an actual camp. He had imagined a grand house or similar.

'We're arriving,' Zoran said unnecessarily.

Drake studied their destination through the window. Beyond the fence he made out several block buildings, most of them one-storey. The car swept past the main entrance and drove around to a side gate where two guards leaned in through the window. Zoran gave them some spiel, and they withdrew. They opened the gates manually and then the black car zoomed through.

'You are getting close to meeting the Colonel,' Zoran said as if it was a spectacular event on the horizon.

Drake leaned forward. 'Any tips?'

'Do not stare at him. Do not hold his gaze. Make no sudden movements. Do not laugh unless he cracks a joke.'

Drake let out a breath. 'Sounds like a great guy. I can't wait to meet him.'

Everything was moving incredibly fast. He felt like the situation had got out of their control, as if they'd flown from Pakistan with one goal in mind and landed in Serbia with quite another. The powers-that-be had forced this to upon them, but that didn't mean it was the right thing to do.

Drake wondered if he should cross his fingers. Maybe that would help.

CHAPTER NINETEEN

Outside the car, the heat hit them again. Drake wasn't sure if it was normal for Serbia, but it was almost arid, as if the sun was sucking the very life out of the air. He stood in his army fatigues, his backpack strapped on, and with his gun close to hand as Zoran waited for them all to get ready. Then, he pointed unerringly at Drake, Hayden, Dahl, and Kinimaka.

'You four,' he said. 'You were agreed upon.'

Drake wondered how he knew their faces, probably by description. Which meant the American government had been doing more than chit-chatting with the Serbs. He pretended to look around at his friends, the ones they were leaving behind, but was really getting an eyeful of the camp.

It was vast, many acres large. Rows of buildings marched off into the distance, most of them relatively small, like storehouses. Several stands of trees and brush dotted the area. Also, Drake spotted parked trucks and vans and cars. Soldiers dashed and jogged and ambled through the whole area, men and women, and there were several dozen guards manning all the entrances. Drake noticed at least one high watchtower in the middle-distance.

'Are you ready?' Zoran asked.

Hayden told him they were. Zoran led the way from the

car along a winding, gravelled path with neat borders. The path looped among trees and then alongside a high hedge until Drake could finally see a dwelling ahead.

It wasn't everything he had expected.

It was another block building, only this one had two floors and a red-tiled roof. The door consisted of black sheet-metal, the windows grimy and unwashed. Drake imagined it might be hard getting a window cleaner around these parts. They crunched right up to the door and then watched as it opened as if pulled from the inside.

A man greeted them. Drake blinked rapidly, surprised. The man was dressed like a butler, complete with a white shirt, cufflinks, white gloves, and a butler's tie. He wore a grey vest and grey striped trousers and bowed as he saw them approaching.

'Very good to meet you,' he said. 'Won't you come inside?'

Drake hesitated. Dahl gawped at the man. Hayden and Kinimaka both stepped over the threshold first, masking the others' surprise and reluctance.

'May I offer you a drink?' the butler asked.

And now another butler approached. This one carried a large, round silver platter, which he held out toward them and politely asked them for their guns. They refused, casting a glance at the silent Zoran who only nodded as if that were enough to shoo the new butler away.

It was. The first butler now asked that they follow him to the drawing room.

Drake didn't like it at all. It wasn't just wrong; it was fucking insane. This man, this colonel, Mitrovic, clearly wasn't running on all twelve cylinders.

'The drawing room?' Dahl asked.

'Yes please. This way.'

The floors were rough concrete, the walls a slightly

lighter version of the same. There were no decorations, no pictures on the wall, no ornaments in sight. It was nothing more than a shell, a concrete box. The only fixtures Drake could see were the light fittings.

The butler led them through an empty room, towards a far door. There were no guards in evidence. Drake was becoming increasingly uneasy. At the far door, the butler stopped, held up a hand and then peered inside.

'Sir,' he said. 'I have the Americans here.'

Drake begged to differ, but said nothing. He could imagine Dahl feeling the same way.

'Oh, send them in immediately,' a deep voice boomed.

Drake steeled himself, not knowing what to expect beyond the drawing-room door. As one, the team was ushered through. Drake took it all in as fast as he could.

Basically unfurnished, the drawing-room was wide and vacant. There were some long curtains across the windows, a couple of free-standing light fittings and a dark oak desk smack bang in the middle of the room. The Colonel was standing behind that desk.

Drake almost cringed when he saw him.

The butler escorted them further inside. Drake felt reluctant. Colonel Mitrovic was a tall and wide man. His hair was black and hung down to his shoulders. He wore a regal robe, golden gloves and shiny golden boots. He carried a gleaming black walking stick with a silver-plated, knobbly tip. As he walked towards them, the walking stick tapped on the ground. The man gave them a hundred megawatt smile.

'My American friends, how are you? It is so good to see you here, in my humble home,' he gestured at the mostly empty room. 'I would ask you to sit but seem to have misplaced all my chairs.'

Mitrovic laughed loudly. There was a large bottle of

liquid on his desk and two stacks of glasses. He stood smiling at them for what seemed like an interminably long time and then turned and started pouring out the liquid.

Hayden stepped forward, face carefully neutral. 'It is good to meet you too, Colonel. What a wonderful home you have here.'

'Isn't it?' Mitrovic said as he poured. 'My manservants keep it in wonderful condition.'

Drake winced. *Manservants?*

'Here,' Mitrovic spread the glasses out on the table. 'It is fifty-year old bourbon. Take yourself a glass and enjoy.' He swilled his down in less than two seconds.

Hayden smiled and clasped her hands in front of her. None of the team moved forward. Mitrovic fixed them with a painted on smile.

'So why have you come here seeking my help?'

Drake tried not to cringe. The colonel knew exactly why they were here, and it wasn't to "seek his help."

Hayden handled it better than he would have. 'A good question, Colonel. Our government has an interest, a profound interest, in a... shall we say... *package* you have recently taken possession of.'

'I come into possession of many packages, miss. What is it you want exactly?'

Mitrovic was being a dick, Drake thought.

Hayden plunged in. 'The nuclear weapon?' she said, sotto voice.

'Ah, yes,' Mitrovic tapped the concrete floor with the tip of his cane. 'The nuclear weapon. No doubt, your government players are wondering what I intend to do with it.'

'It had crossed our mind,' Drake said impatiently.

'Well, the answer is outside, in a shed, under cover. Perhaps I will take you to it. Would you like that?'

Drake couldn't get a proper read on the man. Was he deranged? Was he playing with them, playing a dangerous game? Or was he two tonnes short of a full load? Drake imagined it was the latter.

Hayden said, 'You will show us the weapon?'

'Sure, sure, you are my American friends. Why wouldn't I? Now let me get out of this infernal robe and put on some clothes.'

Mitrovic turned away. He dropped the robe. Drake averted his eyes. The colonel was naked underneath. The next few moments were ill at ease as the butler came forward with an armful of clothing and helped the colonel get dressed.

'There,' Mitrovic said finally. 'We're ready.'

Drake bristled to start shooting. That there were no guards in here, no guards in the *house*, spoke to Mitrovic's state of mind. And, Drake remembered, this guy was in charge. Some said he ran the country. Some said he answered to nobody.

A prickle ran down the length of his spine. His weapon was beside his right hand. The problem was, Mitrovic had an army outside.

Mitrovic was studying them. He offered up that beaming smile once more. He had kept his cane and now swirled it in their direction.

'If you would follow me,' he said. 'I will take you to the weapon.'

It felt all wrong. They were being swept along through circumstance, without a safety net, with no form of backup. The colonel might be manipulating them, taking the piss out of them. He could even be leading them towards their deaths. But what could they say? "No thanks, mate, I think you're a whack job?" Well... maybe.

Drake stepped aside as Mitrovic brushed past him. The

butlers still hovered in the doorway, their white-gloved hands now with Mitrovic's regal robe draped over them. Their faces were blank, their body language neutral. They didn't move as the Ghost Squadron pushed past them.

Mitrovic led them back through the house. At the doorway, Drake now noticed an umbrella stand. In an insane twist, he noticed the stand bristled not with umbrellas, but with submachine guns. Mitrovic paused next to it and took the time to pluck a couple of guns from the rack, study them, and then put all but one back. The one he kept he aimed at the floor. Then he moved to the door.

'Follow me,' he said.

Drake exchanged a glance with Hayden. Her face was unreadable, but Drake knew exactly what was going on beneath the surface. She was just as incredulous as he.

A blistering sun still blazed down outside. Drake shaded his eyes. Incredibly, unfathomably, there were still no guards nearby. They picked up the rest of the Ghost Squadron who were standing around bored and then Mitrovic led them down the curving path, looking as though he was out for an afternoon stroll.

'Pipe!' he suddenly bellowed.

Drake blinked and stared at the colonel as if he was mad. In the next moment, one of his butlers bounded past, holding a pipe between two fingers. The pipe was already lit. He passed it to the colonel and then backed away. The colonel gave the ground a double tap with his cane, puffed on his pipe, and then continued leading the way.

They followed him between low-slung buildings, still walking along the gravelled path. To left and right there was activity, soldiers dressed in green fatigues going about their business, loading weapons, gassing cars and trucks, involved in skilful drills. Some marched and some strolled and others jogged. Drake watched them, seeing quite a mismatch between them. Some were good at what they did, others were atrocious. But he saw no sign of any mercenaries. All these men appeared to belong to Mitrovic.

Ten minutes passed. Finally, they came to a structure built of block that resembled a barn. The double doors were closed and, strangely, there was a horse peering over the top of one of them. Mitrovic nodded at the barn.

'The weapon is inside?' Hyden asked.

'Take a look,' Mitrovic waved his submachine gun at the door.

Drake hesitated to move. He looked around. There were soldiers everywhere, all walking towards them. Their weapons were raised... pointed at the team.

'Take a good look.' Mitrovic raised his own weapon and placed the business end on Hayden's throat. 'Now.'

'We are representatives of the U.S. government,' Kinimaka said.

'I recognise no leadership but my own. And if I rule here, I rule everywhere. You see, everywhere is here, so the rest of it does not exist. If I cannot see it, I cannot own it, so, ergo, it isn't there. What U.S. government?'

Drake's brain hurt trying to follow that logic. He licked his lips. Whatever reality Mitrovic lived in, the *true* reality was that they were standing here, being confronted by dozens of soldiers, alongside a madman.

'Get inside with the horses,' Mitrovic said.

'Where is the weapon?' Hayden tried.

'You will soon see. Now,' he waved his gun. 'Do you see my men? They are real, and they will shoot one of you at a time if you don't all get inside the barn right now.'

Drake watched as the soldiers surrounded them in a semicircle. They could fight, they could attack, but countless weapons were being aimed at them, and Drake doubted they could take them all cleanly. Someone would get shot. It wasn't worth the risk. He trusted the others would come to the same conclusion.

Hayden pushed at the barn door. The horse backed away. The team walked through into the dingy interior as Mitrovic cackled behind them.

'Now,' he said in a loud voice. 'Bring me my slippers!'

CHAPTER TWENTY

There were three horses in the barn, several bales of hay, and a few stables. The place stank. The floor was hard earth; the walls rotting wood. Drake's team stood around, staring at each other.

'What next?' Dahl asked.

'Well, there's no nuke in here,' Hayden said.

Drake had already scanned the space. 'Is it me, or are we dealing with a total psycho?'

Kenzie nodded. 'He's even more whacked out than Alicia.'

The blonde just nodded. 'Have to agree.'

'What the hell does he want with us?' Kinimaka said. 'You can't reason with him. What's his plan?'

'I feel, with Mitrovic, that plans come and go, coalesce and melt away, in a heartbeat,' Drake said. 'His plan depends on what minute it is.'

'The guy's ultra dangerous,' Cam said.

Drake nodded in agreement. The team drew their weapons, looking at the barn door. They could see dozens of figures outside. What would Mitrovic do next?

They didn't have to wait long for an answer.

'We will interrogate them!' they heard the colonel's voice above everything else. 'Find out what they know. Bring the prisoners to me!'

It was typical, Drake thought. He'd just shoved them

into the barn and now wanted them brought before him, wanted them interrogated. It was the flighty, addled, erratic mind of the man they were dealing with.

'We're going nowhere,' Hayden said.

The soldiers grabbed the barn doors and flung them wide open. Light flooded the small space. Drake dropped to one knee, levelled his gun, and fired. Bullets slammed from his gun into the men crowded around the doorway.

He saw the Colonel hopping and laughing as the bullets flashed by. He was skipping and springing from foot to foot like a breakdancer and, miraculously, all the bullets missed him. It was his men who went down, struck on the legs and chest, spinning in place. Drake heard the other's open fire, too. Bullets riddled the air outside the barn.

The horses reared and panicked. Drake felt sorry for them. He inched closer to the entrance. Mitrovic's men were falling, collapsing, spinning away. Drake rose and started making his way forward.

Out of the barn and into the light. It was a fluid situation, and it was deadly. Mitrovic had backed up but was still hopping from foot to foot, still clutching his pipe and cane. Drake knew they had seconds to decide what to do next.

He ran for Mitrovic. There were a few soldiers in his way, so Drake elbowed one and kicked another. A third he kneed in the stomach. All the men went down, and Drake drew his handgun for the close-up shots that would kill them. Shaw was at his back, taking over the attack as Drake arrowed directly for Mitrovic.

When he got close, Mitrovic whirled. Gunfire surrounded them; the soldiers' attentions fixed on those steadily exiting the barn who used its walls and small crates for cover. Drake ducked as Mitrovic swept the cane at his head.

'Oh, darn, missed.'

The Colonel spun and whirled again, this time jabbing with the cane. Drake smashed it away with his left hand.

'Fetch me my slippers!' Mitrovic cried out.

Drake saw he was already wearing them. Somewhere in all this madness, one of the butlers had exchanged Mitrovic's boots for red silk, gold-thread slippers.

'You, my friend,' he muttered. 'Are bat-shit crazy.'

'I know!' The colonel heard him. 'And I love it!'

Drake aimed the Glock at his head. 'Where the hell is the nuke?'

Around them, it was chaos. The soldiers had their attention filled by the Ghost Squadron, who were still firing constantly from the barn, still taking cover. Eight soldiers had already died, more lie wounded, squirming on the ground. More soldiers were dashing over to join the fight.

Drake knew it was a fight and flight situation, and they had to be quick about it. They couldn't hope to stand up to the depth of Mitrovic's army. There was a large truck with a canvas cover not too far away, and he had his eyes on it.

He jumped on the comms. 'When you get a chance, someone hot wire that truck over there. It's our best way out of here.'

And then he turned back to Mitrovic.

'Hey, dickhead, where's the nuke?'

The colonel guffawed at him. 'Isn't it with the horses? Neighhhh. Oh, my, have we mislaid it?'

Drake clouted Mitrovic across the temple with the Glock. Blood sprouted forth. The colonel squinted. The guy was demented.

'What did you do with the nuke?' Drake tried again.

'I exploded it. Yes, it went *boom!* Didn't you hear? Your Washington, DC no longer exists.'

Drake tried centring the colonel with a blow to the ribs.

The man took a puff from his pipe and twirled his cane. The blood on his face trickled down his lips. Mitrovic licked at it.

'If I have to shoot you, I will,' Drake hissed. 'I don't want to shoot an unarmed madman, but I need to know what you've done with that weapon.'

'Did you ask the horses? They always talk back politely to me.'

Drake fired his handgun. The bullet flashed past Mitrovic's face, inches away. Now the colonel blinked and narrowed his eyes.

'You shot at me,' he said in a normal voice.

'I'm going to kill you and put your world out of its misery.' Drake aimed the gun at Mitrovic's forehead.

'Wait, wait. The nuke, yes? That's what you want. It was here. I know it was. I stroked it. I took all my clothes off and rode up and down its solid length. I grabbed my-'

'For fuck's sake,' Drake muttered. 'Where is it *now?*'

Mitrovic blinked. 'Yes, well, it's gone, hasn't it? Is it not there? What a shame. I seem to remember pressing buttons, hitting it with a hammer,' Mitrovic blinked. 'Nothing happened. I think it's a dud. Anyway... what was the question?'

A bullet flew between them. Drake's team was out of the barn now, staying low and firing rapidly. They sheltered behind nearby crates and oil drums and kept moving steadily forward. There were twelve soldiers lying on the ground, but another ten had arrived to back up the initial few. Still more could be seen dashing towards the battle.

Drake slapped Mitrovic with an open hand. This time, the blow stunned him, rocked his brain. The man's eyes flew wide open.

'My manservant will teach you a lesson for that!'

'You were telling me about the nuclear weapon,' Drake said. 'You were telling me where it went.'

'Oh, that. Yes, I moved it on as agreed. General Kerimov of Turkmenistan took possession,' Mitrovic leaned forward confidentially. 'He has his own country, you know.'

'When?' Drake snapped.

'Two days ago.'

Two days. That meant they had caught the nuke up rapidly. Drake asked Mitrovic for a description of this Kerimov, but the man just looked blank.

'He looks... like a man,' the colonel said.

Drake felt a bullet whizz past his face, saw Dahl racing for the nearby truck. The team was keeping Mitrovic's army at bay, but it wouldn't last for long. They'd run out of bullets before they killed all of Mitrovic's men.

'Come with me,' Drake said.

He grabbed the colonel and forced him to walk. He paraded him in front of his men, the ludicrous figure in his slippers, still carrying his pipe and cane. Drake made sure that, if any of his men opened fire, they would hit the colonel first. As he walked past his team, they quickly joined him, heading for the truck.

It fired into life. Dahl looked back through the open window. The team scrambled up into the truck's rear area, dragging Mitrovic with them.

'If you follow,' Drake yelled. 'We dice him up a piece at a time,' he brandished his knife. 'I will honestly throw him to you bit by bit off the back of this truck.'

Weapons lowered. The soldiers looked ashen faced but severe. Drake made sure they could all see Mitrovic.

'Drive,' he said.

Dahl put his foot down. Mitrovic wobbled. If Drake hadn't had hold of his collar, the colonel would have face-planted right off the truck. Dahl guided the vehicle along the track towards the side gates and then straight through. The guards were alert enough to salute as he went by.

'It's Mitrovic,' Drake said, realising. 'The guards don't

know what's real and what isn't. They're used to his insanities.'

'That's why they saluted the people kidnapping him?' Mai asked.

'That's exactly why.'

Drake forced Mitrovic's arm into the air, waving it as they pulled away from the gate. At least one guard waved back. Drake guessed this was the most surreal, most bizarre escape he'd ever pulled off.

It wouldn't last long, though, not when the bulk of the army got involved.

Dahl guided the truck along the gravel path, heading away from Mitrovic's compound. The flat fields were to the left and right again, and Drake hoped Dahl remembered exactly where they'd left the plane. Almost as an afterthought, he radioed the pilot and told him to get it ready to leave at a moment's notice.

'What did he tell you?' Hayden gestured at Mitrovic.

Drake explained what he knew, which was very little.

'The nuke's moved on.' Hayden shook her head. 'It's better travelled than I am, but we do seem to be gaining on it.'

'Two days behind,' Kinimaka cursed. 'We just missed it.'

'But what kind of madman would put Mitrovic in the loop?' Alicia asked.

The colonel turned and frowned at her. 'I get the impression you don't like me, young lady. I will have to chide you for that.'

Alicia saw the plane, stuck her boot out and kicked Mitrovic off the back of the moving truck. The colonel bounced in the dirt and, as they roared away, held up a hand.

'I'm okay!' he shouted.

Drake was already thinking about what came next.

CHAPTER TWENTY ONE

'We're catching up,' Hayden said. 'But this is one elaborate plot. This way of maintaining secrecy and moving the bomb quickly. It's crazy ingenious.'

They were seated aboard the plane, winging their way towards Turkmenistan. They were waiting for a call back from Bryant, but had already anticipated what their boss was going to say.

He would tell them to stick with the mission.

The flight would take around four and a half hours. By then, they hoped to know a lot more about this new player, General Kerimov. Mitrovic had told Drake that he controlled a *country*, but that couldn't be Turkmenistan itself. Perhaps the Colonel was exaggerating. Of course, could they trust anything that came out of Mitrovic's mouth?

They rested, ate rations, and drank bottled water. They sat back with their eyes closed. The mission was weighing on them, feeling like some elongated op without end. Of course, the problem was the nuke. It had always been the problem. They couldn't just stop tracking it. There was still an end user, though that person appeared to be nowhere in sight. The nuke had travelled lands relatively close to each other so far. It had been easily shipped or flown or even transported over ground.

Drake spooned up a few rations, trying not to think

about the taste. They were nasty, but they were calorie-heavy and would give him the energy he needed to get through the next several hours. He looked over at Hayden when her phone rang.

'Bryant,' she said.

It was the same speech as before. Yes, they wanted the Ghost Squadron to continue its pursuit of the nuke. Yes, they would lend all assistance. Yes, they had to work faster, harder, take more risks.

Drake asked Bryant what he knew of General Kerimov.

'For God's sake, tell me he isn't a whacko,' Alicia said.

'No, I think Kerimov is quite normal for a man who's criminally insane,' Bryant told them. 'As far as we can tell, at least. He lives on the eastern outskirts of Turkmenistan. We can get you into the country using diplomatic channels, but after that, you're on your own. Rustle up some transport somehow and make your way to his house.'

'House?' Drake imagined a two-up, two-down with a white picket fence.

'Mansion, palace,' Bryant said. 'The guy owns a sprawling home from which he conducts his business. Kerimov has a wide network of contacts, of men who are beholden to him. Basically, he's a tyrant. Anyone who crosses him ends up six feet under.'

'Not normal then,' Dahl said. 'Just another asshole dictator who wants something he hasn't got and will sacrifice anyone to get it.'

Drake nodded. 'We know a few of those,' he said. 'We've come across a few during the last ten years. Buried a few too.'

'Well, you're going to find it hard to bury Kerimov. The guy has an army around him.'

'So did the last guy.' Mai said.

'We left him eating dirt,' Alicia told Bryant. 'Literally.'

'Well, that's good. I can send you all the information we have on Kerimov. When you land, make your way to his place with all haste.'

'His mansion?' Kenzie said.

'Yeah, his mansion. Find a way inside. The guy has a nuclear weapon.'

'Are we the only team on this?' Hayden asked.

'On the ground, yes. But there's a full office of tech support.'

Drake knew they were up against it. They had been ever since they first took this job a few days ago. Always a step behind, they were struggling to stay on an even keel, to keep up with the machinations of one very shadowy player who, somehow, had managed to set this network up and put it to good use.

Drake wondered who the hell they were dealing with.

CHAPTER TWENTY TWO

Sabrina Quinn put the phone down and ordered her favourite drink from her manservant, John. The heavenly liquid arrived seconds later on a silver platter, was placed on her desk, and left unpoured. John knew she liked to do that. Sabrina didn't allow herself to think until the bourbon was in the glass, the first sip touching her lips.

Where were we now?

Oh, yes, the nuclear weapon was snaking its way nicely in her direction. It was an interesting route, necessarily vague, lorded over by many fake kings – generals and warlords and colonels – self-proclaimed, of course. Nobody ever said they'd earned their ranks. But the progress was encouraging. Sabrina left her desk and wandered over to the picture window that gave her a good view of Knightsbridge. Soon, she would have to leave this place, probably forever, and the thought weighed heavily on her. This was her home, had been for more years than she cared to remember. But the committee had decided that the target was London, and the committee was going to get their way.

Sabrina didn't like it, but that was the job.

Yes, she was the head of the committee, and she could rightly shoot them down in flames. But that didn't make for good bedfellows. If nine out of nine voted to teach a lesson to London, then that lesson needed teaching.

Sabrina watched the people flow by below. London was an enjoyable city, yes, but it was loud and it was noisy and it was unforgiving. There were more sharks navigating the streets of London and nestled in its imposing buildings than she cared to admit. Of course, she was one of them, probably the biggest and most vicious. It was a universally admitted fact. You didn't want to get on the wrong side of Sabrina Quinn.

The shadow network she ran was into everything. Guns, bombs, people trafficking, drugs, kidnap and ransom. To some people in the business, they were well known, to others not even a whispered warning on their lips. The network was called Coda; they used private jets to attend meetings all over the world where they conducted their shadow business; they manipulated high-flyers in all walks of life to aid their interests; they ordered blood be spilled for any manner of slight by their bought-and-paid-for mercenaries from east to west. And it didn't end there. Not by a long shot. They turned over millions a day, wrecked countless lives every minute, increased their holdings by the second. Coda was a well-oiled killing machine, and it made many men and women very wealthy.

Sabrina stood at the topmost pinnacle, eyeing those below her. It wasn't that some jumped-up minister or MI6 boss or scrappy Lord had upset them; it was far more serious than that. There were powerful people in London, *of* London, who were refusing to do business with what they'd started calling 'a terrorist organisation.' How laughable. It boiled Sabrina's blood. Coda prided itself on being a noble business, what might have once been called a *gentleman's* business, and they were always loyal to who they did business with. None of this backstreet, cutthroat dealing. None of this betrayal. If you dealt with Coda, you knew you were dealing with the most reliable and the best, someone who would have your back so long as you toed the line.

She sipped her bourbon some more. The alcohol mellowed her, but it didn't soothe her anger. These people in London, her now *ex* business partners, would find out the hard way that you didn't *ever* stop working for Coda. They were too well connected.

Her phone rang. Sabrina crossed the room to look at the screen. It said caller unknown, but Sabrina had an excellent idea of who was calling her.

'Speak,' she said, answering it in her characteristic way.

'This is Germaine.'

'Yes, I know who it is. Speak.'

'We have been looking into this team that appears to be on the trail of the package. They're getting closer.'

'How close?'

'It would appear they're closing in on General Kerimov as we speak.'

'That's not good, Germaine.'

'I know. We have warned the general, but the situation is incredibly fluid.'

'I know that, Germaine. It's meant to be. That's the whole idea of transporting a... package... as quietly as possible with no blowback on us. You have to be clean. The entire deal must be *fluid*.'

'Like I said, we have warned Kerimov,' Germaine sounded a trifle aggravated. 'But, well, he's not the most stable of individuals.'

'The price of doing business in the world we do business,' Sabrina said. 'These people... this team... what do you know of them?'

'Call themselves the Ghost Squadron. They work for Glacier, out of DC, for a guy called Connor Bryant. He owns the company and runs quite a few mercenaries around the world.'

'So we're being hounded by bloody mercenaries?'

'I guess we are.'

Sabrina took a moment. 'Any ideas who they are?'

'We have some CCTV footage and are looking into it. The facial recognition software should give us a few hits. Until then, all we have is this guy, Connor Bryant.'

Sabrina didn't say anything, but she had heard of Connor Bryant. The guy was a well-respected player in the military security field. Coda's dealings brought them in contact with almost everyone in that field.

'This Bryant is running the team?' she asked.

'He appears to be, yes. From his office in DC.'

'Then kill him,' Sabrina said.

Germaine went quiet. 'I'm sorry... say that again.'

'Kill him,' Sabrina repeated. 'Do it quickly.'

'You want us to put a hit out on the owner of a firm of private military contractors?'

'Is that a problem?'

'Glacier is huge. They have government contacts. They're well-connected to the upper echelons in DC. Even the White House...'

'To me, that's another good reason to get rid of him. Maybe the White House, the military or even the CIA are sniffing around our operation via this team. And they're getting close. Killing Bryant would put them on the back foot, maybe lose them a day or two, give us the time we need.'

'How much time do we need?'

Sabrina narrowed her eyes. 'Don't overstep, Germaine. Do not forget that you work for me.'

Germaine sighed. 'Normally,' he said. 'A hit like this would take weeks to set up. I'm assuming you want it done in a few days?'

'Don't be silly. I want it done today.'

There was a sharp intake of breath. Sabrina waited until Germaine had got his head around her order.

'It won't be perfect by any means.'

'Just as long as they don't trace it back to us.'

'We'll have to use expendables.'

Sabrina nodded to herself. 'Just end Connor Bryant today,' she said. 'He's interfered enough in our business.'

'Consider it done.'

CHAPTER TWENTY THREE

Connor Bryant was running late. He wondered if he should sacrifice grabbing his morning coffee on the way to work, then remembered he was the boss, and decided he'd sacrificed enough for Glacier. He usually worked into the night, was available twenty-four-hours a day and often got in early. Today, it wouldn't matter if he was fifteen minutes late.

It was a bright and breezy DC day. Bryant jumped into his car and backed out of his driveway. He ran through the list of jobs he had planned. Nothing too strenuous, although the current antics of the Ghost Squadron, in line with the government's wishes, had him on edge night and day. He was very aware that he worked for the government at the moment, very much at their beck and call. It unsettled him, made him feel as if the firm he'd built from scratch wasn't his at all. But working alongside those in charge of the country was part of his job, and owning a private military security firm brought him into contact with government officials almost every day.

Keep them sweet.

Bryant drove up to his favourite drive-thru, ordered a coffee and waited for it to be brewed. He didn't check his mirrors, didn't maintain any kind of surveillance around him. Why would he? Yes, recently his office was shot up by a sniper, but all that badness had been aimed at the Ghost

Squadron, not him. And the repair work was progressing nicely. Bryant saw improvements every day and assumed the workers would soon be finished.

He took his coffee, slotted it into a cup holder and drove away from the drive-thru. The streets of DC were busy this morning, traffic jams everywhere. Bryant thought about the job, and that inevitably brought him around to Mai Kitano.

They were enjoying that pre-relationship time at the moment, that time when everything was new and fresh and worries weren't really an issue. Bryant hoped it would pan out for a lot longer; he didn't want to get tied into anything right now. But that was a problem, because he didn't want to lose Mai either. The Japanese woman was definitely making an impression, getting under his skin. He thought about her at least once every hour of every day.

Especially when she was away on a dangerous mission.

And they didn't get much more dangerous than the one they were on right now. Already they'd been to Afghanistan and Pakistan, two war-torn countries that harboured hordes of terrorists. They'd met dictators and stolen the information right out from under the noses of militia leaders. They couldn't hope to succeed forever.

But the Ghost Squadron was a team of winners. Bryant knew that. They were as severe as they were clever, as hard as they were easy-going. He'd never known a team like them, and Bryant had been around security forces for more than a decade.

How the hell did they keep going after all these years?

But Bryant knew the answer to that one. They mentioned it often enough. They were a family as much as a team, and their lives revolved around each other. They respected one another enough to never disparage that bond.

Bryant moved steadily in the stop-start traffic. There was a big truck to his side, trying to inch its way into his lane. There was a motorcycle to the rear that was way too close, its single headlight glaring through his rear-view mirror. Bryant took it all in good humour and phoned the office to tell them he was stuck in traffic.

Half an hour later, he was approaching the office where he worked. It was a tall building, all grey concrete and glass. Glacier had four floors about halfway up, recognisable now from the outside as workers repaired the windows and frames.

Bryant ignored it all, driving in through the underground parking entrance and heading down to the second basement level where he usually parked. There was nothing like being consistent. Bryant stopped the car, picked up his coffee cup and tipped it back, taking a long gulp. He sighed. Time to get through that door, into work, and into the mood.

Game face on.

Lately, that phrase was more and more appropriate. Bryant had always presented a unique personality for work, an image far louder than his genuine, quieter, personal self. At work, he was brash, bold, a lover of all women and a bit of a joker. Bryant had carefully crafted this character through the years as he built his business up. It was what the power players wanted to see. Many people saw him as that type of man.

But, on the quiet, Bryant was quite the opposite.

Not a womaniser with a boorish, loud charisma. But Bryant had played the part too well. He'd almost believed he was that kind of man. Then Mai came along and he wanted to show her what he *really* was, how kind and quiet he could be, how much he respected the opposite sex, how good a person he was.

Alicia had never bought it, he knew. She had a good heart, but she wasn't deep enough for Bryant. But Mai, now there was a woman who had depths you could never fathom, unknown layers.

Bryant shrugged it all off, worrying that he was thinking of Mai way too much, and got out of the car. The parking area echoed to the sound of engines and the quiet squeal of tyres. He took another gulp of his drink. The entrance door that led to the building's lifts was dead ahead, about twenty steps away.

That was when the three men appeared. Bryant saw them out of the corner of his eye. At first, he didn't register them as threats. They were moving too slowly. But then, as they drifted closer, Bryant focused on their faces, their figures, their hands.

Two of them carried guns, the other a knife.

He slowed, looked around. There was nobody else in sight. Bryant had nowhere to run. He was alone.

But he also carried a gun.

He dropped the coffee cup, reached into his waistband, and plucked out the Glock 17 he kept there. It felt alien to his grip, barely used except for target practice. In fact, this entire scene felt alien to him. How could armed men be attacking him in his own parking basement?

Bryant got off the first shot, trying to scare the men away. His bullet went high over their heads. Immediately, they fell to the floor and took cover. One of them peered around a parked car, the others were nowhere in sight.

'What do you want?' Bryant fought to keep his voice steady.

Of course, they were professionals. They didn't answer. They didn't even fire back just yet. Bryant pulled his trigger again, hoping to attract some attention.

One man appeared, scuttling closer, crouch-running

between two cars. The guy with the knife popped up for a second, also advancing. Bryant breathed fast. His heart beat double time. He wasn't used to this. What would Drake do? What would Mai do? They would take the fight to their enemies.

Bryant rose, gun aimed. Just then, a bullet flew past his temple, scaring him and forcing him back down. In the next second, there were running footsteps. Bryant looked up just in time to see the knife-wielder springing close and then hurling himself over Bryant's car until they were face to face.

Bryant brought his gun up.

The knife-wielder slapped it away, stepped in, and thrust with the knife. It passed between Bryant's ribs and upper arm, nicking the flesh. It was a lucky miss. The guy withdrew the knife and made to attack again.

Bryant kicked him, fell back, slid down the car onto his ass. Through luck, he'd actually made some space for himself. His gun aimed upwards. Bryant pulled the trigger. His bullet passed right over the top of the knife-wielder's head.

But the shot gave him pause. The man blinked. By now, Bryant could hear other movements, the sounds of the other two men approaching. When they arrived, Bryant was done for.

He lashed out, tripped his attacker, and then kicked him in the face. The knife clattered away. Bryant saw the guy looked dazed and rose to his knees.

Just in time to see the other two men rounding the car.

Bryant's blood was pounding, rushing to his brain. He fired quickly, two shots, missing both men but making them dive for cover. One of them got a shot off that missed Bryant's shin by three millimetres.

Bryant got a view underneath the cars. He could see

both his opponents; at least he could see their legs, and got the idea to shoot under the vehicles, maybe disable one of the men. He angled his gun under the vehicle and pulled the trigger.

Someone cried out. A man fell. If Bryant had fired again, same position, his bullet would have killed the guy who fell, but Bryant was no killer. He was barely a fighter. How many bullets had he fired? Yes, he should know, but he didn't have a clue. Bryant wasn't wired that way.

A body slid over the car above him. It landed next to him, two feet planted. The man held a gun, which pointed unwaveringly at Bryant.

'No,' he said.

But the man opened fire. Bryant felt the white heat enter him, felt the agony. Two shots as the attacker moved quickly, both fired into his stomach. Bryant lost his grip on the gun, curled up, and groaned.

Someone dragged the man with the knife to his feet. Then, both men vanished from sight and went to help their shot colleague. There were some groans and a scream, and then the three men started limping away. Bryant lay in agony, clutching his stomach, trying to stem the flow of blood and keep pressure on the wound. He heard the screech of tyres, saw the passing of a vehicle, but he just lay there.

Slowly dying.

CHAPTER TWENTY FOUR

The pilots said they would wait for one day only.

Drake and the rest of the team clambered quickly down from the body of the aircraft and looked around. They were slap bang in the middle of an airstrip, in the middle of a forest, somewhere in eastern Turkmenistan. According to Bryant's information, they were a solid two-hour drive from General Kerimov's mansion.

At this stage, they didn't know how much of the area Kerimov controlled. Mitrovic had suggested a *country*. Drake very much doubted that.

'We need a vehicle,' Kenzie was saying. 'I can see several along the edges of the airstrip.'

Drake saw them, too. Small, 4x4 off-road vehicles capable of cutting through the forests and dirt tracks without issue.

'You got some dosh ready?' he asked Hayden.

She dug into her backpack. 'The supply is getting low, but let's try it.'

'We only want to borrow them,' Dahl said.

'That depends if you're behind the wheel,' Drake said. 'Often people see you and just think "target practice."'

Dahl didn't react. Instead, he just said, 'You're not wrong,' and followed Hayden towards the trucks.

The team spent half an hour negotiating a reasonable price for the borrowing of two trucks. They piled in, stashed their gear, and kept their weapons handy. Kinimaka drove the first in line, Kenzie the second. They checked Kerimov's position on the sat nav and then started off weaving among the dirt roads that spider-webbed the area. Drake ducked as they passed under low-hanging boughs, the branches slapping at the roofs of the trucks. He made a face as they squeezed in between narrowly spaced trunks, sure they were going to scratch the vehicles and incur more costs. He held on tightly as they bounced from rut to rut, following whichever road ran in the right direction.

They drove flat out for an hour before slowing down. Drake felt battered and bruised from the rough travel, hanging on with one hand, feeling almost sea sick. Their journey took them along one track, between stands of trees, and then onto another via a series of monumental ruts. Twice, the lead vehicle got stuck, its front wheels caught between deep delves in the ground, and had to be nudged along by the second vehicle.

The second hour, they took it easier.

The GPS led them unerringly to the right area, but it was easy to spot the noisy trucks. As they came closer, they ditched them by the side of the road and would return for them later. Drake helped drive them off the road and then cover them in branches and other foliage to hide them from prying eyes. Twenty minutes later, you couldn't tell the surrounding forest from the trucks.

The team started off through the forest on foot, a half-hour walk from General Kerimov's residence, or at least where American intelligence pinpointed his abode. After studying the aerial photos, Drake had a better idea of what they were up against.

Kerimov's mansion was sprawling, sitting in the middle of a thick stand of trees, and looked to have been built on frequently. There were many extensions, offshoots, and smaller outbuildings. There were sections that looked like they didn't belong, and the team could only guess at the extent of the basement levels.

'We're gonna search all that whilst we hide from an army?' Alicia asked, amazingly without a touch of sarcasm in her voice.

'It'll take an army to guard it,' Mai said.

'If we can make a covert entry, we may stand a chance,' Drake said. 'The problem is all those outbuildings.'

He could count at least six, any of which looked large enough to house their nuclear bomb.

They trudged on, spread out through the forest and remained vigilant for guards. They bypassed one man half-asleep on his feet, another taking a piss as they crept through to his left. Knowing they were within the perimeter of Kerimov's guards, they slowed down and started creeping along. The last thousand yards took them the best part of an hour.

Finally, atop a tree-lined mound that overlooked the mansion, the team bedded in to observe. They all took out their binoculars and got their first proper look at the place.

'I see guards everywhere,' Mai said.

'Stationed outside the house, the outbuildings, the steps, the bloody windows.' Drake shook his head. 'This Kerimov is a complete paranoid.'

'I see more coming and going,' Kinimaka said. 'In and out of the house. Look, at least two of the outbuildings are being used as mess rooms for the guards. That at least rules them out.'

'And I see another is a storage hut,' Cam said. 'Over to the right near that clump of bushes.'

Drake was pleased. They seemed to be getting somewhere.

'If Kerimov has the nuke, I doubt he'd keep it outside,' Hayden said. 'Not now. I've seen the size of his mansion.'

Alicia looked over. 'You think he's compensating for something?'

'Big time, so to speak.'

Drake took another long gaze at the enormous mansion. 'The house may be big, but that nuke ain't too small. If it's in there, we'll find it.'

'Maybe it's in the swimming pool,' Dahl was focusing on the back.

Drake shook his head. 'Funny, but I wouldn't rule anywhere out. The calibre of people who've taken possession of this thing isn't exactly high.'

'Or even half sane,' Hayden added.

'I wonder where Kerimov is?' Shaw said.

They spent several more minutes studying the house and grounds. Drake took it all in. The built-up surrounding walls, the gardens, the statues, the non-working fountains that had taken on a decidedly greenish tinge through mould.

'Check out the gate,' Dahl said after a while.

Drake shifted his focus. He was already thinking that there seemed to be a lot of comings and goings down there.

'Vans, trucks, you name it. They're in and out all the time.'

'Are you thinking what I'm thinking?' Dahl asked.

'There isn't a lot of room for my balls in these trousers?'

'No. That we can hop aboard a truck and drive it right into the grounds.'

Drake knew what Dahl meant by "hop aboard." He nodded. 'It feels like the best way in. We could drive it right up to the house. And those guards can't know everyone who's doing the driving. There's too many of them passing through.'

'Sounds like a plan,' Hayden said, packing away her binoculars.

The team started making their way around to the front of the house, sticking to the heavy foliage and taking it slow. They were here now; they didn't need to rush too much. Drake was hyper aware that any of those trucks might be here to remove the nuke, of course, but the journey around to the front of the house had to be done in silence. Twice, they passed guards, circumvented them, and continued.

They moved to a place down the track that led up to the front of the house and watched two more trucks bounce along. Finally, they were in position and ready.

Dahl raised a hand.

CHAPTER TWENTY FIVE

'Wait,' Kinimaka said.

Dahl lowered his hand. There were just three of them waiting by the side of the road, the rest of the team concealed in the brush and trees up the slope above. A truck was coming down the track, headed for the house. The only problem was that a truck was coming the other way too, headed *away* from the house.

They waited. The two vehicles struggled to pass each other on the narrow track, both squeezing into the foliage with their wheels churning up grass and mud as they inched past each other. Dahl crouched lower, hidden from sight by a sprawling thorn bush that stood about three feet high. Soon, the trucks had passed each other and were gone. Dahl waited as another passed them by, leaving the house. Five minutes passed. Then fifteen. Finally, there came the roar of another engine approaching.

'Ready?'

His companions, Kinimaka and Cam, nodded. They saw the truck coming, faded green with a tarpaulin stretched over the rear, and waited just enough time to make sure it wasn't loaded with troops. They had deliberately chosen a place on the road where it narrowed, so that the passing truck would have to slow. Now, as it did, Dahl stepped out from one side, Kinimaka the other. Dahl grabbed the door handle and wrenched, yanking the door open. The man inside, in the passenger seat, looked startled. He yelped when Dahl leaned in, grabbed his jacket and pulled, but the noise didn't stop him from flying out of his seat, through the air, and then hitting the ground hard with his spine.

The guy groaned, the sound of him hitting the ground loud even over the noise of the truck. On the other side, Kinimaka was dealing similarly with the driver. Dahl knelt with his knee on his enemy's solar plexus and smashed a fist into the man's temple. He didn't last long after that, sinking quickly into oblivion.

The truck was still moving.

Cam had slipped around Kinimaka and jumped into the cab. He grabbed the wheel and goosed the pedals, slowing it down. Dahl and Kinimaka gripped their victims by their jackets and dragged them further into the brush. At that moment, the others appeared, slipping and sliding down the slope that led to the road.

Drake checked the back of the truck. It was empty, save for a load of crates haphazardly stacked. Many had come loose in the journey and were lying on their sides. Drake and the others climbed up, made a space for themselves behind the crates and next to the cab, and then crouched down.

Drake slapped the partition three times, signalling that they were ready.

Cam, in the driver's seat, threw the truck into gear and put his foot on the accelerator. The gears ground together. Drake heard Cam complaining. The truck still moved forward, now gaining traction and speed. Drake could imagine Dahl and Kinimaka sitting in the two passenger seats, jostling each other for space.

It made him smile just a little.

The truck picked up more speed. Cam was getting the hang of it. Drake held on as best he could, constantly jarred and falling against his teammates because of the unexpected ruts in the road. Twice, he wondered aloud why Kerimov just couldn't see his way to tarmacking the damn thing.

Then Cam shouted, 'We're approaching the gates.'

Drake readied his weapon.

The truck slowed. Drake turned around and put his eye to a hole in the partition. He could see the front of the truck and the windscreen, and whatever was outside. Currently, that was a high, thick, wooden gate topped with rolls of barbed wire. The gate was closed. Four men stood on each side, all with weapons and that glassy thousand-yard stare in their eyes that attested to early morning drinking or drugs or just plain, unadulterated boredom. Hard to say which at this distance.

Drake watched. Cam stopped the truck just before the gate. Two of the guards yawned and came across to the driver's window. What these men saw were three mercenaries driving a goods truck, just like many before them and even more that would come after. They held their weapons loosely and leaned in with blank expressions.

'What are you carrying?' one of them said in broken English, no doubt recognising that they were European.

'Crates,' he said quickly, and then added, 'Food and drinks.'

Drake winced slightly. Cam was embellishing, and that didn't usually go well on a dangerous mission.

'We just had food and drink truck a half hour ago,' the guard said.

Drake made a face, gripped his weapon tighter. The last thing they needed right now was an all-out gunfight at the front gate.

'Kerimov must have ordered more,' Dahl said, leaning

over. 'You know what he's like. C'mon, man, we're just doing our job here.'

The guard sent a jaded look at the back of the truck, then retreated and slapped the engine cover. 'Move on through,' he said. 'Take it easy inside.'

Cam nodded and quickly wound up his window. He pressed the accelerator as the gates opened. They were inside. The problem now was where they would end up parking. Would they have to start unloading the truck? Drake wasn't sure, but he was ready.

Cam drove through the mansion's sprawling grounds. They passed the outbuildings one at a time and tried to get a better look inside, but noticed nothing new. Tension filled the truck. They might need to make a move at any moment. They were all prepared as best they could be, but the relentless jostling of the truck constantly spoiled their readiness.

Cam didn't have the luxury of following another vehicle. He had to guess where to go. At first, the road wound in just one direction, but then, as they passed the side of the house, it branched off into several different routes. As he hesitated, Cam saw someone beckoning him from the back of the house.

'Deliveries to the rear,' Dahl said.

Drake waited as Cam bounced them along nearer and nearer the back. As they rounded the corner, Drake saw several trucks and vans parked, their cargos being unloaded. Others were doing the opposite, accepting crates and items that were wrapped in large sheets and other packing materials.

'Quite the little enterprise the General's got going,' Dahl said.

There were men everywhere. One look at them, and Drake knew they would blend in perfectly. Most of the men were European. All carried guns across their shoulders or holstered at their waists. The only problem was...

'There are no women,' he said. 'None that I can see.'

'So the sudden arrival of five might draw a bit of attention,' Alicia said. 'Especially three beauties, and Mai and Kenzie.'

Drake heard Mai hiss, but there was no other reaction. They decided the women should stay hidden for as long as possible. They all had hoods, in any case, and it wasn't a long walk from the truck to the house.

Cam backed into a parking space. They were right outside the rear of the property now, flanked by other trucks and men, and with their backs to a pair of French windows that had been thrown open.

Cam turned the truck off. The sudden lack of noise was loud in Drake's ears. They sat for a moment and then waited as Dahl climbed down from the passenger seat and jumped to the ground.

'Time to unload this mother,' he said.

CHAPTER TWENTY SIX

Drake jumped down and walked to the back of the truck. He shouldered his weapon and grabbed a crate, picking the heaviest, and handing it down to Dahl. The Swede moved to the side and waited, since they all wanted to enter the house together. Drake passed Cam a crate and then Kinimaka. As he did so, the women readied themselves, drawing up their hoods. Drake jumped down from the back of the truck, his boots splashing in a dirty puddle. He turned around and reached up for the crate that Shaw was passing down.

Hefted it. Stood to one side with the others. Cam would lead the way into the mansion. Alicia and the women all jumped down holding a crate. Cam didn't waste any time. He set off in the house's direction, climbing a set of steps to the wide open French windows. Dahl and Kinimaka followed him closely. Drake let Alicia and Mai go next, hoping they would go unnoticed in the crowd. To his left and right, other drivers and passengers offloaded their cargo, carrying it into the house. It was a slow and steady procession, which suited Drake and the others just fine.

Cam entered the house. Inside, the room was furnished like a massive study, with a desk in one corner, a leather chair, and several rows of bookcases filled with hardbacks. Drake wondered how the hell someone like Kerimov had come to own this mansion, and then decided he didn't really want to know. The original occupants were long gone now. Drake felt sorry for them.

The room was plushly carpeted, though the constant tramp of boots across it was wearing the thread count down a bit. The team carried their boxes through it, finding themselves in a wide, marble-walled corridor. Other mercenaries were ahead of them. Some rooms they passed were occupied, the people within tearing open crates and boxes and distributing whatever stuff was inside. Drake saw well-packed grenades alongside rows of fruit and piles of body armour standing next to pre-packed ration boxes as he walked by. They didn't slow, didn't veer from their path. They ventured deeper into the house.

'No clue where we're supposed to go with these,' Dahl whispered from the corner of his mouth. 'At this point, we're just wandering with a load of boxes in our hands.'

'You see anything suspicious?' Alicia asked.

'Are you kidding? It's *all* suspicious.'

'No, I meant-'

'I know what you meant. All the boxes I've seen so far have been opened. No nukes.'

They went down the corridor and then through another room, a wide unfurnished space that might once have been a ballroom or a very large dining room with one of those huge, imposing dinner tables, but Drake saw nothing to tell them what it was now. There were some crates stacked in one corner, though, which instantly drew their attention.

The crates were unopened. Dahl put his burden down, grabbed a wrecking bar that was lying beside the crates and levered all the lids up. After a minute, he shook his head.

'Ammo,' he said. 'Kerimov has enough military supplies to start a minor war.' He held on to the wrecking bar.

They weren't challenged. They blended in well with all

the others mercs wandering around. The general's men were in evidence too, many of them opening crates and handing recently sealed boxes over to waiting mercenaries.

'Quite the little industry he's got going on here,' Kinimaka said.

They pressed further inside, pushing their luck. Finally, they came to an area of the house where there were no boxes, no mercs, no guards. They stood in a hallway, a flight of stairs to their left, a long march to what looked like a kitchen area to their right.

'What next?' Cam asked.

'It's a big place,' Alicia voiced the issue that was on all their minds.

Drake put his crate down. It was time to come out of the shadows and start to push this thing.

'Let's move,' he said.

The team threw their crates to the floor, unhooked their weapons, and started for the stairs. They pounded up two at a time. They hit the first floor landing, turned right, and saw two guards ahead. The men looked bored at first, then alarmed.

'Who are you?' one said.

Drake ran at him, smashed him across the face with an elbow. He disarmed the man and said, 'What do you know about a nuclear weapon?'

The guy shook his head vigorously as Drake and Mai covered his friend.

'Kerimov?'

The guard gestured upwards with his eyes, indicating the next floor.

'He's always up there,' the other guard, now in Kinimaka's grip, said. 'Playing his video games.'

Drake shook his head in disbelief. Was this the modern version of Nero fiddling whilst Rome burned? General

Kerimov mashing the buttons on his PlayStation whilst his enemies infiltrated his hideout? Drake looked over at the next flight of stairs, saw them winding up to the next floor. There were no guards stationed at the top.

Quickly, he knocked out the guy they were talking to. Kinimaka dealt with his friend; then they dragged both guards into a nearby closet. They would be out cold for a while.

Dahl went first, starting up the next flight of stairs. The others followed closely. The stairs wound in a half circle, giving them an expanding view of the next floor the higher they rose. Drake saw a wide corridor with several rooms, their doors closed.

At the far end, they'd stationed a couple of guards outside a door.

Drake slowed them all down, let his team catch up. They raised their weapons. There would be no easy, quiet way to do this. If finding the nuke wasn't so imperative, they'd choose another plan, but time was of the essence.

'No backing down,' Dahl said.

They rounded the corner, saw the guards. Alarm registered in the men's eyes and crossed their expressions. Drake was already sprinting, hoping to reach them before they had time to fire their guns. It worked, almost. He reached the first guard and swung his weapon at the man's head, caught him a crushing blow across the temple. The man spun against the doorway, leaving a blood trail. The second guy was set upon by Dahl, who hit him with a flying kick. The impact caused him to jam his finger against his trigger, letting loose a burst of bullets that flew up at the ceiling. It was a brief burst, but it was loud in the enclosed space.

Kinimaka hit the room's double doors, splintering them. They flew open, shards of wood flying everywhere. Inside,

Drake saw men and women lounging on large sofas, a thickset man seated on a red rug in the middle of the floor, a black controller clutched in his right hand. The TV played some video game that involved swords and dragons. Bottles of beer were everywhere and plates with half-eaten items of food, bowls full of crisps and peanuts. A warm sun blazed in through several floor-to-ceiling windows and there was the low thump of rap music, something that immediately set Drake's nerves on edge.

The team dashed into the room. Men and women turned in surprise, their faces just visible over the tops of the sofas.

Drake raced for General Kerimov.

There was something else in the room too, an array of weapons. These men and women all carried firearms and had placed them down nearby. They would need subduing before they reached for their guns.

Drake smashed Kerimov on the top of the head, sent him tumbling forward. The man didn't utter a sound. The controller fell out of his hand, tumbling to the floor. To his right, Dahl and Kinimaka hit two men on the run, knocking weapons from their hands and pushing them back so hard they fell to the floor. Alicia, Mai and Kenzie subdued more men, hitting them hard and throwing them down. Which left Cam and Shaw to overcome the three women.

Cam took no prisoners. A blonde came at him with a snarl, her long hair flying. Cam hit her in the mouth, the impact sending her head backwards, almost snapping her neck. She fell and was out like a light before she even knew what was happening. The other two women came at Shaw, knives in their hands.

Shaw blocked a thrust and used the butt of her gun on her opponent's temple. The other woman struck Shaw across the face, leaving a mark. Shaw took the blow, stepped back and then caught the hand holding the knife. With a jerk, she broke it at the wrist. The woman screamed.

Dahl's and Kinimaka's opponents were no pushovers, either. They had fallen to the floor but were soon back on their feet, bulky and threatening. Dahl grabbed his opponent by the shoulders and tried a headbutt, but the man ducked out of the way and brought a knee up into Dahl's midriff. The Swede grunted, took firmer hold of his opponent's shoulders and tried to heave him off his feet. The problem was, the guy was thickset and heavy, too heavy to move easily.

To Dahl's right, Kinimaka threw punch after punch into his opponent's midriff and ribs, using him as a human punchbag. At first the guy covered up and took the punches, probably hoping that Kinimaka would tire, but the Hawaiian just kept coming, kept punching, kept on smashing blows into his enemy's torso. The guy was backing up swiftly, bumping into the tall window at his back.

Now, Dahl's opponent grabbed him too, so now both men had hold of each other's shoulders. They had their heads down too, trying to avoid the headbutt. They heaved and lurched and pitched each other from side to side, trying to get the upper hand.

Just then, Dahl tripped. His opponent instantly hurled the Swede straight at the window, using all his strength. The glass shattered, the shards raining down like a waterfall. Dahl hit the window and then – to Drake's shock and despair – went flying straight out.

But he kept hold of his opponent and took him with him.

Both men tumbled out into the day, sharp pieces of

glass pricking at their exposed skin. Dahl's heart was in his mouth. He knew they were on the third floor. It was a super long drop to the ground. He tumbled, unable to stop himself. He couldn't see which way was up or down, but made sure he kept a tight hold of his opponent. He used the momentum of the tumble to make sure his enemy rolled until he was beneath him.

Sooner than expected, both men came to a sudden halt.

They hit a balcony. Dahl was on top. His opponent was winded, probably with broken bones too, since Dahl had come down on his ribs. Dahl saw an instant opportunity. The guy was shocked and groaning, leaving his face unprotected. Dahl threw several hammer blows at it, knocking it left and right until the eyes closed and the man passed out.

Then Dahl sat up, looked up, and started climbing.

Drake was hauling General Kerimov to his feet, unable to break away. Kinimaka had finished with his opponent and now started towards the broken window, shock registering on his face. Hayden had been helping Cam and Shaw. Now, she too ran for the window.

Drake's entire team was focused on the shattered frame.

And then, incredibly, Dahl's face filled the hole. It was like seeing a man rise from the dead. Drake blinked, unable to believe his eyes. Dahl reached out, accepted Kinimaka's outstretched hand, and let the Hawaiian haul him inside.

'I'm back,' he murmured.

Drake couldn't imagine what had happened, but he was grateful for it. Somehow, the Swede had been spared the long drop to the ground and had made his way back up. Typical Dahl, really. Drake should have expected it.

Kerimov twisted in his grip. Drake gestured at the TV. 'You wanna carry on with your game? That's fine, but first I need a few answers.'

'We are an army!' the thickset man growled.

'Do I look like I give a shit? Listen, you are Kerimov, right?'

'Fuck you.'

Alicia moved in and slapped the general with an open hand. His eyes went wide. She gripped his trachea between her fingers.

'Tell me, general,' she said. 'Are you attached to your balls?'

The general swallowed heavily. 'I am Kerimov,' he blurted. 'What do you want?'

'Preferably not your balls,' Alicia answered. 'But I can arrange that the moment you stop answering our questions.'

Drake shook the man hard. 'You took possession of a nuclear warhead from a madman called Mitrovic. From Serbia. He says he sent the nuke to you. Now, general, we are here to collect it. Where is it?'

Kerimov stared at Alicia with fear and dread on his face. 'I'm sorry,' he said. 'The nuke is not here.'

Drake tried not to close his eyes in disappointment, tried not to let the frustration show. 'What do you mean?'

And now General Kerimov laughed. He spat on the floor. 'I don't care what you do to me,' he said. 'I have cast the die. The weapon is with one of the most terrible people in all the world.'

Kerimov couldn't stop laughing. Drake broke one of his ribs to shut him the hell up. 'Is it the end user? Explain yourself.'

'I don't explain myself to anyone.'

Now, Drake rammed the barrel of his gun into Kerimov's broken rib. 'Honestly,' he said. 'I'd sooner shoot you than talk to you.'

'How can you have passed it on so quickly?' Alicia asked.

'It stayed here for less than half a day. The speed of transfer was important to... the end user. It has to fly through the hands like hot butter,' he laughed. 'That's what they said. *Fly* through the hands.'

'What end user?' Drake asked.

Kerimov shrugged. 'I do not care. I do not know. Nor would I tell you if I did.'

Alicia dug her weapon into Kerimov's groin. 'Listen, General. I'm gonna blow these peanuts all over your fucking TV if you don't start answering our questions.'

'I do not know who the end user is. Why would I? They set the network up. They are crazy powerful people who I, nor anyone else in the chain, would dare to cross. They have immense reach, as you can tell. Clearly, you understand they wish to stay anonymous.'

'All right,' Drake said. 'Then tell us, who did you hand the weapon over to?'

A smug expression came over the general's face. 'Flux,' he said with a grin.

Drake narrowed his eyes. He'd heard the name. 'Flux?' he repeated.

'Oh, yeah,' the general said. 'And now how much trouble are you in?'

Drake tried to keep his voice level. 'What the hell do you know about Flux?'

'Are you kidding?' Kerimov looked genuinely puzzled. 'If you're in this game, you know about Flux. He's the worst terrorist on the planet.'

Drake had heard the stories, they all had. Flux was evil personified. No morals. No maxims other than slaughter. Even his own people feared him. Flux was not above massacring them to prove a point. Somehow, though, he always ended up on top. The thorniest problem Drake could visualise off the top of his head, apart from the man's

reputation, was that no one knew where Flux was based.
'Where'd you deliver the bomb to?' he asked.
Kerimov grinned. 'Iran,' he said.

CHAPTER TWENTY SEVEN

Iran?

It wasn't good. Of all the places they'd been on their quest for the nuke, Iran would probably be the worst in terms of danger.

'When did he take delivery?' Dahl asked.

'Yesterday,' Kerimov couldn't stop grinning.

Alicia soon stopped that with a swift blow to the groin. 'You think it's funny? How funny is it now?'

The nuke was still travelling, still out there, still en route to the end user. Drake couldn't think of anyone worse than Flux to be in control of it, even the mad Mitrovic.

'Is Flux the end user?' he asked.

Kerimov was bent double, groaning in pain. He flipped Drake off until Alicia threatened him once again.

'I do not know for certain, but I doubt it. Flux said something about passing it on when I spoke with him.'

'You terrorists chat with each other?' Mai said. 'What is it – a gossip line? A Facebook group?'

'I am *not* a terrorist. I am an entrepreneur.'

It was Drake's turn to laugh. He glared at the general and wished there was something he could physically, morally, do with the man, some way he could depose him of all his power. The actual truth was he'd be back in business as soon as the Ghost Squadron left.

They were done. Drake nodded at Dahl, who was about

to smash Kerimov over the head, fixing to put him to sleep for an hour, when there was a commotion at the door.

Drake looked over.

Kerimov's men were piling in, weapons up.

Drake dropped and fired. Dahl dealt with Kerimov harshly, putting him to sleep. The rest of the team opened fire on the newcomers. Men thrashed as bullets struck them, limbs flailing, collapsing at the threshold of the room. Still more came, shooting as they appeared, their bullets flying erratically around the room.

The Ghost Squadron dropped low, not wanting to catch a stray bullet. They darted to cover, using the sofa and overturned tables, though they knew the items were flimsy at best. Dahl held up Kerimov in front of him as a shield.

'Shoot me now, you bastards,' he said.

Some of them ceased fire, others didn't realise and just kept coming. Drake looked behind him to the window.

'Could that be our way out?' he yelled.

Dahl looked over. 'Balconies,' he said. 'A few, all the way to the ground.'

It would have to do. Drake let off an extended burst, blocking the doorway with bodies, and then ran to the window, shouting for his team to follow. Dahl stayed in place, still holding Kerimov in front of him. Hayden and Kinimaka stayed low, maintaining their fire. The others all followed Drake to the window.

He looked out, feeling the tug of a breeze as it flowed past him. The balcony was about ten feet down. Drake didn't waste any time. He lowered himself until he was full length, then let go, landing sure-footed on the external balcony below. He moved immediately to the edge. Cam came next, then Shaw. Drake looked down.

There was another balcony directly below and, underneath that, a flat patch of grass that would soften their landing.

'Come on,' he said.

Beyond the grass, he saw one side of the general's mansion, though with all the extensions it was difficult to determine which particular side it was. A fountain stood to the right, a flat expanse of grass and then concrete all around it. The grounds extended straight to a chain-link fence and then a treeline. Three outbuildings dotted the area below, two with their doors propped open. Drake saw no sign of any men down there.

He sensed the others coming, heard them land. The balcony was getting crowded. He climbed over the railing, dangled, and then dropped inwards, landing boots first on the next balcony, now just ten feet or so from ground level. He leaned out, looked up.

It was like a supply chain up there. Dahl and Hayden coming over the top balcony, Kinimaka covering them. Cam and Shaw climbing down towards him from the second. Drake turned around and viewed the grass below.

It all looked good. Of course, when everything seems to be going in your favour, then something rears up to go against you. Drake knew that. He didn't see it coming, but he certainly heard it.

There was a hiss like steam escaping and then, half a second later, an explosion. Drake fell to his knees. The entire building shook. Something impacted high above and sent a rain of mortar pouring down, a mushroom cloud of smoke billowing out. Drake looked up, unable to believe what he was seeing.

And then he looked through the rails of the balcony.

Eight men stood in the middle of the grounds. One of them held an RPG that was even now being reloaded. The explosion had been a rocket, fired by one of Kerimov's own men. Yes, they were launching weapons on their own house, trying to pick off the infiltrators with a rocket-propelled grenade.

Drake stuck his gun through the railings and opened fire. Bullets struck among the eight men, most of them missing. Cam and Shaw were above him, leaning over the top rail with their guns aimed, also firing. The guy with the RPG didn't move an inch, just raised the weapon to his shoulder once more, aimed and pressed his trigger.

Drake ducked. The grenade flew at them, launched by a gunpowder booster charge and emitting a cloud of light grey-blue smoke. It flew at an initial speed of 115 metres per second, the rocket motor igniting after ten metres and carrying it with an even greater velocity. Drake saw none of the flight. He had his head burrowed in his arms.

The rocket hit the side of the house, ten feet to the left of the upper floor balcony. The building shuddered again. Dahl and Kinimaka held on tightly, covered in debris and momentarily hidden by the cloud. Drake looked up and saw a river of brick and block pouring down the side of the building.

He fired again. This time, his bullets hit. Three men went down, folding beside the RPG carrier. The shooter himself ducked and started looking wildly around him, looking for cover.

Drake used the distraction to climb over the balcony and then leap down to the grass. He landed and rolled, still clutching his gun in the ready position, coming up on one knee. He sighted on the running men.

Opened fire. Two more went down.

Cam and Shaw landed lightly beside him, still firing and making Drake wonder about their advancing skills. They had learned a lot in the training camp that they'd attended. Their bullets riddled the running men.

All but the RPG shooter. He must have seen his men falling around him and now span and fired his weapon for the last time.

The rocket flew high, way over Drake's head, and smashed into the side of the house. This time, it struck the top balcony.

Dahl and Kinimaka were jumping off it.

The grenade hit with a sound like thunder and exploded. A surge of debris erupted from the wall, this time mixed with iron railing and wooden window frame and shards of glass. The plume of smoke enveloped Dahl and Kinimaka as they leapt down to the next balcony, then mushroomed out and over the top of them.

The side of the house seemed to groan.

Then Drake saw the top floor slump; he saw rows of bricks pouring from the wall in a stream, plummeting to the ground. He saw the roof slip just a few inches, and then the guttering pull away. There was a deep, resounding rumbling sound.

Mai and Alicia were on the bottom balcony, climbing over the railings, the others just behind her. Bits of debris dropped down on them. A twisted railing passed by Mai's head, arrowing down inches away from her and then sticking upright in the grass.

Cam fired the shot that took the RPG shooter out. By then, more men were arriving, running around the corners of the house. Too many for Drake to calculate.

They were in trouble here.

Hopefully, the general was still out for the count. That would distract them a little. Just then, Mai, Alicia and Hayden came running up and crouched with them.

'Don't fire yet,' Drake murmured. 'They just arrived and haven't spotted us. They don't know what to shoot at.'

They raced over to the fountain. Dahl and Kenzie and Kinimaka were still waiting beside the house in an exposed position. Kerimov's men saw them easily.

And turned on them, weapons aimed.

Drake and the others rose as one, concentrating their fire on the soldiers, rifling them with bullets. Confused, they turned and then fell, dead or screaming. In the middle of it, Dahl, Kinimaka, and Kenzie set off running towards the fountain.

Drake span, trying to figure a way out of this. There were too many enemies, even for his team to manage. The trick was to keep moving, keep searching for a way out, stay on top of the situation. He bellowed out an order as Dahl and the others reached them.

'Move!'

They ran from the fountain across the grass, using the carved stone water source to cover them. Drake ran low and fast, letting those at the back guard them with some covering fire. He got a quick glimpse of the general's house now, saw the damage the rockets had done, the great hole gouged in its side. Bricks and blocks and mortar still poured from the third floor to the ground. It was hardly stable, and there were men leaning out of the blasted window hole, staring across the estate as they sought their enemy.

Drake slowed as the grass disappeared and he came to the road that curved around the general's estate. It made sense to follow it to the front. Everywhere else would be surging with men.

They raced along the road, taking it in turns to provide cover and then reload. Ahead, the road curved as it ran towards the front of the house. Drake hoped they would soon come across a miracle.

Behind them, the soldiers were grouping, starting to get a better idea of what was happening, or at least learn that they were supposed to be chasing a group of interlopers. Their confusion was Drake's ally. Meanwhile, Drake could already see the front gate.

And the truck stopped in front of it.

'Come on,' he hissed.

They ran with their heads down, pouring on as much speed as possible. Four soldiers manned the main gate, all of whom were now staring at the men and women running towards them.

They raised their weapons. Drake fired first, winging two of them. The idling truck suddenly roared its engine. Hayden and Kinimaka opened fire, shooting the other two guards just as they opened fire, their bullets whizzing through the air above their heads. The truck, their only way out of here, started to move forward, its wheels turning slowly. It roared, it jerked, smoke billowed out of its exhaust.

'Don't let it get away!' Drake cried. 'Without that truck, we're dead.'

CHAPTER TWENTY EIGHT

The truck drove through the main gate.

Drake and his team were on its tail, just running past its rear quarters when gunfire rang out behind them. The soldiers were chasing hard now, having pinpointed their adversaries and received their orders. Even as he ran around the side of the truck, Drake heard bullets pinging off its bodywork in his wake.

He increased his speed, reached up, and grabbed the door handle. He wrenched it open. Inside, a seated man wearing jeans and a t-shirt pointed a handgun at him. Drake instantly dropped and rolled as the weapon fired, the bullet passing over his head. Drake lost momentum, came up again, and continued to run along the side of the truck.

On the passenger side, Alicia was doing the same thing. She opened the door, let it swing wide open, and saw the gun pointed at her head. Luckily, hers was already aimed and firing. She shot the passenger in the leg as he opened fire; the agony making him miss his shot and shoot high into the air. The man clutched at his leg, screaming.

Alicia grabbed him and hauled him forcefully out of the moving truck. He hit the dirt with a thud and an even louder yell. Alicia left him for one of the others to take care of. She took a quick look inside the truck, getting a view of the driver.

He fired at her instantly.

The bullet flew by inches from her skull. Alicia knew Drake was running along the other side. She didn't want to fire blindly in case the bullet penetrated the vehicle's shell and hit him. But there was another way. She ran slightly faster, then faster again, until she could almost see the driver's legs. The trouble was the truck was picking up more and more speed by the second; it was outdistancing her.

But just for a few seconds, she got a glimpse of the driver's legs.

Alicia fired off two shots, saw her bullets strike flesh and heard the man cry out. The truck slowed immediately. The guy clutched his right leg, the gun in his hand forgotten. Alicia saw Drake reach in, grab hold of the man, and haul him out of the cab.

Now it was empty.

Drake jumped up into the driver's seat, Alicia into the passenger's. The others unhooked the tarpaulin from its stays along the back and jumped up as the vehicle gently rolled to a stop. Behind them, the soldiers drew nearer. Their bullets whipped among the trees and pinged off the truck, mercifully for now missing flesh and the vehicle's tyres.

Drake slammed his foot on the accelerator before the truck stalled. The engine roared. The tyres gripped and propelled it forward. They picked up speed. The truck bounced and jolted them from side to side. Drake tried to avoid the worst ruts, but one evasion just sent him swerving into another delve in the earth. The truck groaned. In the back, the rest of the team took cover behind the crates that were stacked inside.

Drake drove fast, giving no quarter. He couldn't afford to drive at anything but top speed. To both sides, the forest flashed by, branches reaching for him and scraping along the side of the truck. Drake was so concentrated on the driving, it took him more than a minute to close his door.

'Get your fucking foot down, Drakey!' Alicia yelled.

'I am! This is as fast as the bastard will go!'

Through the side mirror, now that the door was closed, he could see that they weren't being closely followed. Not yet. That wouldn't last. He could already imagine the soldiers commandeering the nearest truck.

The road swung left and right. Thick forest whipped by. The truck bounced and rolled slightly and made noises that told Drake it was about to fall apart. The suspension groaned as if it was about to give way. To top it all, as he drove, the passenger side wing mirror fell off.

The rear partition suddenly slid open. Hayden's face appeared. 'Push it, Drake. We've a fair way to go to the plane.'

Drake knew it. But now, the road was smoothing out in places. The truck flew along it, eating up the miles. After fifteen minutes he made out the telltale signs of someone following: a boxy shape, the glint of sunshine on glass, the blurry outlines of a speeding truck, but he couldn't slow down enough to be sure.

Instead, he drove as fast as he could.

The track became a road, albeit a bumpy, potholed one. But Drake was used to driving around potholes - he'd lived in England for many years. He negotiated the hazards and kept the truck flying along. By now, the sun was waning towards the west but still gave off a broad swathe of yellow-gold and a powerful blast of heat. The truck, inside, was sweltering as both Drake and Alicia thought to wind the windows down.

Behind them, three trucks were gaining.

Drake saw the airfield ahead. He powered the truck

around a heap of tyres, through a gap in between piles of machine parts and then through an open iron-framed gateway. Hayden had already radioed the pilots to be ready for takeoff. The truck jolted its way along the potholed road, closing the gap rapidly to the plane. As he peered through the windscreen, Drake saw that the rear cargo hold was wide open.

'Get ready to bail,' he shouted through the rear partition.

Just then, gunfire erupted. Dahl and Kinimaka and the others fired from the back of the truck into the engines and windscreens of their oncoming pursuers. It was all carefully calculated – now that they were approaching the plane, they needed to create as much of a gap between the pursuers and the pursued as possible. The bullets smashed amongst the following trucks, pounding through bodywork and engine blocks and pulverising windscreens. The trucks veered wildly, swerving all over the road.

Drake drove arrow straight for the rear cargo hold. The pilots must have seen the action happening behind them. The plane was already moving, its engines starting to roar. Drake hit the accelerator, stamped on the brakes and drifted the bouncing truck right up to the edge of the dragging cargo hold door.

Doors flew open. He and Alicia jumped out. The others leapt from the back of the truck, firing as they jumped. The plane picked up speed. Drake and Alicia ran onto the rear cargo hold door as it scraped across the concrete.

Halfway up, they stopped, turned, and fell to one knee. They opened fire, covering their friends as they, in turn, ran and raced for the cargo hold door.

Drake hit the following trucks once more, sending them veering wildly. By now, the drivers had had enough of being hit and pulled up. Soldiers poured out of the vehicles, so many Drake wondered how they'd all survived the rattling journey on board. Maybe they'd been so tightly packed the jolting hadn't bothered them. He quickly strafed the air surrounding them.

The team scrambled on board the plane. Dahl, the last man, almost could not keep up with it as it quickly gathered speed. Once he was on board, Drake ran up the ramp and hit the big red button, the one that lifted the cargo hold door. The pilots had timed it just right for, as the door lifted and blocked any chance the pursuers had of firing inside, the aircraft's wheels left the ground and the plane took flight.

Drake let out a long breath and turned to his colleagues. 'Everyone okay?'

There were several nods and affirmatives. Cam and Shaw threw themselves into seats. Hayden and Kinimaka leaned against the side of the plane, whilst the others just stood in place, panting.

'Much too close for comfort,' Kenzie said.

'I'd say we pissed that general off,' Dahl said with a smile. 'Hope the bastard's house falls down.'

Hayden was already kneeling and rummaging in her backpack. She came up quickly with the sat phone. 'We gotta call Bryant.'

The phone rang and rang. Drake let the tension and adrenaline ease its way out of him and sat down. He took a bottle of water from a nearby basket and drank it before hunting for some rations. They weren't exactly tasty, but they were calorific enough to keep him going.

Hayden looked surprised when a female voice eventually answered Bryant's phone.

'Who is this?' the woman asked.

Mai frowned and walked over. Alicia was quick to notice and perked right up. Drake expected her to say something derogatory but, for now, she stayed quiet.

Hayden explained who they were and asked to speak to Bryant immediately.

'We've been waiting for your call,' the woman said in a sad voice. 'I'm sorry to tell you that Mr Bryant has been shot. He's in hospital, in intensive care.'

Drake felt his world shift. Hayden just stared at the phone. *'What?'*

In his shock, Drake barely noticed the terrible expression that crossed Mai's face: the fear, the terror, the dreadful hurt and suffering.

The woman went on. 'I'm putting you through to Mr Sutherland.'

Drake was even more surprised. This wasn't the right operation for the assistant director of the FBI to be directly involved in.

Seconds passed, maybe a minute. Mai was staring at the phone as if it was a living, writhing snake. Her eyes were blank, her face slack. Drake stood up and went over to her.

'I'm sorry,' he said.

'He's in intensive care?' Mai questioned, barely able to believe it.

'Is it related to the mission?' Dahl wondered.

Alicia leaned forward and put a hand on Mai's shoulder. Drake had always known there was a deeper bond between the two.

A deep voice came through the sat phone's speaker. 'This is Sutherland. I'm sorry about what happened to Bryant, but he's in the best place now, in the best care. You must move on with your mission.'

'That's why we called,' Hayden whispered, still in shock. 'Is... is Bryant going to be okay?'

'He's stable and strong. He'll pull through. What have you got for me?'

'Can I ask, sir, why are *you* dealing with this?'

Sutherland accepted the question because he knew them well and had worked with them a few times before. 'Not my choice, believe me. I'm Bryant's liaison. He came through me to reach the military chiefs, as I was the easiest choice because of our past liaisons. An excellent move on Bryant's part, I guess. Not so good for me. Now that Bryant's injured, I'm your point man. There just isn't time to get anyone else up to speed.'

'Well, thanks,' Hayden said and then caught Sutherland up on events that had transpired in Turkmenistan. When she was done, Sutherland stayed quiet.

'Sir?' she questioned after a while.

'Flux?' he questioned, his voice taut. 'Are you sure?'

'Yes, sir. I know it's bad. We've all heard of this guy.'

'And he's the end user?'

'We don't think so. Not according to Kerimov.'

'Well, thank god for small mercies,' Sutherland said. 'Flux would as soon explode that bomb as make his morning coffee. He's the worst kind of evil.'

'He took delivery of the bomb yesterday,' Dahl said.

'That's a little more encouraging. If I recall correctly, Flux operates out of Iran.'

'That's what we're told, sir.'

Sutherland told them to sit tight as he made further enquiries. He also told them he'd order the pilots to make a beeline for Iran, despite the obvious issue that might cause. Drake wasn't too worried. Iranian airspace was at least ninety minutes away.

The line went dead. Mai still hadn't moved. Drake couldn't hide the shock over the news of Bryant and didn't know what to say. He, like Dahl, wondered if it had anything to do with their current mission. Maybe it was the end user, showing their reach. Maybe, somehow, they knew that the Ghost Squadron was chasing the bomb around the globe, chasing their network down. Was Bryant's shooting a retaliation?

Drake ate as they waited for Sutherland to call back. He felt the plane make a turn, now headed for Iran, wondered briefly what the hell would happen next. He wondered about Flux. The man's very name stood for instability, liquidity, and unrest. His reputation was fearsome. It surprised Drake they hadn't come across him yet on their travels around the world, but you couldn't police everyone. There simply weren't enough hours in the day, and there was always another bad guy to catch.

'We have to remember that Bryant is strong,' Hayden said into the oppressing silence. 'He'll pull through this.'

Mai nodded, speaking for the first time. 'They say he's stable. He's through the worst of it.'

Drake spoke up quickly. 'Like you say, he's a strong character. He's been with us on a few missions, even saved our asses. By what I know of the man, he'll survive this.'

Mai smiled gratefully. Dahl turned his attention to the mission, perhaps trying to take their minds off the Bryant situation.

'We need to talk about this guy, this new asshole,' he said. 'Talk to me about Flux.'

CHAPTER TWENTY NINE

'Flux,' Hayden looked from face to face. 'Is a whole heap of badness. Well connected, well travelled, well funded. Yes, he works out of Iran, but he can pop up anywhere. He seems to know how to use the dark byways of the world to flit from place to place. He's a vile killer, a leader, all the bad things you could name. He's one of those things that crept out of Pandora's evil box that we haven't been able to catch or kill. The guy's a living nightmare.'

Dahl made a face. 'We'll see about all that,' he said.

'The guy is prominent in Iran,' Hayden said. 'Supported by the state. That obviously makes him harder to pin down. Unofficially, they conceal and protect him and allow him to operate.'

'Which brings us to the problem of operating in Iran,' Drake said.

'Not gonna happen,' Kinimaka said. 'Not without careful planning, tech support, some kind of mobile command centre. Flying as we are, we're not getting into Iran.'

Drake had been on enough ops to know the Hawaiian was right. The group sat glumly for a while, every second taking them closer to a country they could not officially land in and, if they entered its airspace, would shoot them down.

'We wait for Sutherland.' Hayden said.

The minutes ticked by. The plane flew on. Tension

thickened the air. They were all very aware that Flux had taken possession of the bomb just yesterday. They were closer than they had ever been. Just an hour from Iran, then fifty minutes, then forty-five.

At last, Sutherland rang back.

'Change of plan,' he said.

Drake sat forward on the edge of his seat. 'What does that mean?'

'It means I can't smuggle you into Iran. We don't have enough time to set up an op, let alone position men on the ground, in the right place, to facilitate your arrival.'

'Do you know where Flux is?' Alicia interrupted.

'I'll get to that. Right now, you have to listen. The closest I can get you to Iran is Kuwait.'

Drake knew the assistant director was doing his best, but still couldn't stop the disappointment from showing in his voice. 'Is that the best you can do, sir?'

'It's a short skip and a jump from Kuwait to Iran,' Hayden said lightly.

'It may be,' Sutherland said. 'But the entire logistics operation will be up to you. I can't help you at such short notice.'

Drake wasn't surprised. They were bordering on Kuwaiti territory as they spoke.

'Assets on the ground?' he said.

'All prepped, primed, and told to watch out for you. Just in case.'

Sutherland signed off then, leaving Drake with an empty feeling. It felt as if they weren't being backed up to the fullest, despite the target. It felt as if the government was fighting against itself. Maybe some didn't believe the threat was real. And there were people, Drake knew, in the upper echelons who wouldn't be interested if the threat wasn't directly aimed at the United States.

'Kuwait military strip landing in ten minutes,' the pilot's voice came over the tannoy system.

Drake made sure his weapons were clean and fully loaded, that his backpack was replete with rations, ammo, and a dozen other items as he felt the plane start its descent. He met the eyes of the man sitting across from him.

'We ready to take out this terrorist wanker?' he said.

'I'm looking forward to it.' Dahl said.

'No one's taken him out yet,' Hayden said with a hint of warning.

'That's because he hasn't come across the SPEAR team,' Alicia said.

'We're the Ghost Squadron now,' Drake said.

'I lose track.'

'Too much going on in her fluffy blonde head,' Kenzie said with a grin.

'How'd you like it if I stick you with one of your trademark knives?' Alicia growled.

'I can think of better things.'

Mai was hanging her head in a corner of the plane, ignoring the pilot's seatbelt warnings. 'We take this guy out not just to recover the nuke,' she said. 'But for Bryant, too. They're all part of the same network, moving it on and on. They all deserve to die.'

Drake nodded solemnly. 'Agreed,' he said. 'Bryant is one of us. We're doing this for him, as well.'

'First, we have to get into Iran without being detected,' Shaw said. 'Any idea how we're gonna do that?'

'We'll find a way,' Mai said. 'We always do.'

Drake turned his gaze to Hayden. 'Has Sutherland sent through the coordinates for Flux's camp?'

'Yes, just now. Don't forget they're *rough* coordinates. Based on second-hand intel. It's come from informers,

people looking to make a few dollars here and there.'
'How up to date is it?'
Hayden looked up at him. 'Just a few hours old.'
And Drake smiled. 'That'll do,' he said.

CHAPTER THIRTY

They landed with a screech and a few bounces, waited for the plane to taxi to a stop, and then climbed out after thanking the pilots. The plane wouldn't wait for them now. It would be gone after a quick refuel.

There was a man waiting for them on the tarmac, an American who went by the name, Robbie.

'What's the plan?' he yelled above the dying roar of the jet engines.

Drake walked up to him. 'Can you get us a couple of fast boats? And then transport us to the Persian Gulf?'

Robbie nodded immediately. 'This is a military base,' he said. 'I can get you exactly that. And the Persian Gulf's right over there,' he pointed.

Drake shielded his eyes from the fumes the plane was kicking out and looked to his right. The evening sun was just setting over Kuwait, throwing a blood-red streak across the land that painted the western horizon to his left. Where the Gulf was, to his right, there was only shadow. He fancied he could see the rippling waters.

'That's perfect,' he said. 'Do you start many missions from here?'

Robbie smiled quickly. 'It has been known.'

'Won't they be on the lookout for that?' Dahl asked, nodding toward Iran.

'It's a damn long shoreline.' Robbie said.

Drake started walking past the American, trying to get him moving. 'The boats?' He asked.

'You're not American, sir. Where are you from?'

'International coalition,' Drake said. 'And I'm from God's own country, mate. Sunny Yorkshire.'

'Never heard of that.'

Drake shook his head as he walked. What was the world coming to? Dahl was grinning. They followed Robbie into a vast hangar like a treasure cave. Stacks of boats stood alongside crates of ammo and weapons, tactical gear and even a couple of helicopters. There was everything from uniforms and boots to grenades and rocket launchers and electrical equipment. Drake's eye settled on the pile of boats.

'The Zodiac Commando 470,' Robbie said. 'Also known as the Combat Rubber Reconnaissance Craft, used by the Navy, the Marines and the Army. We have a tonne of them, sir.'

Drake could see that. He told the guy they needed two, then waited as they were brought over to him. The team wandered over to a docking area and waited for the boats to be placed in the water.

'You sure you wanna go right now?' Robbie asked. 'There's fresh chow in the mess hall?'

'As appealing as that sounds,' Alicia said. 'We can't wait.'

Drake checked that the 55 horsepower, two-stroke engine worked, and that the paddles they would need as they came closer to the far shore were on board. With that, he climbed into the first boat and watched as Dahl started it up. Kinimaka took charge of the other, his hand close to the tiller arm.

Soon, the boats were heading away from the dock and out into the darkness. Drake had a heading on his phone, the soft glow barely illuminating his face. They were all running on the barest minimum of tech — they were moving too fast to slow down and make use of the better instruments. For now, speed commanded them.

The heavy swell of the Persian Gulf soon enveloped them. Drake clung on to the side ropes, his face occasionally coated by a salty spray. The craft rode the troughs and the peaks well, water occasionally splashing over the side of the boat. It had been a while since Drake rode a Zodiac, and it took him a few minutes to get used to the sensations again.

Darkness surrounded them. Drake had the coordinates for a spot on the far shore to guide them. Above, the arc of the sky twinkled with stars and the sliver of a moon barely risen above the horizon. Even so, it cast silvery slithers across the waters, reflecting off the boat's dark hull and the clothes of the team. They stayed as low as possible, hunched over, holding on, powering ever closer to the Iranian shore.

'We are just over a hundred miles from Flux's supposed camp,' Hayden whispered to them at one point. 'Thanks to Sutherland for coming through with the intel.'

'Is that from the Iranian shore?' Drake questioned.

'Yes, sorry, from the shore.'

Time passed in a rapid flow, just like the waves that bore them along on their journey. The night deepened. It took a long time to make the crossing, but Drake's training had taught him to use the downtime to relax, to switch off, to let the long minutes and hours pass by without too much conscious thought. He was alert, ready to act, but also mentally untroubled, saving his adrenalin for what was to come.

A few miles off shore, they switched to paddles. The waters whispered to the sound of the oars parting them. The boats drifted silently into shore.

And grounded on a stony beach. Robbie had told them the best place to land based on the latest intel, even programmed the coordinates for them. It seemed Robbie was right. There was nobody there to greet them, a good thing in Iran.

Drake helped pull the boat up and hide it alongside the other at the top of the shore. There was some underbrush there, a thick tangle of it, and soon Drake didn't think anyone could easily see the boats, even in daylight. They dropped a marker on their GPS so that they could find the boats later.

If they came back this way.

Drake led them away from the shoreline. They had one hundred miles to cover. It could have been far worse, but it still wasn't ideal. The first thing he looked for was a village.

'There's a settlement about five miles away,' he said, looking at his phone and the up-to-date satellite maps Robbie had downloaded there. 'If we hustle, we can be there in an hour.'

It would be perfect timing. They'd be hitting the lonely village in the dead of night.

They ploughed on through the dark. The terrain was rocky and sparse. Dense bush dotted the landscape. They found a path and tried to stick to it, heading in an easterly direction. To their right, a low set of hills marked the horizon. To the left, it was flat and open, nothing but a vast stretch of land and then the night sky arcing down to meet it.

They held their weapons ready and stalked through the Iranian night. It was a sweaty, hard hour, running with their packs on, heads down. Cam and Shaw ranged out to right and left, checking for dangers, but finding nothing. Drake went ahead a few clicks, but all he found was darkness and more darkness.

Finally, they reached the village. It was a small settlement, unlit, just a collection of huts and block houses clustered around a main road. Drake saw no movement as they approached. Taking advantage of the inactivity, they split up and spent just a few minutes scouting the area, the size of their crew a definite advantage in this situation.

'Found one,' Kenzie said after a few minutes.

She pinpointed her position on the GPS. Drake and the others scrambled over to her, staying silent. Soon, they were all looking at the dark pickup truck parked on the side of the road outside a low slung house.

'Get ready to hot-wire it,' Drake said. 'I'll leave some money.'

None of them felt right about stealing a truck, hence the cash. Drake left it wedged under a rock on the house's doorstep and then returned to the vehicle. Dahl had broken in and already had the wiring loom in his hand.

'Do it,' Drake said.

They set off as quietly as they were able, but the truck was a diesel and made more than a little noise. They sat three up front and the rest in the rear bed, hanging on. Drake wasn't sure how many Iranian patrols or check points were in the area, but he imagined there'd be a few.

This was the most dangerous part; the drive through the night, not knowing what they might come upon. Again, it was all determined by speed. They couldn't rest, couldn't pause, could barely slow down because they had to stay on the trail of the nuclear weapon. There were no other options.

Drake guided the truck along the rutted road, leaving the town far behind. A mountain range, picked out by the stars, grew until it dominated the way forward. Hours passed and soon the dawn rose, spreading like a fresh painting across the land ahead, flashing through the highest peaks. Drake was grateful that they had survived the night unscathed.

Taking risks, they continued on.

'Wait,' Hayden suddenly said. 'Stop.'

Drake pulled up and looked at her. 'What do you see?'

Hayden glared hard through the binoculars. 'Some way ahead, there's a checkpoint. I see two trucks and the blurry shapes of soldiers. You're going to have to go around.'

Drake swore. He had seen an alternate path a few miles ago, but the detour was going to cost them time. Still, they had no option but to go around.

An hour later, Hayden stopped him again.

'Another one,' she said. 'Is there an alternative route?'

This time, Drake had seen no dissecting road. He took some time to study the intricate maps. 'If we go back here,' he pointed. 'A road loops around and through that mountain pass. It's remote. We'll just have to hope they don't have patrols up there too.'

They set off. The truck laboured as it started up the slopes, its wheels spinning on the loose gravel. But it stuck to the task, turning out to be a dependable warhorse. They wound up into the mountains. The air up here was thinner and clear, as fresh as Drake could remember air being. They were just passing under a low overhang when Hayden shouted out for the third time.

'Trucks coming this way,' she snapped. 'Get off the road.'

Easier said than done. Drake had to drive towards them and hope that they weren't being too observant before he found a steeply inclined slope down which he could take the truck and hope to hell they could make it back up later. The slope was sharp and angled; it would hide them from the road.

They waited. They readied their weapons. In the back,

because of the angle, the team was forced to hold on tightly for fear of tumbling over the top of the cab. Soon, they heard the trucks approaching.

The crunch of their tyres gave them away, the roar of their engines. Drake couldn't see anything; they were blind down the slope. He stayed at the wheel whilst the others jumped out and guarded the slope, hidden away from the main road. Drake listened carefully, detecting no slowing down of the passing trucks, no lessening of the engine sound. Soon, the small convoy had passed and continued down the mountain.

Hayden took the team up to the road and watched their enemies vanish, only returning when she gauged the way on, up and down, safe. Then, it was up to Drake to back the truck up the steep slope and drive it back out onto the road.

Hours passed. They hid from two more patrols, avoided another checkpoint. All the consistent veering off their route cost them the day. They had hoped to arrive at Flux's camp by nightfall. Instead, they were still twenty miles distant.

Drake found a place to hide the truck. The team had no choice but to spend the night in discomfort, or at least those in the back did, jostling for a place to lie. They slept fitfully, posed guards, and were wide awake by sunrise. They met on the rocks for a quick breakfast of rations and coffee warmed over a tiny campfire as the sun threw its new rays across the land.

'Last leg of the journey,' Drake said, standing and emptying the dregs of his cup.

'Flux hasn't ever seen anything like us before,' Dahl rose.

'Let's hope he's at home,' Kinimaka said.

'Same goes for the nuke,' Cam said.

'This one's for Bryant,' Mai said. Drake could tell by the strain in her eyes, by her expression, that she was desperate for news, but knew full well she couldn't contact anyone at home. She was resigned to completing this mission without further information.

'Do we have a plan?' Alicia asked lightly.

'Yeah, improvise,' Drake said.

'What we always do,' Dahl said. 'We make it work.'

'It's a straight shot to Flux's camp now.' Drake was studying the map. 'Down out of the mountains to the north and then a long stretch of relatively flat ground. There are a few hills we can get lost in if we need to, along with a bumpy row quite close to the terrorist camp. They should help get us closer.'

The team nodded and rose to their feet. They made their way back to the truck, only Alicia complaining about the cramped space. Drake jumped back in the driver's seat and started the vehicle up.

It was time to finish this thing.

CHAPTER THIRTY ONE

Hayden received a message through the sat phone as they neared Flux's camp.

'Just an update from Sutherland,' she said in the loud confines of the cab. 'More information about Flux. Nothing we didn't already know. He's owned up to several bombings in the past, proudly it seems. He's wanted all across the world and is in the top ten of the FBI and Interpol's most wanted lists. I guess he's a terrorist head of state. He flaunts it. Wants his enemies to know who he is. The guy has a vast network and is loved by all those he leads. They must be proper fanatics.'

By now, Drake was slowing the truck as they came in sight of the far hills, the ones that bordered Flux's camp. He didn't want to get too close for fear of being seen by a random patrol. Soon, he found a place to leave the truck where it would remain out of sight for a few hours to all but the most determined of searchers.

After that, they were on foot.

They stayed low to the landscape, studying the terrain ahead carefully through their binoculars and seeing no sign of activity in the hills. Soon, they had reached the rocky slopes and started pushing their way through the tightly packed boulders, heading up and up. They stopped often to check the route and search for antagonists. Nothing untoward appeared. Drake trod through loose shale and gravel. When he leaned against one boulder, he felt it shift and shouted out a warning to those below. The boulder gave way and rolled at speed all the way down the slope. After that, and a few dangerous looks from his friends, he didn't lean against any more boulders.

They topped the rise and lay down on their stomachs. They crawled to the edge of the slope that should lead down to the valley where Flux had his camp. Drake expected to see a makeshift expanse of tents, maybe a few houses fashioned out of blocks, maybe even a village with a few dusty roads.

What he saw made him close his eyes for a few seconds and then open them again. He couldn't believe what he was seeing.

Someone, not Flux surely, had built a palace out here in the Iranian desert. On the outside, it looked abandoned, the crumbling, dirty walls, the broken down gates and roofs, the untended gardens that might once have consisted of green grass but were now nothing but rough scrub. The palace walls had once been white, a lot of it marble, but were now unrecognisable as the desert threw its weight against them. Sand and shale piled up against most of them. There were paths around the gardens, paths that led to the gates and to the doors of the main house, or palace, as Drake saw it. There were a couple of minarets, a couple of turrets.

Men wearing desert garb walked the paths and passed through the doorways. They came out of many tents set up on the grounds, ducking between dwellings. They were mostly armed, most of them looking well-cared for and smiling. They didn't look at all like a desperate terrorist company, not like Drake had been told.

'What the hell?' Hayden said.

'This casts a new light on things,' Dahl said.

'Much more difficult to infiltrate than a camp,' Cam said.

Drake kept his eyes on the activity. So it seemed Flux lived like a prince. He slept in a palace, kept guards and lorded his status over everyone. The Iranian state kept him in excellent conditions, it appeared.

As he lay in position, Drake checked the surrounding hills. There were a few scouts out and about, several men trudging through the scrubby wilderness. Drake and his team had come up between them, a nice slice of luck. He saw one man stationed at the top of the highest peak, sitting cross-legged and eating a meal.

'The hills have ears,' Kenzie said.

Drake nodded. 'Stay low, guys.'

They continued their surveillance of Flux's compound. At first, it was mostly men wearing desert garb and battledress and carrying guns, everything you might expect from a terrorist's palace, but Drake also saw marble columns and waterfalls and two large pools, a hot tub and a jacuzzi. He then saw women in robes carry trays to the various guards and then, hardly able to believe his eyes, saw several women wearing swimsuits emerge from one of the doorways. The women proceeded to the pools, took luxurious deckchairs, or just jumped in and started swimming. The men paid no attention to them.

After a while, a figure emerged who really grabbed Drake's attention.

It was a man, about six feet in height. He wore a silk dressing gown, open at the front, and carried a big Smith and Wesson handgun stuffed down the front of his swim shorts. He carried a bowl of food in one hand and twirled a knife in the other, and walked about like he owned the place. Twice Drake saw him issue orders to the guards.

Flux.

It had to be. The man put down the food and the gun, shed his robe, and started doing laps. The women smiled and waved at him. A guard came over and offered him a mobile phone, which he yelled into for about thirty seconds. Then he threw the phone across the puddle-strewn patio. The guard hurried off to collect it. Drake took in the face of the man they'd come to see.

'Definitely Flux,' he said.

'Not a minion,' Alicia agreed.

'How are we gonna get down there?' Kinimaka asked, switching his attention from left to right.

'Yeah,' Kenzie said. 'I forgot my bikini.'

'You could pass for one of those bitches,' Alicia said. 'Even wearing your fighting clothes.'

Kenzie screwed her face up, unclear whether Alicia was paying her a compliment or handing out an insult.

'Whatever it is, it has to be today,' Hayden said. 'Or tonight. You can guarantee Flux has a plan for that nuke.'

CHAPTER THIRTY TWO

Connor Bryant drifted, lying in the lap of luxury. He had a vague idea that the painkillers were really kicking in, but he didn't care. His vision was blurry, a warm, soothing feeling crept through his head. Reality took on a cloudy edge, faded away. He felt himself sinking deeper and deeper into the arms of some sweet dream.

Bryant knew nothing more for a while. When he woke again, he was slightly more lucid. He recognised he was lying on a hospital bed, that there were tubes hanging around and attached to him, that he was in a private room. He saw a window and a corridor to his right, people in doctor's and nurse's uniforms passing by.

He was in a hospital.

Why?

Bryant tried to dredge it up from his memory. The drugs were doing a good job of clouding his brain. Bryant wondered why that was. Was he hurt? In pain? Even... dying?

It was a sobering thought, and it helped him find a touch more clarity. There was some deep agony in his gut. He could sense it, but he couldn't feel it. Perhaps that was something to do with all the tubes. He was comfortable. Nobody came to check in on him, which wasn't necessarily a bad thing. It meant he was stable. But he wasn't himself. He knew that... but he couldn't figure out why.

Trauma.

Yes, of course. He'd heard that trauma victims blocked certain events from their memories, chiefly the shocking events that put them in harm's way.

What happened to me?

The good part was that he could remember who he was, where he worked, who his friends were. Mai's face floated before him, making him smile. But he could barely move, and he got the feeling that he shouldn't.

Just then, something happened. The warm, syrupy feeling started closing over him again. He could feel its soothing advance creeping through his veins, no doubt from one of the drips. He must be on some kind of regimen, painkillers every hour or something like that. It wasn't uncomfortable, though, far from it. Bryant enjoyed the sensation, though he had the feeling it might be wasting his life away.

But at the moment, it was necessary.

The deep ache in his guts told him that.

Bryant slipped away. The ride down into oblivion felt good. He zoned out for quite a while. Daylight disappeared and then came back, flooding through the curtains of his room. Bryant woke a while later, once more reaching up through the gooey darkness for reason and clarity. This was the third time he could recall waking, and still he hadn't seen a soul in his room.

This time, Bryant shifted. It didn't feel so bad. He pushed himself backwards on the bed, tried to raise himself a little. The tubes shook and joggled this way and that. Something clamped deep in his gut. Bryant didn't like the feel, so he stopped moving. He turned his gaze towards the window that overlooked the corridor.

A nurse clad all in blue passed by, hurrying. Bryant tried to shout at her, but it seemed his mouth was full of cotton wool. That wouldn't do. He tried to summon up some saliva, to wet his lips. He cleared his throat.

He tried again.

This time, a squeak came forth. Nothing more than that. He saw another nurse pass by and then a doctor, none of them even glancing his way. Something occurred to him then, and it was a good thought because it proved his brain was still firing on all its cylinders. He remembered that these hospital rooms had an emergency call button.

But where the hell was it?

Bryant didn't want to turn onto his side for fear of doing himself damage. He turned his head as much as he was able, first left and then right, searching for that big red button, anything that might scream out *Emergency!*

Nothing swam into focus. Bryant let his eyes adjust. There was something blocky and large perched on the bedside table. He wondered if he might be able to reach out for it. He hadn't seen his arms and hands yet. Did he want to? Could they be injured, lacerated... worse? Bryant shuddered. Did he really want to see what was wrong with him?

But his limbs felt fine. At least, he thought so. It was a tough choice, but Bryant finally made it. He was going to reach out for the blocky thing.

Right then, he heard a door opening. Relief flooded through him. At last... at last... someone had remembered he was here.

He cast his eyes down to the bottom of the bed, towards the door.

But it wasn't a doctor or a nurse who had entered his room. It was two men wearing civilian clothing, one clad in jeans and a big black jacket, the other wearing all denim. He could tell by the looks on their faces that they weren't here to give him a sponge bath.

And by the guns that suddenly appeared in their hands.

Bryant's hearing was fine. He heard the door closing, heard their footsteps as they walked over him, even heard suppressors being screwed into the barrels of the guns. Bryant tried to let out a yell, but his voice still wouldn't work, his throat hoarse.

The men were smiling now as they came to stand over him.

'Quinn sends her regards,' one man whispered.

What the hell did that mean?

'The boss lady wants you dead,' the other muttered. 'You must have really fucked up big time, friend.'

They aimed their weapons at his head.

Bryant, helpless, flashed once more on Mai's face. It was the last thing he would ever see, the last thing he wanted to see. The face of the best thing in his life.

'Shame the boys couldn't finish the job properly in the first place,' the first man cast his eyes down Bryant's body as he spoke.

'Yeah, but they aren't nearly as good as us,' his companion said.

'You got that right, bud.'

Fingers squeezed triggers. Bryant saw the last second of his life about to expire. If only he could rise, fight back, do something about it. But he was helpless, somewhere alien, for a reason that he couldn't even remember. Where was Mai anyway?

There came a loud bang, the noise ripping through the room. Bryant saw his death approaching. He'd thought it was the gun going off. But, as he blinked, he realised it was the door smashing inwards, splintering away from its hinges. Beyond the two gunmen, Bryant could now see four more figures barging into his room.

First, I have no one for hours. Now my room's fucking

full. The errant thought whisked through his head.

The newcomers had guns too. Everyone had guns but him. He watched as bullets started flying above him, feeling strangely emotionally detached. He could hear it all, hear the loud discharge and the smashing glass and the fragmenting wood and plaster. Bullets whacked into flesh. Bryant flinched as the agonised sounds of those struck by the streaking metal filled the tiny room.

The gunmen twisted away, their blood flying across the broken window, across the plaster walls, across Bryant's bedsheet. One moment they were there, standing menacingly over him, the next they dropped like logs and were gone.

Bryant stared at the newcomers. They wore suits, carried police issue handguns and were running towards him. Two of the four turned to him whilst the other two bent down towards the victims.

'Are you okay? Did they hit you?' one man asked.

Bryant didn't know how to respond to that. He couldn't speak, and the answer required both a nod and the shake of a head. But he managed a smile; he was grateful for their intervention.

Who were they?

As if in answer, the same man who'd spoken bent over and talked directly at his face as though afraid Bryant couldn't hear him.

'Do you know Matt Drake and Hayden Jaye?'

Bryant managed a nod this time.

'They called in a favour. A big one. With assistant Director Sutherland. The FBI has your back now, Mr Bryant.'

The man holstered his weapon. The other man went back to the damaged door. Outside, Bryant could see the faces of dozens of doctors and nurses, all staring at him.

Now they came. If only he could remember why he was here.

But it all seemed important. Bryant smiled again, and tried to speak, the rasp in his throat now finally giving way to real speech.

'Thank you,' was the first thing he said.

The FBI agent nodded. The others rose from their inspection of the gunmen and grimly shook their heads.

'No need to call a doctor,' one said with a bit of dark humour that Bryant appreciated.

Bryant was sure of one thing now. All of this went back to Drake and Hayden and the Ghost Squadron. Someone was trying to kill him because of them. And on the back of that, he wondered just how much trouble they were in?

And Mai? How much trouble was the woman he loved in?

Bryant wondered if they might increase the dose of painkillers.

CHAPTER THIRTY THREE

They saw no sign of a bomb, of any weapon other than the guns the guards were carrying. They saw no crates, no boxes, no packages of any kind. Flux was behaving as a pampered, protected, spoilt, greedy terrorist should. He was doing laps of his pool, sipping champagne, eating triangular sandwiches and playing grab-ass with the assorted women who lounged around on their deck chairs. He was sitting in the water with his back to the far side, reclining lazily, soaking up the rays of the sun.

Drake found it an odd scenario. Here they were, in the middle of the desert, in Iran of all places, studying a scene that might have come straight from Beverly Hills.

'It's kind of surreal,' Alicia said.

They were all lying flat, hidden among rocks, staring down at the palace. They hadn't moved a muscle in about an hour. Only once had the passing patrols bothered them, coming within about one hundred feet, but much further down the slope behind them. The guards never stopped walking and didn't scan their surroundings too much, either. It was all to do with complacency, Drake knew, a complacency that started right at the very top with Flux.

'This man's supposed to be the world's worst terrorist?' he murmured. 'I don't see a lot of that.'

'Maybe once,' Dahl said. 'He's something else now.'

'Yeah, protected by the state,' Kinimaka said. 'The

illusion they conjure for him – maybe it's a veil they hide behind, committing the acts themselves.'

'The government, you mean?'

'Agents of the government. They do something atrocious, lay it at Flux's door. All the while, Flux is sunning himself and doing laps. The Iranians are free to do whatever they want.'

Drake thought is sounded plausible. 'The question is...' he said. 'Would this Flux, this man, have taken delivery of the nuke?'

'Kerimov seemed pretty certain that it was him.' Mai said.

Drake nodded. 'So maybe Flux keeps his hand in,' he said. 'Shows his face, flies things in and out. It's an even better cover for the Iranians because Flux still appears active.'

There were no outbuildings below that Drake could see. The only place to hide the nuke was the palace itself. He could see only one option.

'What's our way inside?' he asked everyone.

Dahl sighed. 'The good news is that they've left the palace to rot,' he said. 'Do you see the various piles of desert debris heaped against the walls, crumbling them in places? That's our way in. Of course, we don't know how well they keep the grounds lit during the night, but it's the only way I can see short of strolling through the front gate.'

'Covert infiltration,' Shaw said. 'I like it.'

'All of us?' Can asked doubtfully.

'Good question,' Drake said. 'I'm thinking two or three at the very most.'

'We've been trained for this,' Shaw spoke up immediately. 'Trained by the ninja.'

Drake looked over at both her and Cam. 'How long were you there? Three, four months?'

'I'm sure we can do this.'

'I'm not sure exactly what *this* is,' Cam admitted.

Drake fixed the young man with a gaze. 'Infiltrate the palace. Find Flux. Interrogate him. Find out what he plans to do with the nuke.'

'Right,' Cam said. 'Well, I can definitely do that.'

'And I'll go with them,' Mai said. 'To make sure they don't die.'

Drake felt better about that. He hadn't wanted the youngest members of their team, the newest, to feel as though they weren't trusted – especially since they'd recently come back from Japan – but the thought of sending them alone into the dragon's den had definitely unsettled him.

'It's decided then,' he said. 'We wait until dark.'

Hours passed. The team kept their heads down. The patrol passed by once more, this time a tad closer but still way down the hill, nowhere near the top and close to Drake's position. Flux and his women got bored with swimming. They climbed out of the pools, sent servants off to find food, and were soon tucking into local delicacies, still drinking their champagne. Drake saw Flux work out using an outside gym. He saw the man field several calls, all of them seemingly frantic before turning back to lounge by the side of the pool. He was putting on a good show.

Darkness fell. A few lights came on around the palace grounds, not many. Flux and his women had already retired somewhere. When they went inside, Drake tried to keep track of their passage through the various windows, but it was of no use. All he could see was that Flux went up to the second floor.

Still, they waited. Mai, Cam and Shaw made themselves

ready, preparing their weapons and their clothing and blacking out their faces. They pulled on black hats and gloves and, even lying next to the team, blended into the darkness.

'It's time,' Drake finally said.

A few stars sparkled above in the endless vault of the night. Darkness stretched to every horizon, and the sky felt huge. The temperature was plummeting. Drake and the others first made sure the patrol wasn't anywhere near and then pulled out thicker jackets in which to spend the night, black blankets too that they could drape over themselves. If the patrol didn't see them during the day, it certainly wasn't going to see them during the night.

But they stayed alert, kept their weapon ready in case Mai, Cam and Shaw needed their backup.

Nobody said good luck. The words weren't in their team's vocabulary. Luck didn't come into it. Mai led Cam and Shaw down the slope, careful not to dislodge any stones or piles of gravel. They stepped between boulders and then along a deeply riven channel, finally reaching the base of the hills.

Mai looked up at the once-white palace walls.

There was a pile of debris to her left, one they'd earlier marked as their best way into the palace. There were few internal guards on this side; the closest being many hundreds of feet away. Mai pointed and then ran ahead of Cam and Shaw.

Together, they melded with the shadows. They were mere flitting shapes, climbing the pile of sand and stone and other debris. Keeping a low centre of gravity, they emerged atop the rubble and paused for a moment on the palace walls.

In front of Mai, there was a long drop to the ground. If they jumped from here, they would probably break their ankles or legs.

But directly ahead of her was another reason they'd chosen this place.

A gnarly old tree, sparse and twisted, grew directly beside the wall. It wasn't green, and its branches were empty of any leaves, but it looked strong and sturdy and perfect for climbing.

Mai reached for the closest branch, clung to the trunk, and then slithered down. She could see the nearest guard from her vantage point. He was smoking and looking off to her right, the red glow of the tip of his cigarette giving him away. She was a blot of darkness sliding to the ground, indistinguishable from all the rest.

Cam and Shaw followed her.

They crouched at the foot of the tree, getting the lie of the land all the way to the palace. The main and only issue was the guard in their way.

He hadn't been there before. Now, it seemed one of the guards had decided to take up a post close to the door they'd chosen to go through. Of course, they could choose a different door, but the guy's vantage point allowed him to see most of them, or at least hear something passing close by.

Mai turned to Cam and Shaw. 'We take him out,' she said without emotion. 'See that foliage there? That's his new home.'

They nodded. They stayed low to the ground, crouching and walking, sticking to the shadows as they approached the man. As close as she could get, Mai lifted her knife and flicked an arm. The blade flew unerringly true, lodged into the man's throat and made it impossible for him to make a noise as he died. She then raced forward to cushion his fall.

She caught the dead man in her arms, waited for Cam, and then the two of them carried him to a scrubby, thorny expanse of brush. They laid him down in the middle and watched him sink out of sight. When Mai turned back to examine the place where she knew Shaw was waiting, she couldn't see the woman.

Perfect.

They were on the comms system. Mai used it to alert Shaw that they were headed for the side door. She ran in gracefully and quickly, stopped before it and used her lock picks to finesse the lock. She needn't have bothered. The door wasn't secure. As soon as her hand touched the handle, it turned. The three infiltrators pushed their way into the house.

The first room was dark, embracing their figures with shadows. They felt at home in it. They slipped through it, part of it, an extension of blackness, and reached the far door just a few seconds later.

'We're inside,' Mai said for the benefit of Drake and the others. 'Heading up to the second floor.'

She cracked open the door. There was a woman clad in a flimsy robe padding along the corridor, holding a bottle of champagne by the neck. She was weaving, bouncing off both walls. Mai waited for her to vanish down the corridor.

She opened the door wide, slipped through. Cam and Shaw followed. Ahead, the corridor ran straight, dimly illuminated. To the left, a flight of stairs led up to the second floor. It was well lit. Mai saw a light switch and flicked it, plunging the entire area into darkness. If anyone noticed, they wouldn't think anything of it, not with all the activity in and around the house.

Steadily, the team made their way up the long flight of stairs. They hugged the wall, keeping an eye above and below. Soon, they were on the first floor landing. Mai turned to her companions.

'Stay stealthy,' she said. 'Check every room.'

They split up. Mai went to the first door, reached out for

the brass handle and turned it slowly. She stayed low, opening the door an inch at a time. On the other side she found a storage room, full of brooms and boxes and a Shark hoover. Quickly, she closed the door and moved on to the next. She repeated her action and found herself staring into a bedroom with two women lying fast asleep on the bed. They were snoring lightly, their faces turned away from each other.

And then Mai's comms system erupted in her right ear.

'I've found him. Hurry. I've found Flux.' Cam's voice.

Mai raced towards him.

CHAPTER THIRTY FOUR

Mai entered the bedroom and took in the scene in a flash. Flux was lying between two women, the silk duvet barely covering his form. He was fast asleep, head cradled in his arm, and looked extremely unthreatening. His beard was trapped between his arm and the bedsheet, his naked thighs and legs crossed over. The women beside him were in a similar state of peace, both dusky and long-legged and snoring gently.

Mai hesitated for a few seconds. They needed to do this just right. Cam and Shaw stayed close. Together, they crept into the bedroom, using hand signals as they moved toward the women.

Mai leapt at Flux. She landed atop him, legs to either side, and delivered a hard finger strike to his throat. Flux woke in agony, eyes bulging, clutching the area where she'd hit. Cam and Shaw dragged the women out of bed and made them kneel silently on the floor with their hands over their heads.

Mai struck Flu again, this time a palm strike to the nose that came close to breaking it. Flux's eyes, big and round, watered profusely; he was gasping for breath.

Mai, astride him, bent down to whisper in his right ear.

'We've come for you, or the nuclear weapon. Your choice.'

As she spoke, she withdrew a knife and laid it gently across Flux's throat.

'Be careful how you answer,' she whispered.

Flux went very still. His eyes, flicking from side to side until now, stared straight at her and reduced to their normal size.

'I am just a prince living in the countryside,' he said in perfect English. 'I do not know what you're talking about.'

Mai checked that Cam and Shaw were in control of their own situations before turning her attention back to Flux.

'Okay, I'll play,' she said. 'Mr Flux, we know you're a terrorist. Even if we didn't, we've seen your armed guards and know you are not just a prince. I'm part of a team come to kill you if you don't cooperate. I'm happy to complete that mission. I've got this far, haven't I?'

She nodded Flux's head for him, letting the sharp blade caress his throat.

'Bitch,' Flux spat. 'Filthy whore, get off me.'

Mai felt surprised at his words, considering the company he'd been keeping when she got here. 'You took possession of a nuclear weapon,' she said. 'From General Kerimov. Yes, he gave us your name. If you tell me where it is, you live.'

Mai pressed the knife in hard enough to draw a thin line of blood. Flux's expression of disgust and disdain twisted into fear.

'I... I passed it on,' he said.

Mai's heart skipped a beat. 'What? To who? How many of you bastards are there in this chain?'

Flux's mouth turned up at the edges. 'He's the last one.'

Mai leaned forward. 'The end user?'

'No, the last in the chain, you dumb bitch. Just like I told you.'

Mai had to force herself not to cut any deeper. The urge was strong. 'Where did you send it?'

Flux laughed in her face. 'How dumb are you people?

The bomb was never *here*. Do you really think I'd risk bringing it to my palace? It landed in my mountain hideout to the east where my men quickly passed it on.'

Mai tried not to let her disappointment show. Flux's words showed just how wrong they could be, how wrong the intel could be, how even the best of them got it wrong sometimes.

'The bomb was never here?' Shaw repeated.

'Idiots,' Flux hissed.

Mai took the knife away for a moment and broke Flux's nose. She could only take so much.

'Owww,' he now spoke in a deep, nasally voice.

'Keep it up,' she said. 'See where it gets you.'

'You bwoke my dose.'

'You got off lightly. It's gonna get a lot worse if you don't tell me who you sold the nuke to.'

Flux's eyes were watering so badly Mai thought he might be crying. He was shivering, his naked body trembling all over. Mai wasn't sure if it was from the cool air con in the room or fear of death. She hoped it was the latter. Flux might be the big, bad terrorist, but anyone sane feared imminent death.

'Deng. A Chinese businessman.'

'Businessman?'

'All right, he's an arms dealer. Same difference. Deng's a big deal. He'll pass your nuke on in double quick time. Get it straight to the end user.'

At least now they had double confirmation that this Deng was the *final* go-between. Mai pressed the tip of the dagger into the hollow of Flux's throat.

'Full name. Where can we find him?'

'Jen Deng. Like I said, he's a fucking arms dealer. How the hell would I know where to find him?'

'How did he collect the weapon?'

'Chopper flew in and took it away. I only had the damn thing for a couple of hours. Didn't even have time to look at it.'

'Why would an asshole terrorist like you give a nuclear weapon away?'

'Finally, a good question. Hey, I know what the end user has planned for it.' Flux let out a nasty little laugh.

Mai dipped a finger in the man's own blood and held it up for him to see. 'And what is that exactly?'

Flux started laughing harder. 'I actually don't know everything. But let me tell you this. One of these days, very soon, they will scratch London off the map.'

And his laughter filled the room.

Two Minutes to Midnight

CHAPTER THIRTY FIVE

They raced for the coast.

Time flew by, hurrying past on swift wings with all the hopes and dreams of the population of London dependent on speed. Mai had trussed up Flux and his two cohorts, knocked them all out, and then rushed back to Drake and the others. A quick whispered conversation on the hoof, and then they were all running. Flying back to the trucks. As they ran, they called Sutherland and filled him in with the latest information. The truck started immediately, the roar of its engine initially loud but settling to a dull rumble. The vehicles jerked and bounced their way along the road; Drake driving as fast as possible.

The team felt frustration like a thick blanket settle over them. The miles passed them by; the minutes flashing past way too fast. They were not only conscious of racing to catch up to the arms dealer; they also knew that Flux would send his men after them the moment he was found and released. They'd trussed him up pretty good and gagged him, but it was only a matter of time.

The truck ploughed on through the remainder of the night, taking them unerringly towards the coast. Darkness gave way to a crimson dawn, the flash of sunlight a deep red gash that first lit up the east and then started spreading its tendrils cross the arid, rocky land. The team hung on tightly as Drake slowed for nothing and waited for Sutherland's return call.

Finally, it came.

'Of course, we know about this so-called Chinese businessman,' were his first words. 'the bastard's well-known in the intelligence community. He's a slippery one, able to cover his tracks and never get caught. Always a step in front. But, as with all of them, we keep tabs. Deng's always mobile, always fluid.'

'Does that mean we can't track him?' Drake was holding on to the wheel and guiding the truck between ruts, watching as the front engine block bounced up and down, trying to keep traction in the wheels as the rutted road wound left and right through the blasted landscape.

'Of course not.'

'Do we know where he is?' Hayden asked.

'That's on ongoing op,' Sutherland told them.

'And what of London?' Kinimaka asked.

'We've passed the information on. The Brits are understandably jumpy and cagey. By the sounds of things, this hasn't come at them like a bolt from the blue. They'd already heard some chatter. With such a wide network transporting the bomb, it's hard to keep that sort of thing quiet.'

'But it's brought them no closer to finding the bomb?' Dahl asked.

'They're struggling, just like we are.'

Drake gritted his teeth as the landscape flashed past. That was the last thing he wanted to hear. 'If Deng delivers that nuke, it's gone,' he said. 'It'll be in London within days if it's not there already. The next thing we hear of it will be the bloody explosion.'

'I agree with you. And that's why I've laid on the best transport when you get back to Kuwait. Where are you, by the way?'

'Iran,' Kenzie said.

Drake said. 'We're close to the coast.'

'Don't take too long,' Sutherland said.

Drake said nothing, driving with a grim, hard look on his face. Around the truck, the others held on tightly.

'Do you have a location for this last asshole?' Alicia asked.

'It's not that simple. Like I said, we're working on it. Deng is... notorious for his movement. It's one thing that's kept him free all these years. Most of the time, he's afloat.'

Drake frowned. 'Afloat?'

'Yeah, on a boat.'

'I know what afloat means. It just surprises me, that's all. He stays off the radar?'

'Well, there's the factor of international waters. And just like with aeroplanes, there are byways you can plough that flow between radars and conventional travel lines. If you know them, you can remain invisible.'

Drake had heard of these so-called byways before. There was a time he'd thought them a fallacy, but no more.

The truck ploughed on, now storming through the early morning. The landscape flashed past to both sides, the road behind them empty. Kenzie and Shaw were keeping an eye out of the back, but so far there were no tell-tale mushroom clouds of following vehicles.

'Like I said, there's a fast chopper waiting for you on Kuwaiti tarmac. Don't hang around.'

Sutherland ended the call. Drake threw the truck around bends and over ruts. The vehicle groaned in complaint. The team was mostly silent, concentrating on staying in their seats and digesting everything that Sutherland had told them.

It was a harsh, unpleasant journey. Finally, though, the rolling sea came into sight ahead. Drake dropped down a track towards the expanse and aimed their truck for the spot where they'd left the boats. When they found it, Drake slammed on the brakes, making the tyres grind in the shale. The truck went on for several meters, slewing at the back. Finally, it stopped, and the team piled out.

The rising heat struck them gently. The wind off the gulf rippled through their hair. Quickly, they found the boats and dragged them down the beach towards the whispering waves. Climbing on, they used the oars for a while until they could start the outboard. Then, they put their heads down and went full speed, Kinimaka and Dahl at the tillers', following a dot and a route on their GPS back to the Kuwaiti airbase.

Their phone rang again. It was Sutherland, sounding anxious. He told them they'd tracked Deng down and that speed was now very much of the essence. There was a force of men standing ready, but he really wanted the Ghost Squadron to be part of the mission after everything they'd accomplished so far.

'We're in the middle of the bloody Persian Gulf,' Drake told him.

'Not for long,' Sutherland said.

The cryptic statement was explained ten minutes later when a buffeting sound came over the horizon. The sound was accompanied by a little black dot that soon grew larger and morphed into a large transport helicopter. The aircraft grew even bigger, but they didn't slacken their speed as it raced towards them. Soon, it was hovering overhead as they waited below, special rope lines looping towards them. The team wasted no time climbing the ropes and clambering into the chopper. The pilots welcomed them with nods.

'Go,' Drake said when they were all aboard.

The chopper banked and flew westward. Drake still found he was counting the minutes, though Sutherland had saved them hours with the helicopter stunt. Soon, they made out the contours of Kuwait ahead, and then the military base grew clearer. The chopper came in to land, bounced its landing skids twice off the ground and settled. Instantly, the team was jumping down to the ground, boots now landing on Kuwaiti soil.

'Where to?' Hayden yelled.

A soldier clad in all black ran up to her. 'Miss Jaye?' He addressed her. 'All of you, come with me.'

The soldier broke into a run. They followed; racing across the Kuwaiti tarmac with the sun beating down above. It occurred to Drake at that moment that they'd just visited the lair of one of the world's most notorious terrorists and hadn't had to use their guns once. A reflection of their abilities, he knew. Still, it would have been nice to take a few of them out, Flux included, and destroy their network.

He didn't slow. The soldier led them towards several choppers, but these were proper attack aircraft rather than transport helicopters. They split up and jumped into separate ones. Drake threw his pack to the floor between his knees and buckled in. They were running blind, unsure what they were headed towards and who they were travelling with. Drake was hoping for an update.

The choppers roared, ready to take off. Drake counted eight of them. Still, soldiers were climbing aboard, even as one chopper started to take off. There was a crackling in Drake's ear, and then he heard Patrick Sutherland's voice once more.

'You're in Kuwait, in the choppers, I hear. Right where we want you.'

'It's quite a force,' Hayden said.

'And we're gonna need you all. Deng has been found, his yacht floating in the ocean, but he's surrounded by a flotilla of boats. We're assuming it's his armada of guards. You're heading into quite the naval battle.'

'It's where we usually end up,' Drake said with resignation in his voice. 'In the thick of it.'

'Yes, well, if Deng still has that nuke, then at least we know he's not the final recipient. He won't use it.'

'And if it's gone?' Hayden all but whispered.

'Then God help London,' Sutherland said.

'How far away is Deng?' Drake asked.

'From you now? An hour, maybe a touch longer.'

'We hitting them hard from the get go?' Dahl asked. 'No negotiations?'

'Deng won't negotiate. It's not in his nature. Even if you captured and tortured him, you'd get nothing out of him. That's the reason for the eight choppers and several zodiacs.'

'Zodiacs?' Dahl repeated.

'Launched from the nearest vessel we have; they're timed to hit the flotilla around the same time as you. It's a full on assault.'

'Our primary objective being the nuke,' Hayden said.

'Yes, and Deng, of course. Maybe he'll tell you who he handed the weapon off to, if he has. Maybe he'll drop a hint or a clue by mistake. Don't underestimate grabbing the bastard.'

Drake held on tightly as the chopper took off. The sound of all eight rising like predators under the blazing sunshine was tremendous. They climbed slowly in sync, large black marauders filled with men at arms, bristling with weapons. They rose and rose until they cleared the surrounding buildings, until they all hovered menacingly in the morning, until their pilots received the final word to go.

It came soon enough. Drake felt the chopper bank, heard its turbine roar, and held on as they started winging their way towards Deng's flotilla. It was a sudden, fast, almost desperate change in circumstance for the Ghost Squadron. Drake did not know where they were headed. He knew only that a ragtag team had been assembled to go take out a notorious, well-guarded arms dealer.

And the Ghost Squadron was a part of it.

The chopper flew at the heart of the pack, surrounded by other aircraft on all sides. The formation was tight, fast, noisy.

'Fifty-five minutes,' the pilot said over the comms system. 'Make ready.'

Drake hefted his weapon.

CHAPTER THIRTY SIX

Drake held on as the choppers swept over the topmost swells of the ocean.

They were so low that spray coated their windows, streaking in formation across the waves, staying as near to the water as possible so they could avoid detection until the very last second. Drake had his gun in one hand and a rope clasped in the other. He was ready to jump out.

Ahead, Deng's flotilla came into sight. It was quite a spectacle. The enormous yacht, surrounded by smaller vessels, motorised sailing boats mostly, but also tenders and dinghies and other rubberised craft, all bobbing on the ocean. The convoy spread out far and wide, leaving quite a space between vessels.

The choppers came in at high speed. To the right, Drake could see a wide, black shape skimming across the waves; the wedge of attack zodiacs, planned to arrive at the same time that they did. The shape was in menacing formation; the zodiacs moving at frightening speed.

The choppers swept in. Drake's team, tasked with capturing the main yacht, saw their choppers aiming for that target. All around them, other helicopters headed for smaller boats.

From the right, the zodiac taskforce pounded in across the waves. The array of boats darted through Deng's boats, flying left and right and banking hard as they whizzed alongside. The waves churned and slapped angrily at the bows.

Drake felt the chopper descending, saw the deck of the main silvery yacht flying up to meet them. He could see figures too, darting left and right. Looking across the waves, he saw boats coming together and men rappelling from the choppers, holding on tight as they plunged into battle.

And then the gunfire began, resounding across the waters. The entire area was choppy, full of troughs and valleys, the gunfire travelling between the swells.

Drake rose, grabbed the rope, and sent a quick glance at those members of his team who were there. Hayden, Dahl and Alicia. The rest were aboard the other chopper, which was even now descending towards the rear of Deng's yacht. The ropes slithered out of the door. Drake leaned out, used the mechanism to slide down the rope, and landed boots first on the deck of the yacht. A man was holding a gun about three feet to his right. That gun, trained up at the chopper, now swivelled towards him. Drake shot the man down with a burst of his automatic weapon. More of Deng's men were opening doors, guns in hand, and rushing out on deck. Drake protected his descending teammates by sweeping the enemy with gunfire. Parts of the hull shattered or were shredded. Bullets thudded into the yacht's bodywork. Dozens of pairs of boots hit the deck. The attack force landed and swept outwards.

Deng's men opened fire now, both on the yacht and all across the ocean. There were zodiacs taking bullets, their men hidden beneath the gunwales. There were pockets of enemies taking cover behind cabins and crates, leaning out to take potshots, men descending on ropes, firing downward as they came. Other zodiacs darted through the armada, picking defenders off one by one.

Drake waited for his colleagues, then started along the top deck. Ahead, Deng's men hid in a room, popping out to fire and then retreating. Drake treated them to a full burst of automatic fire, shattering the door they were hiding behind and sending them flying backwards amid a hail of blood. He heard running footsteps from the rear, turned quickly to see the rest of the team arriving.

'Deng.' Drake said.

They nodded, entering the boat and training their guns ahead. A man charged at them, carrying a kitchen knife. Drake shot him through the leg and moved on. The walls standing all around them felt wrong, insulating them from the wider battle. They didn't want to be insulated; they wanted to be a full-on part of it.

But this was their mission. They came to a set of stairs and ran down quickly, finding themselves on another deck that opened out into a stateroom at the back. They didn't waste any time checking all the rooms, a small kitchen, a closet and a library complete with rows of books and a gilt-edged desk.

Another set of stairs. There were men at the bottom, firing up at them. Drake rolled a flash bang down there, waited for it to explode, and then started down at double speed. The men were squirming on the floor or sitting, holding their heads. The team quickly relieved them of their weapons and tied them up. Drake soon saw that this was the first of the bedroom levels. He saw three doors on each side. The team split up, took them quickly and efficiently.

The bedrooms were empty, apart from one where a beautiful woman with auburn hair slept on her side, covered by a satin blanket. Drake tried not to stare at her serene, striking face and let her be.

Drake soon came to another set of stairs. By now, he

knew Deng would be holed up somewhere below, well protected. That didn't matter. The guy was going down and the team would waste no time getting the job done. They barely stopped for breath, barely hesitated for more than a few seconds. Every obstacle took them moments to overcome.

At the next set of stairs, they used flashbangs again. Some of Deng's men had been standing further back and didn't succumb, so Drake and the others had to drill them full of holes in order to continue. The inexorable progress continued. They left dying, captured, and dead men in their wake. Above them, on deck and across the water, the battle continued.

Drake came to a porthole. He looked out, saw that he was almost at sea level. The choppy waves were outside, and he saw part of the battle that was continuing. Helicopters still circled overhead, men using machine guns to fire down into Deng's boats. Fire was being returned from the deck by men holding their own automatic weapons and standing in the face of the withering barrage. Around them, soldiers ran and defenders fought. The attackers had overrun several boats. On others, hand to hand combat was happening. Drake saw an airplane fly over the scene, low and sporting rockets. Sutherland had really outdone himself with this one. Boats crashed together as they came too close, glass fibre and carbon smashing and splintering. An enemy vessel was sinking, men leaping over the bows straight into the water, screaming and drowning. Aboard another, a fire had broken out, flames leaping towards the skies and darting at the seas as if taunting the churning waters.

Drake drew a deep breath. It was mayhem out there. He hurried on, determined to find Deng and then join in.

There were only two bedrooms left on this level. Hayden

and Kinimaka headed for one, Alicia and Dahl the other. As they put their hands on both handles, the rooms to both doors suddenly opened inwards. There were men in the doorways, all armed. The team fell to their knees and fired, sending men spinning back into the rooms. Blood flew out into the corridor and coated both doors.

The team waited, not wanting to rush into a bombardment of bullets. Hayden kicked at the side of the door. Someone opened fire, the shots shattering the frame and sending a wood chip into her temple that Kinimaka had to lever out using two fingers. Hayden looked a little dazed, but she didn't back down.

Drake took out another flashbang, but Alicia, impatient, had beaten him to it. She hurled her grenade through the open door, stepped back, and waited. In seconds, there was an explosion and a flash of light. Men yelled out in shock and surprise and there was the sound of falling bodies.

Drake rushed over the threshold. Inside, it was a mess of figures. Two were trying to defy the flashbang, remaining on their feet and attempting to level their weapons. For them, it was suicide. Drake shot them first, then swung his weapon around as his team burst through the open door at his back.

Four men were on their knees, another on the vast four-poster bed that dominated the room. All had their hands over their ears or eyes and were head down. That was except for the guy on the bed, who was lying on his side with his face scrunched into one of the fleur-de-lis pattern pillows.

Alicia, Kinimaka, Dahl and Hayden attended to the four fallen gunmen, smacking them across the head until they were unconscious and then zip-tying their hands and ankles. Drake dashed across to the bed.

Wary, he gave himself space and jabbed the guy in the

ribs. He couldn't see his hands properly. When he rolled, Drake was ready to open fire. But, luckily for the guy, there was nothing in his hands except a TV remote.

A lesser operative might have spied the black plastic object, assumed it was a gun, and opened fire. Not Drake. He recognised it and held his trigger finger.

'Who are you?' he yelled in the man's face.

Drake noted he was Chinese. A good start.

'Servant!' the man yelled. 'I serve these people. They make me work or they kill my family.'

Drake narrowed his eyes. This guy was entirely too clean cut and fancily dressed to be a servant. And, in any case, they had a picture of Deng. He called Hayden over. 'Is this Deng?'

'That's the scumbag,' Hayden pulled out her phone and flicked to an image. 'Larger than life.'

Drake took a moment to scan the room and their surroundings. The only personal effect he could see was a framed photograph of a woman, the same woman he'd left sleeping in the bedroom upstairs, the beautiful auburn-haired female. He grabbed the man's arm and pulled him to the edge of the bed, made him stand, and then prodded his ribs with the barrel of his gun.

'You're Deng,' he said. 'The prick we're here to see. Tell me Deng. Where's the nuclear weapon?'

If Drake had been expecting any reaction, it wasn't the one he got. Deng, staring impassively into his face, suddenly burst out laughing. His entire body shook, his knees trembled as if he was going to fall. The man could barely hold his head up, and there were tears rolling down his face.

Drake stepped back, caught unawares. Deng continued to belly laugh, the mirth flowing from him in waves. Drake wanted to smash him over the head, but couldn't risk knocking him out. Not just yet.

Hayden stepped up, put her hands around the guy's neck, and throttled him until he shut the hell up. 'That's better,' she said. 'You shouldn't be laughing, Deng. Your answers measure the length of your life.'

Deng attempted to sober up. Hayden's hand around his throat helped. After a few moments, he gestured for her to remove it.

'You people are so funny,' he said. 'You soldiers. Always a day late and a dollar short. *Where's the nuclear weapon?*' he imitated Drake, speaking in a deep voice without the Yorkshire accent. 'You're just so funny.'

Drake punched him in the gut, doubling the guy over. 'How about now?' he asked.

'Still funny,' the guy gasped.

And then they ran out of time.

CHAPTER THIRTY SEVEN

Footsteps pounded down the corridor.

They'd left Cam and Shaw on watch out there and now there came a sudden volley of gunfire. Cam yelled out a warning. Bullets strafed the air and crashed into the doorframe. Both Cam and Shaw disappeared from sight, forced to dive into the empty bedroom across the hall.

Drake took charge of Deng, hauling his hands up behind his back. He rested his gun momentarily on the man's shoulders.

'Talk to me,' he said. 'If I fire this thing, you're going deaf.'

'I laugh at you Americans.'

Drake saw figures flashing past the doorway. Somehow, Deng had managed to get reinforcements in the middle of the naval battle. For a moment, the newcomers did nothing, just got into place, but then a voice rang out.

'Send him out and we let you live.'

Drake shook Deng as hard as a dog shakes a play toy. 'Come and get him. He's the first thing you're gonna see.'

In the room, they'd spread out, crouching or kneeling, ready for the onslaught they knew was inevitable.

Only it didn't happen immediately. Next, Drake heard a whispered conversation outside. After that, there was a deep silence and then an object arced into the room.

Fuck it.

'A bloody flashbang,' Dahl said. 'They're playing us at our own-'

'Shut up and duck,' Kenzie yelled.

The team scattered, turned away, tried to bury their heads in their arms. They knew exactly what to expect. With foresight, Drake was about to throw Deng onto the flashbang when Kinimaka hurled one of the trussed up soldiers atop it. An excellent move. When the grenade went off, the soldier's body was covering it.

Even so, the noise was deafening. Drake kept hold of Deng, but only just. The others had covered up, but now, expecting an attack, fired at the doorway.

Figures, racing through the open threshold, twisted and fell. Drake used Deng's shoulder as a support, firing and trying to ignore the flashbang's ringing in his ears, the bright light scorched onto his retina. The good news was, he could see the attacking figures; the bad news – only their outlines.

But he saw them sprawling to their deaths. The soldier's body had sufficiently muted the flashbang to allow his team to operate almost at full capacity. The attackers were running into a slaughter.

And they fell in the doorway, piling on top of each other. The whole thing took about ten seconds, and then there was an abrupt silence.

'Can we come out now?' Cam asked through the comms.

Drake shook Deng again. The man was holding his ears, a look of pain engraved on his face. His eyes were closed.

'Not laughing now, are you, bastard?' Drake muttered.

'We should get him out of here,' Hayden said. 'His men all know where he is. Interrogation will have to wait.'

Drake agreed. They were sitting ducks in this bedroom-cum-stateroom. They had to move fast.

The team grabbed Deng and dashed back into the

corridor where Cam and Shaw were waiting. They held their weapons at the ready, expecting an attack. None came. Together, the Ghost Squadron ran back along the polished floor to the set of stairs and then started up, reaching the higher level in seconds. Ahead, there was movement.

Drake dragged Deng low to the floor. They spied three men rushing between rooms, racing as if they were looking for something, or someone. The gap between them was closing swiftly.

Dahl rose to his feet. 'Put your guns down,' he yelled.

The men stopped and stared and then raised their weapons. It was a narrow corridor. Dahl was standing, gun prepped; Alicia was kneeling in front of him. Both opened fire simultaneously, riddling the new aggressors with bullets. The men twisted and fell, dead before they got a shot off.

'Move,' Dahl said.

They dragged Deng up the rest of the stairs and then started along that level, moving fast. Soon, they reached another set of stairs, raced up it, and came out into a stateroom with large glass windows on all sides. Drake pushed Deng along and flattened his face against one of the windows.

'Look, Deng,' he said. 'Take a look at your empire being destroyed.'

The Chinese arms dealer gawped disbelievingly through the glass. Outside, helicopters hovered over numerous boats; rappel lines dangling from them to the embattled decks. There were men fighting, taking cover, shooting, falling overboard. There were soldiers rounding Deng's men up, tying their arms behind their backs. Drake saw besieged boats rising and falling on the rolling swells, zodiacs flitting in between them, making sharp turns and racing from vessel to vessel, choppers backing up those fighting below with small arms fire, men and women still abseiling from on high. The sound of heavy gunfire echoed across the white tips of the waves.

Deng gawped at it. 'My boats,' was all he said.

'Your entire network is going down,' Drake said. 'This is the end. Do yourself a favour and tell us where the nuke is.'

Now there was no laughter. Deng turned and spat at them. 'I am not your lap dog,' he said. 'You will never domesticate me.'

Drake smashed the man's face once more into the glass, leaving a bloody smear. 'We're gonna take you apart,' he whispered.

'Fuck you,' Deng growled.

Dahl went to work on the man, throwing a few punches, a few threats. Deng winced and grunted and took it all. Even when Kenzie, the ex-Israeli, started whispering in his ear and squeezing pressure points, Deng resisted. He ended up in a heap, blubbering, but he told them nothing.

'This isn't working,' Drake said. 'He's not gonna break.'

'Never,' Deng muttered. 'I am no informant. I will die first.'

'Wait,' Drake said as a memory hit him. 'The woman. The redhead. She was sleeping below.'

'You noticed her?' Alicia smiled. 'I noticed her too.'

'Not that,' Drake said. 'I mean, there's a framed photo of her on Deng's dresser. They're together. Maybe married.'

Hayden was glaring at him. 'You can't mean...'

'This is a nuclear *bomb,*' Drake growled at her. 'Just go grab the woman.'

Dens was looking up at them from the floor, his eyes hooded. He'd barely moved, but his eyes followed Hayden and Kinimaka all the way out of the room.

Drake made a show of taking his knife out and

sharpening it a few times. He didn't look at Deng. Dahl hauled the man to his feet and wiped his bloody face.

'Last chance,' the Swede said. 'Spill it.'

Deng glared at him and said nothing. Two minutes later, Hayden and Kinimaka appeared, dragging the auburn-haired woman between them. The woman wore a silk kimono and had clearly been hiding. Her hair was still hanging down, her eyes rimmed red.

As soon as Deng set eyes on her, Drake saw his face change. Hayden played her part well, dragging the woman along and then throwing her at Drake. The Yorkshireman grabbed her, raised the knife, and then shrugged. Instead, he threw her to Alicia.

'You do the honours,' he said.

The Englishwoman shrugged. 'No skin off my nose,' she said. 'But it'll be more than a few slithers off yours.' She laughed, imitating Deng's mirth of before. She made a show of withdrawing her own knife and holding it close to the woman's face.

'Do you care for her?' Dahl asked. 'We don't. She's gonna get cut unless you talk, Deng.'

Alicia introduced the point of her knife to her captive's right bicep. The blade split the silk kimono and drew a drop of blood from the white skin. Hayden drew a deep breath.

'Alicia,' she couldn't help herself give a warning.

'This is a nuke,' Drake said again. 'Nothing's off the table.' He turned to Deng. 'Last chance, asshole.'

Deng's eyes were wide. His gaze fixed on the woman's face. She was crying, looking back at him from under her hair. Deng's fists were clenching and unclenching at a rapid rate.

Alicia dug the knife in harder, splitting the skin properly. The woman screamed. Blood ran freely.

'Wait,' Deng said, his voice agonised. 'Just wait.'

'You have one chance to put this right,' Dahl said.

'It's not here. Please don't hurt her. The nuke got moved on almost as soon as it landed. I didn't want that thing hanging around, you can understand. That was part of the deal. Yeah, I'd take it. I'd be part of the chain. But I wouldn't hold it for long.'

'So it's gone,' Drake said, trying to hide his disappointment.

'You are far too late.'

Dahl grabbed the man by the throat and forced him to look at the auburn-haired lady. 'Tell us now,' he said. 'Where did you send it?'

Deng's mouth curled up, despite himself. His eyes glittered. 'London,' he said. 'To the end user. The final destination. I wonder what they intend to do with it.'

He guffawed. Alicia made the auburn-haired woman gasp with a twist of her knife. Deng raised his hands. 'No!'

'Talk,' Drake hissed.

'All I know is the weapon is now with its end user. I was told that I was the final link in the chain. London is the target. This woman, this crazy bitch, she will use it, I guarantee you.'

'Woman?' Drake echoed.

'I spoke with her. I do not know her identity, only that she is a woman and that she runs a shadowy entity she calls Coda. I have never heard of it before.'

Coda. Neither had Drake. He urged Deng to continue.

'What else can I tell you? It's already there. It has a timer trigger. And, oh, I was told to stay away from London tomorrow.'

Drake listened to the words and tried not to react as his stomach plunged through the floor. *Tomorrow?* The word hit him like a death knell. It froze the blood in his veins.

'Fucking hell,' Alicia said for them all.

Drake leapt at the arms dealer. 'Details,' he growled. 'Start talking now. Shipping that bomb will have taken permits, export permits. Other admin issues. The cargo sailed on a small but fast container ship straight from here to London. It must have done. Transit time is short. Tell us everything, Deng, and you might get out of this alive.'

CHAPTER THIRTY EIGHT

Sabrina Quinn knew the weapon was, finally, in London.

It was a *pinch* moment, as she called them. A moment to sit back, take a deep breath, and pinch yourself. She too was in London, in her cosy Knightsbridge apartment, which she would soon have to leave. There wasn't a lot of time.

She'd sent men to the dock and the container ship, men who knew how to unpack the special cargo. They would transport it to its next destination which, may or may not, be its final one.

Sabrina paced the plush-carpeted floor. Her bare feet sank deep into the yarn count. She had a glass of whiskey clinking with ice in one hand, a piece of paper in the other. The piece of paper contained information on where and when the ship had recently docked. She was checking it for the fifth time.

Yes, her men were going the right way.

She checked the time. It was early evening in London, the skies darkening, the sunset stretched like a bright lipstick smile across the horizon. She had yet to speak to Coda one last time, to apprise them of the situation. They had all done well. The bomb, even though it was being pursued by American Special Forces, had made its way from one country to the next, and to the next. It had flitted through countless hands, stayed out of Coda's sphere. The only person who knew Coda was involved was the arms dealer, Deng, and Sabrina knew he would never open his mouth. Deng would rather die than risk the wrath of Coda. He knew exactly what they represented.

Coda.

Sabrina was proud to be its leader. Few organisations could stay firmly behind the scenes as they did and remain ultra powerful. They were mostly unheard of, unknown. Of course, some fresh upstart always came along, ready to challenge them, and that upstart then had to feel the power of their reach, their seriousness. That was what the London bomb was all about – the upstart being the UK government.

They needed to learn exactly who was in charge.

Sabrina spent a few minutes talking to her board members. She didn't linger. There was too much to do. She was in constant contact with the men headed for the container, knew where they were at any given moment. And right now, they were on the dock. They were close. She found it hard to concentrate on anything else.

But she did her duty and ended with the words everyone expected.

'Stay clear of London tomorrow.'

There were the appropriate guffaws, the smiles. No one thinking of the mass casualties. Why would they? London had brought this on itself and, as with all wars, the innocent always suffered the most.

Not those at the top, those calling the shots. Never those.

Sabrina had more work to do. As soon as the conference ended, she took a gulp of the whiskey, felt the cold ice against her lips and then put the glass down. She sat behind her desk, plucked her mobile phone from its shiny holder. She dialled a number.

'Yanny, is that you?'

'Yes, I am here.'

'The time is upon us. Are you ready to do what you have to do?'

'It is a difficult time.'

'What the hell is that supposed to mean?'

'I drown in guilt.'

'We spoke about this. We agreed it was necessary.' Sabrina knew Yanny had always been reticent about what he had to do. It was why she'd decided to make the extra call to him before the weapon turned up on his doorstep. The trouble was, Yanny was her nuclear physicist. Only he could do the necessary business to arm the bomb and then send it on its way. Yanny was waiting for the weapon in a truck just a few blocks from the container yard.

'It is time to be strong,' she said evenly, knowing how fragile his state of mind was. 'Time to do your duty. You owe us, Yanny. You owe *me*. I got your family out of Croatia in time, *just* in time. If I hadn't acted, they'd be dead now.'

Yanny sounded like he was crying. 'I know.'

'Are you waiting near to the warehouse? Can you see the truck?'

'No.'

Sabrina felt a surge of rage. Somehow, she quelled it before blasting Yanny's ears. Somehow, she didn't snap.

'You know where to go,' she said. 'It's the first step. Just head out the door, go to the warehouse. Meet Vinny. You remember Vinny. He'll look after you. And then the weapon will arrive. You'll arm it on the move, and then you're done. Debt cleared. Family safe.'

'My family is already safe, thanks to you.'

Sabrina licked her lips. 'Are they, Yanny?'

There was a profound silence. Yanny was still crying,

but now he knew exactly what he had to do. 'I can be at the warehouse in eight minutes,' he said dully. 'But it will take quite a while to do what you require of me.'

'I know. Take your time. It is not required until the morning. Good boy.'

Sabrina ended the call, sat back, and sighed. She still didn't trust the little bastard, but he was all they had. Yanny would come through. She had to believe it.

Still in contact with the men seeking the container, she knew they had located the right one.

It was all coming together. Now that the moment had arrived, Sabrina felt her own trepidations. The explosion would take out a good part of the familiar London that she knew and loved so well, damage quite a bit of the infrastructure. That was a loss more important to her than the expendable souls that would perish.

Of course, the damage wouldn't be as big as it might have been.

Yanny would break the weapon down into a dirty bomb, something mobile and smaller and easily transported. That was the whole point. Ground Zero was highly important. A dirty bomb, she knew, was a radiological weapon that combined radioactive material, the kind Yanny would extract, with conventional explosives. The bomb would contaminate the area around its dispersal point. It would also cause a massive explosion, though not a full-on nuclear eruption. Hopefully, Sabrina thought, it would take down the entire area around it.

The civilian impact, the immediate casualties, would be huge. But not only that. London would have a headache on its hands for years. Long-term health issues. The psychological impact. The economic effect: it might crash. Sabrina hoped it would. The signs and sight of it would make her laugh from her new home all the way across Europe in Geneva.

Fuck you, UK government. We – Coda – really do own you.

She received a text, checked it quickly. The container had been properly identified by her men and was being loaded onto a truck. This was the tricky point. She wasn't aware how good the radiation sensors were at the dock, nor how well the shipment had been guarded. Yes, it was travelling identified as medical supplies, so a little radiation was expected. Yes, it had been shielded in a lead case. Yes, it had external warning signs all over it, the kind that made inquisitive guards want to stay away. Yes, it had already supposedly passed its scrutinizations and had all the necessary papers.

Sabrina waited with bated breath.

Finally, she got the text.

The nuclear weapon was loaded and on its way to the warehouse where Yanny would be waiting for it.

Boom, she thought.

Two Minutes to Midnight

CHAPTER THIRTY NINE

In London, a thick fog had rolled in with the coming night. It swept through the old, busy streets, moving along pavements like a physical presence, brushing past shoppers and business executives, tourists and day-trippers. It swirled along the roads, slowing the traffic, creeping through half-open windows and caressing cars and windows and block-brick structures. London's streetlights shone dimly through the gloom, their illumination diffused.

At Piccadilly Circus, the traffic was snarled up, a thick snake of cars standing end to end from the traffic lights and along Piccadilly. Very little was moving, the cars' engines muffled by the fog. The Westminster bridge was heavy with road-and-foot traffic, thick all along its impressive span, the waters below churning softly. Harrods sat amid the mist, embattled, its golden lights shining through the night with a more mellow tinge; its vivid window displays bastions against the swirling vapours. Shoppers pulled up their collars or fitted hats as they left the store; some turning around and going straight back in, back to the brightness, perhaps hoping that the murkiness would burn away before they reappeared. Oxford Street bustled noisily under the confusion, its shops hectic, its underground station emitting streams of men and women, its long, shining, straight length a lonely stronghold against the onset of the eddying dark. Hyde Park lay gripped by the churning haze, an alien, solitary place with stark monuments and leafless, twisted trees clawing at every horizon, an open space seemingly cut off from reality.

Matt Drake arrived into this soupy arena with his team around 19.45 that night. The plane touched down with a squeal and a bounce and then taxied up the runway to the nearest terminal. Ten minutes later, they were cleared to enter the country, whisked along by waiting crews, now part of a massive, concerted effort to save the city. Their backpacks weren't checked; they were barely spoken to, but they were part of the team on the ground. As far as anyone knew, the nuclear weapon was already here.

And all they had to go on was the arms dealer's words: *stay clear of London tomorrow.*

They had time. Tomorrow hadn't yet come. And to say they had nothing else to go on wasn't strictly true. The British authorities had spent the time while Drake and the others were in the air to find and track the container ship Deng had sent to London. Yes, it had all the right papers, the export licences, the appropriately signed documents. Nobody would think to question it. And it hadn't been easy to trace. Thousands of containers entered London on any given day and Deng, being the man he was, hadn't known the shipment ID, the type or number of the container, not even the right ship.

Tonight, London was on the highest alert.

Drake found himself in a room, standing among a large number of officers and agents, as a bigwig gave some kind of speech about protecting London. Right then, there was no more information. The bigwig looked stressed and spoke in a clipped manner, his eyes averted from everyone. Drake could tell that he didn't want to be questioned.

Nevertheless, at the end, the hands went up, and the man answered brusquely, his gaze never far from the assistant at his side, who seemed to be listening to the latest flow of information through an earbud. The whole thing lasted about twenty minutes, and then Drake and his team were pulled aside, assigned to a team, and left to their own devices.

'What do we do now?' Alicia asked. 'This thing has grown exponentially.'

'The whole of the city's resources are behind this,' Hayden said. 'They have to be. It's gonna be hard to keep it quiet.'

'Are you kidding?' Kenzie said. 'In my experience, this will spread like wildfire. But, I agree, they have no choice. They have to throw everything they've got at it.'

Drake looked around. The room they occupied was small and windowless. There was a table and chairs and eight other men and women. Most were dressed in police tactical gear, a couple just in their civvies as though they'd rushed here from home and hadn't had a chance to throw anything practical on yet. Nobody spoke to them. They all knew each other and he guessed the Ghost Squadron was currently the third wheel. He didn't blame them. He checked his watch, saw time marching on.

Pretty soon it would be 'tomorrow.'

He waited impatiently, didn't speak much. The entire team was on edge. They shuffled their feet and drank coffee and checked their weapons. They received an earbud communications system to use and fitted it quickly. Nobody – not even Hayden, who was the most sociable of all of them – sought to make conversation with the other team. It was too edgy, the entire night a badly balanced blade that threatened to fall and cut you at any moment.

Finally, at 23.30, a man ran into the room.

Breathlessly, as though he'd visited many rooms before this one, he blurted out his information.

'They tracked down the container to the Port of London, the eastern extent. We're moving out there now.'

The room exploded into action, everyone moving at once. Drake stowed away his weapons, shrugged his backpack on, and followed a line of men and women out of the room. This was what they had been waiting for.

He had no idea of the hellish shitstorm they were walking into.

CHAPTER FORTY

They arrived just before midnight.

The timing struck Drake as odd, memorable. There'd been a great old Dinorock tune called '2 Minutes to Midnight' by Iron Maiden that he used to enjoy. He remembered thinking that it evoked something terrible, a catastrophe, an explosion, the end of all things. He recalled thinking about the Doomsday Clock and how, once back in 1953, it had been set at two minutes to midnight.

That was about 70 years ago.

It was much closer now. If Drake was right, the symbolic clock was now set at ninety seconds to midnight.

Still, 'two minutes' symbolised it well enough for him. When they arrived they leapt out of their cars and raced along a dock, surrounded by countless, high-stacked containers of all colours that formed entire alleyways, a street map of their own, and moving yellow cranes and rushing fork lifts and workers wearing hard hats and hi-vis vests. They ran among the commotion, all heading for a container perched at the far end of the dock. It was waiting for them.

And it was empty.

Drake could see it from a long way away. The container was light blue, rusted, battered about the edges. Its front doors were hanging wide open.

They raced up to the team that was already on site.

'What do you have?' someone shouted.

Drake could see countless agents and police of all variations hanging around. Metropolitan, British Transport, Ministry of Defence. The Civil Nuclear Constabulary. Droves from the covert operations group, SO10. There were more cops around than Drake had ever seen. But there was nothing they could do.

The guy in charge of the scene came over. 'All empty, as you can see,' he said. 'We're trying to find out when and who right now. Hopefully, we can track the vehicle that arrived here and then the men who unloaded the cargo. We discovered trace radiation, but the whole crate's marked up as medical equipment.' He shook his head. 'Even items like x-ray machines, fluoroscopy units, CT scanners and linear accelerators produce some radiation. They marked the crate up with foresight and expert knowledge. A fact that doesn't bode well. We're checking all the CCTV feeds now.'

Drake knew they'd need the CCTV images to track down the truck, or whatever vehicle had been used to transport the bomb. It would give them exact timings, too. It didn't matter how careful the enemy had been, there had to be a timeline of them getting off this dock.

Men and women ran everywhere, their faces sweating, their weapons hanging from their shoulders. It was mayhem, noisy, chaotic. There wasn't a lot to do except stand among the floating tendrils of fog that started congealing, obscuring the surrounding dock, blotting out the cranes and rows of containers as if they'd never been there and Drake stood in some kind of otherworld wonderland. The fog blocked out the sky too, painting away the moon and stars with its ever-thickening brush strokes. Sounds became muted – the rushing and the running and the darting around were almost soundless, the figures just shadows flitting through the swirling murk.

Drake held on to reality.

'This is surreal as shit,' Alicia said, nailing the description for them all in her own way.

'Nothing feels real,' Mai said.

But Drake knew it was all very real. As real and as bad is it got. They were on the proper countdown now – all of London's security forces searching for a bomb that could explode at any moment.

Time passed. It marched on with the speed of an Olympic sprinter, inexorable, deadly. Drake and his team stood in the fog, isolated. Drake was used to waiting; he could stand or sit or lay immobile for hours. The SAS had taught him the art of waiting. Often, back then, years ago, you waited for action – and you waited – and just when your adrenalin was high and you were about to move out, the whole op got cancelled. You had to learn to live with that, to accept it and let the moment go. Right now, he was flying high on adrenaline, ready to move out and fight and chase and kill at a moment's notice. He would save London; he was ready to run head up into the gnashing jaws of the battle, into the very face of the bomb.

The CCTV people did their job, running through hundreds if not thousands of feeds to pinpoint the right truck. Hours of waiting turned into more hours. The police stood around, on edge, sometimes walking back to their vehicles as if expecting a call, sometimes walking to the edge of the docks and staring into the lapping waters below. It was a cold, miserable night, and it passed with all the slowness and cheer of an old person's drawn out, inevitable, lingering death.

'It's not like this in the movies,' Shaw said at one point deep in the night.

Drake said nothing, but nodded. She was right. In the movies, they clicked a few buttons, pinpointed their mark and were off within minutes. It didn't work that way in real life.

Eventually, though, there came a shout. The assembled throng looked up. A man wearing a suit and with a bald head was racing towards them.

'We got it!' he bellowed. 'We got it. Gather round!'

The entire assembled fighting corps came together.

'It's a big, grey transit!' The man yelled. 'We got the plates. We got the make and model. We're tracking it on the roads. Well, what the hell are you waiting for? Get in your vehicles and go find this thing!'

Dawn broke over the horizon.

CHAPTER FORTY ONE

It was a crazy moment.

The entire assembled security force broke and ran for their vehicles. Everyone, including Drake and his team, were getting information through their earbud systems, information about where the transit van might be. There was no concrete information yet, but with the vast array of street cameras bristling throughout London, it was only a matter of time before something broke.

The Ghost Squadron leapt into two separate cars. The engines roared and their drivers took off, following other cars, sweeping through the alleyways made by crates and containers as they sought to clear the dock. The sound of cars revving broke through the early dawn like the charge of a hundred dinosaurs. It was loud and smoky and it assaulted the lazily drifting fog with its urgency.

Dozens of police cars, both marked and unmarked, raced through the Port of London as a rising red ribbon started burning off the worst of the fog. London grew clearer, but it didn't grow any less dangerous. The police sirens were screaming for now as they sped through the city, negotiating the sharp turns and red lights and closing off streets where morning travellers sat and stared in alarm, where pedestrians trod more warily and slowly if they had any sense, where people stared out of café windows and office buildings with interest. *What was happening out in the world today?*

Hopefully, they would never know.

Drake fretted with the rest of them. It was now painfully obvious that their time was running out. The grey transit van had been on the move for a while, probably because its cargo was being worked on, possibly to keep it off someone's radar. A moving object was always harder to hit.

Drake wondered about the shadowy entity called Coda. Would they really go through with this? Was it the most terrible threat of all time? Was it truly real? Even now... there remained unanswered questions.

He sat in the car, leaning forward, eyes focused on the streets that they passed. London was going about its business – just another busy day. Life was good, or if it was bad for the people passing by, they were dealing with it. But they could never hope to deal with what Coda had in store for them.

The comms system squawked in his ear.

'We have spotted the grey van on camera,' a professional voice said. 'Travelling at twenty miles an hour along Kensington Road, sticking to the rules of the road. It's in no hurry. You have a green light to engage.'

The driver put his foot down. Drake suddenly realised they were close to Kensington Road, which threaded through the northern part of Knightsbridge. The driver switched off his sirens and light and started threading smoothly in and out of traffic. He didn't say a word until he blasted through a red light, turned slightly, and spoke just two words.

'Get ready.'

Drake turned to look through the back window. The other car was still there, carrying the rest of his team, but it wasn't by any means alone. Drake saw three or four more cars back there, all converging on the transit van.

They swept through traffic, weaving between cars and

buses and lorries, their unmarked transport slowing them a little and drawing angry looks and honking horns and unsavoury hand gestures.

A moment later, Drake could see the grey van ahead of them. It was currently stuck in traffic, caught close to a red light. A big blue sign on the back told everyone it was MCWP Security Services, the bright logo of a lion and a pair of crossed swords reinforcing the sham. Drake slid forward as the driver slammed his brakes on.

'That's as close as we're gonna get,' he said. 'Go!'

And out into the London streets they went, dozens at the same time. Men and women leaping from roaring cars, doors flinging open, back wheels slewing under braking pressure. They ran at top speed, guns in hand, threading through the vehicles waiting in line at the traffic lights, streams of armed men and women running between the cars, drawing attention from the drivers, passengers and those pedestrians walking along the street. They ran hard and fast, closing in on the grey van.

Drake led the way, his Ghost Squadron spread out behind him. They couldn't be in a better place at a better time. This is what he'd been born for. The answer to the question – *why do you run into the face of danger?* - was all around him. It was sitting in cars, in the back seats, dressed for school. It was driving massive trucks. It was walking along the pavement, moving in and out of shops.

Drake came up right behind the grey van. Alicia and Dahl were with him. The morning sun blazed down from a blue sky as they pressed against the back of the van that might hold a plausible nuclear weapon. Facing the way he had come, he saw the incredible sight of dozens of armed officers racing towards him, running in and out of vehicles, their faces set, their minds intent on only one thing.

Stopping that explosion.

'Do it!' the comms system in his ears burst into life.

Drake was first on the scene. He took a deep breath, slipped around the driver's side of the van, and ran for the front door. He grabbed hold of the handle and yanked it open. A face stared at him, shocked, the eyes wide. Drake pointed his weapon at the man's O of a mouth.

'Get down. What's in the back?'

'Fuck you!'

The guy reached for something, probably a gun nestled in the centre console. Of course, this was the UK and people weren't allowed guns, but where the civilian population weren't allowed to own them, the criminal element got hold of them easily.

This was no moment to mess around or ease off. This asshole had had his warning. Drake fired one bullet straight through the man's face and sent him flying back into the cab. On the other side of the van, Dahl was yanking the passenger out, shoving his gun in the man's face without pulling the trigger. Unusual for the Swede. Drake knew his team was attending to the van's rear doors.

Alicia lifted the handle on the right door, pulled it open. She wasn't quite ready for what happened next. Men fired through the rear, bullets smashing through the air and whistling past her face. Alicia dived to the side. One bullet hit Kinimaka in the centre of the chest.

The Hawaiian went down hard, falling backwards. At his side, Hayden dived out of the way but still received a stinging bullet to the ribs. Both of them wore body armour and felt the shots as painful strikes to the chest. Kinimaka groaned and tried to sit up. Hayden continued to roll out of the way, ignoring the agony.

Alicia, Kenzie, and Mai all had stun grenades in their packs. They unleashed them now, throwing them inside the trucks. The bombs exploded with a debilitating sound and a blinding light, but still the bullets came surging through the back doors.

'How the hell are they still conscious?' Alicia said.

But the bullets were random, clearly fired by men who were crawling, falling about but still trying to defend themselves. The lead smashed into nearby cars, destroyed the grille of a truck. Splintered the glass of a windscreen. Civilians screamed and fled the area; those in vehicles either lay down or threw open their doors and ran.

Alicia fired blindly inside the truck. There was a groan, and the reply of a dozen bullets fired with an automatic weapon. Alicia heard the click of a magazine running dry.

She opened fire again. Her shots rattled around the interior of the van. She aimed deliberately high, at shoulder level, knowing her bullets wouldn't set off the nuke but taking no chances.

Even so, the enemy fired back. Drake and Dahl appeared around the sides of the van.

'Fuck this,' Alicia said, and fished out another stun grenade.

Mai already had one in her hand. Together, the two women hurled them inside the truck and waited for them to go off. There was another minor explosion, a white flash of light, and then silence.

Kinimaka was back on his feet. Hayden ran towards them. Both wore pained expressions but were still in the fight. Kinimaka had his gun trained on the back of the van.

'No movement,' he said.

Now Cam and Shaw ran and leapt up into the van in one fluid movement. Alicia and Mai followed them. Drake stayed in place, keeping the doors wide open. Around them, the rest of the security forces ran up, milled around, kept the scene clear. There were guns pointed at the van, aimed at the sky, pointed at the ground. There were black-clad men and women wearing body armour and black visors everywhere. And even now, even after all the gunfire and explosions, there were still civilians filming from the pavements along the side of the road.

Drake watched as Cam and Shaw ran inside the back of the truck. There were four men on their stomachs or their knees. Cam dragged one to the back and threw him out the door; Shaw dragged another. Then they grabbed one more each and held them up against the right side of the van.

Drake jumped up, letting his companions take care of the two men who'd been hurled out onto their faces. He ignored the captives and Cam and Shaw, and stared hard at the wooden crate that filled the centre of the van. It was large and oblong and it had had its lid levered off and its sides collapsed. What Drake saw now was horrendous.

It was a long metal tube about three feet high and four feet long. It was silver, with black seals and edgings. Thick wires looped along its length and were clustered on top, where at least one compartment lid had been removed. Drake feared what he could see. Fighting, putting himself in harm's way, didn't bother him, but the sight of that bomb made him shiver.

'Is it armed?' Alicia asked.

Drake felt elation. They had finally found it. He ran alongside, bent down and tried to understand what the hell he was looking at. Just then, two men climbed up into the back of the van and approached.

'Stand aside,' one of them said. 'We know what to look for.'

Bomb techs, Drake thought. Thank God for that. He stepped back to let them do their work, still haunted by what he'd already seen: a number pad, a green display that currently, scarily, read: 00:00, and a bundle of snipped wires with exposed ends. When Alicia and Mai turned questioning eyes upon him, Drake shook his head.

I don't know.

But a minute later, he did. And it was worse than horrendous.

'The nuke is dead,' one man said. 'The actual bomb, I mean. It's unusable. But they've removed the plutonium core.'

'Removed?' Drake repeated.

'Yes, that's what all the driving around was for. To give someone, probably a nuclear physicist, time to extract the core from the bomb. You know what that means?'

Drake did. 'A dirty bomb,' he said.

'Yeah. Someone's walking around London with a dirt bomb in a rucksack. Someone out there still has the capability of destroying a good part of this city.'

Drake turned to stare at his team, all clustered around the back of the van. 'This is far from done,' he said.

CHAPTER FORTY TWO

It was 9 a.m. Drake was standing in the road, outside the grey van with the nuke inside, gun pointed at the floor but still prepped and ready. People had hauled off the truck's occupants by now, thrown them into several cars and sped away. The scene was being taped off as much to give the soldiers space from the civilians and the news trucks as anything else. It was still a fast, fluid situation.

Information flew lightning fast through the comms system.

Drake struggled to keep up with it. First, there was the call for CCTV Enforcement to get their asses into gear, track this truck and find out who had climbed out of it before they caught up with it in traffic that morning. Because someone had taken possession of the plutonium, strapped it to a conventional explosive device, mated it, and was even now strolling around the streets of the capital with a massively destructive weapon strapped to their backs.

There were calls to arms, most London boroughs mobilising their police forces and sending them out onto the streets. There were orders flying up and down the chains of command, commissioners and commanders, superintendents and then generals and colonels, all trying to get their ducks in a row, their men to work as one. The security services flooded the byways of London.

Two Minutes to Midnight

Drake waited for some news. Eight o'clock turned into eight thirty and then eight forty-five. There was dried sweat on his face. All they needed was one lead... a clue, any indication that someone had jumped down from that van and made off.

Somewhere. Anywhere.

'We have it,' the comms system suddenly squealed, making Drake rigid with anticipation. 'We have it. A young man, thirties, long brown hair, wearing a black leather jacket and jeans and black gloves, and carrying a light blue large rucksack, jumped out of the grey van at 07.33 this morning, just before we spotted it. He proceeded to walk along Kensington Road and then turned right down Exhibition Road, moving into the heart of Knightsbridge. We lost him there for a while. He popped up again on Brompton Road, walking in the direction of Harrods, crossed the road multiple times, and visited a Caffe Nero along the way.' The speaker sounded perplexed. 'He stayed inside the Nero for a while, after which we lost him. There's fifteen minutes of dead space. Then he pops back up, still carrying the rucksack. He's now doing a loop of Knightsbridge and has been for the last fifty minutes or so.'

'A loop of Knightsbridge?' someone questioned.

'Yeah, walking from Brompton Road, down Lowndes Square, looping around Cadogan Place and then onto the main drag of Sloane Street. He then walks up Hans Crescent and wanders back to Brompton Road before doing the circuit again.'

'He's killing time,' Drake said. 'Waiting for something.'

'Or a certain time of day,' Dahl said. 'Do you have him now?'

'Yep. He's popping off cameras along the entire route. We have him in real time.'

'How far from our position?'

'If you can get through the traffic, five, maybe ten minutes.'

Drake's heart leapt. He would get through traffic. The entire assembled throng parted as if a tsunami had hit it, every man and woman racing off to their vehicles. They leapt inside, kept their sirens and their lights switched off, and started the engines. A deep roar filled Kensington Road. Their driver was professionally trained and roared off by reversing away from the traffic jam, and finding them a route to the right, using Trevor Place. Taking the fastest route meant turning the wrong way along one-way streets and cutting corners. He flung them from left to right, made them crack their heads on the windows and the bulkheads of the car. He drove with his foot hard on the accelerator and then on the brake pedal, waving cars and people out of the way, stopping for nothing. It was a breakneck, no-holds-barred race, and it had Drake's heart pumping. Behind him, the other cars were speeding along in pursuit, sometimes inches from their back bumper, the trust these drivers had in each other showing through. All along the route, shocked faces stared after them.

They reached Sloane Street in five minutes. Here, the drivers parked at the side of the road and let them all out, trying to stay as unobtrusive as possible, but the sudden sight of dozens of armed police and special forces filling Sloane Street wasn't exactly subtle, and was quite a sight to behold.

'Where is he?' Mai asked.

'Temporarily missing,' came the reply through the comms. 'Hold on.'

Drake cursed silently. He walked along Sloane Street. Hans Crescent was on the other side of the road. The Millennium Hotel was a little further along the street. Droves of people, out early morning shopping, packed the pavements. The road itself was full of two-way traffic. He waited. It felt like there was a knife jabbing at his nerves. This young guy could literally set that nuke off at any time and here they were, tooled up and ready, kicking their heels at the side of a road, waiting, watching, hoping someone would spot a face in the crowd.

'Jesus Christ,' came the voice across their comms system.

Drake winced, not liking the sound of that, sweating as the last sun some people might ever see climbed higher into the sky. 'What the fuck is going on?'

'Figured out why we lost him. The bastard's ducked into a department store, a big one. Fucking hell, this has to be it. He's going to detonate the nuke *inside* the store.'

Drake started running as they mentioned the name. He knew exactly where it was. So did the rest of his team and all the assembled agents and police officers. They set off like a swarm of bees, rushing across the road, racing between cars and then people and buildings, readying their guns as they went, eyes and minds and hearts set on one thing.

They ran as fast as they could, conscious that the bomber was exactly where he wanted to be, *when* he wanted to be, and ready to detonate any moment. The flagstones flew by beneath them. People dived out of the way. They didn't manoeuvre their way around the parked cars; they just jumped and slid and bounded over them.

It was a rapid chase, a sprint to save lives. They passed doors and windows and buildings and finally came to the big double doors that marked the entrance of the department store in question. By now CCTV Enforcement had liaised with the security of the store and had access to all its internal cameras. Drake knew there was some kind of password, some kind of phrase, that they used to convey just how dangerous and imperative their needs were. He slammed into the shop, shoving the door back so hard it smashed into a glass window beside it and shattered the glass. He ran on, darting down the aisles, looking for an escalator. Their quarry was on the second floor.

A guard directed them to the nearest escalator, which Drake and his team raced up, three steps at a time. They span right at the top, found the next escalator and ran up that one too. They were sweating, heaving, nearing their prey. They levelled their guns. Men and women and children, all vulnerable, darted desperately out of their way.

Now there were people yelling, screaming, rushing left and right. They were on their knees, trying to hide from the men with guns, rushing to the far sides of the store. Straight towards the bomb. Drake didn't slow, he didn't veer from his path. He hit the second floor at a sprint and raced towards where intel told him the bomber would be.

And then the figure was right there in front of them, a youth wearing a leather jacket, standing tall, the rucksack still strapped to his back. The ghost squadron fanned out, facing him in a semicircle, with other officers and agents at their back.

There was a moment of terrible silence that stretched like a taut elastic band. Everyone was panting, sweating, trying to calm their racing heartbeats.

'Take off the backpack,' Hayden told the youth. 'Do it slowly.'

It was a nightmare. They couldn't shoot him. Couldn't wound him. They couldn't shoot at the backpack. They had to wait and hope he didn't have the trigger clasped in one of his clenched hands.

The youth then raised both hands, which were empty, and put them through the straps of the backpack. He said nothing. His eyes were black and calm and serene. He might as well have been waiting for a bus to arrive. His facial expression was blank.

'What do you want with me?' he asked placidly.

'Rucksack. Off. Now. On the ground.' Dahl said.

The youth complied. He unhooked the pack from his shoulders, bent over to lay it on the ground, and then knelt before it. He undid the straps quickly, reached inside, and brought out a large metal package. Drake saw the plutonium core, the explosives, the sets of coloured wires.

'Say goodbye,' the youth said.

CHAPTER FORTY THREE

Drake could see the red button that was the trigger. He could see it clearly. The youth's hand was three inches from it. It was all that close – the crazy journey they'd been on, the chase from country to country, from warlords to generals and more, from madman to madman, from bad to far worse – it all came down to three inches of space.

Drake fired at the youth's head, but the guy was already throwing himself to the floor. It was a surreal scene. There was a display cabinet of high-end watches to the left and a row of stands holding facemasks to the right. Drake's bullet shot over the bomber's head, missing by another three inches.

It was far closer than two minutes to midnight. Closer even than ninety seconds. Midnight was here.

The youth fell on the bomb, on the red button. It disappeared beneath him and then squeezed out from underneath his body. It now lay a foot in front of him. He reached for it, face suddenly a mask of hatred and anguish, the red button so close...

And he reached out a finger to press it down.

Dahl was on his knees; he was sighting his weapon. As the youth reached out, one finger outstretched, Dahl blew it off with one shot from his gun, reduced it to a mangled, bloody stump. Drake could have cheered. He had been sighting too, but the Swede beat him to it. The youth screamed and pulled his hand back, cupping the injury. He wailed at Dahl, cursed him for what he'd done.

Dahl lined the bomber's head up in his sights.

And then the youth braced himself, shrugged off the pain, and threw his entire body forward. Drake fired twice, saw bullets punch through a shoulder and a ribcage but, simultaneously, in that same instant, the youth brought a finger down onto the red button.

He pressed the detonator.

Drake saw it and his world fell away. He saw everything in minute slow motion; the finger coming down; the button then descending all the way. He heard the click of the bomb as if it was the last movement of the hands of the Doomsday Clock reaching midnight.

Drake cringed. He drew a breath. His friends, all around him, waited for Armageddon.

But nothing happened.

Nothing... happened.

Drake found he could still move. His limbs worked. He forced them to propel him forward. The youth was lying next to the bomb, not breathing. But his finger still lay directly on the red button.

'Fuck me,' Dahl said. 'The button's not a detonator. It's an arming device.'

The youth hadn't detonated the bomb. He'd armed it.

And now it was ticking down.

Drake knew they'd been given a second chance, but it didn't feel that way. The display currently read 03.59. That meant they had less than four minutes to diffuse the bomb. He looked from it to the assembled men and women.

'Bomb tech?' he asked. 'Can anyone here diffuse this bomb?'

Nobody stepped forward, not straight away. They all knew the basics, but in this situation? Right now? With everything at stake? Could they put everything on the line?

Torsten Dahl could. He waited only two seconds before sinking to his knees and addressing the bomb. Drake sat there with him, Alicia alongside. Mai and Hayden and Kinimaka were at their backs, Kenzie, Cam and Shaw behind them, as if forming a protective shield that might save lives. Dahl bent down to examine the bomb.

'Plutonium core,' he said. 'Wired to an explosive and a detonator. The simplest thing to do is to power down the device. Sometimes, they're linked to the crudest of timers, a kitchen timer for example,' all the time he talked he was probing the bomb, making his colleagues wince, pulling on wires. 'You remove the battery or disconnect the wire. But that's simple. This isn't that.'

The timer was at 02.57.

Drake knew the Swede was carrying out the necessary protocols as he spoke, talking himself through the process. It was then that he realised the entire group of agents and police officers had come up selflessly to join them, to stand around the bomb and offer their support, to watch over them as they bent to their lethal task. It was as poignant a moment as it was surreal.

Drake looked at Dahl. 'What next?'

'BIP,' the Swede said. 'Blow in place, though obviously that's not gonna work here.'

'Ya think?' Alicia said.

The timer clicked past 01.59.

'It has to be kept intact,' Dahl said. 'That means interrupting the bomb. Messing with the switch that connects to the blasting cap. Like this.'

He reached out with one hand, delved deep into the bomb. Drake's gaze filled with the bright green haze of numbers, now clicking past 01.31... 01.30... 01.29...

Dahl drew his hand back quickly, uttering a curse. The

bomb clicked and whirred. Their lives were being measured by the minute. Dahl looked up at the assembled group, his eyes shrouded. 'I can't reach it,' he said. 'Anyone got a set of long-nosed pliers?'

It was a crazy request, the kind of question that made jaws drop, but one man reached into his pocket and extracted a multi-tool. On the end was a set of long-nosed pliers. Dahl reached out for them gratefully.

00.49.

Forty-nine seconds.

Dahl clicked the pliers to get a feel for them, then reached directly into the innards of the bomb. Sweat gathered on his brow. His wrist brushed against taut wires and the conventional explosives. Drake reached out to ease them out of the way, making as much room for Dahl as possible.

The Swede twisted the pliers inside the dirty bomb.

Thirty-two seconds.

'Damn,' Dahl said.

Drake closed his eyes briefly. It was hot work. There was no air, not anywhere. His knees and legs ached. His thoughts were clear and ice cold as they focused on what Dahl was doing.

'You got this?' he asked.

Twenty-five seconds.

Dahl clipped something. Drake held his breath. The collected men and women didn't dare move a muscle. The bomb started whirring loudly, its green display clicked past twenty seconds, still counting down. Dahl sighed deeply and sat back, pulled the pliers out, and closed his eyes.

'I thought that was it,' he said. 'I interrupted the bomb. I don't know what else to do.'

Fourteen seconds.

Drake gritted his teeth. Alicia leaned forward. 'You hit

the last one with a hammer,' she said. 'Can't you do that?'

'Different kind of device.'

'But you can try.' Alicia said.

Nine seconds.

The green glow continued to count down. Dahl didn't give up. He reached once more into the body of the weapon, tried once more to interrupt the flow. The pliers gripped a new wire this time. Dahl stared at it, then gave Drake a last look, and then shrugged.

Four seconds.

Dahl pulled hard on the wire.

CHAPTER FORTY FOUR

Everything stopped.

Drake didn't dare breathe, didn't move a millimetre. Not a sound passed through the department store's second floor. Hundreds of pairs of eyes stared at the green glow of the dirty bomb.

00.02.

Two seconds.

Drake thought: *how many minutes to midnight?*

The display had frozen. The bomb had stopped all its whirring and chirping and rattling. It was quiet, dead, but still deadly. Drake was the first to sit back on his haunches. An air of incredible tension gripped the room.

Alicia broke it. 'For fuck's sake, Torsty,' she said. 'You timed that right down to the fucking wire.'

People gasped. They straightened. They let out deep breaths they'd been holding on to for almost a minute. Dahl wiped his face, and so did Drake. The others pulled away. Nobody moved too far. Drake turned from where he sat, looked over the room, and tried to smile at everyone who was staring back at him.

'Job done,' he said.

After relief, there came the cheers. The rafter-lifting shouts and bouts of clapping and laughter that filled the whole of the second floor. The assembled men and women, bound by their own selfless actions, clapped each other on the back and grinned and stepped forward to shake hands with Torsten Dahl.

Real bomb techs arrived soon after and set about making the weapon entirely safe. They stared at Dahl, their eyes full of respect.

Drake drifted away from the throng, headed for one of the floor-to-ceiling windows that looked down over the busy streets outside. It was jam-packed with pedestrians down there, street-vendors, cars, buses and vans. They would never know...

How many times had a civilian never known how close they'd come?

Drake pondered the question as he laid his head on the cold window to cool off. He was happy to let Dahl claim the limelight. The Swede had won the day. Above the rows of buildings outside, a pristine, fresh morning was taking hold, the skies a deep, cloudless blue. Drake felt a smile stretch across his face.

'What the hell are you smiling at?' Alicia's voice came from his right side, her tone still a little tense. 'It's a bit too early for that.'

'Oh, I don't know. A babe looked up from below, caught my eye.'

'Yeah, of course. Next you'll be telling me I'm not the best member on the team.'

Drake turned to her. 'Are you really, though?'

'I'm telling you now, Drakey, if a babe caught your eye, my boots are gonna catch your bollocks.'

By now, the others were crowding around, some gazing out the window and taking in the panorama outside, others just looking at each other.

'We stopped Coda,' Hayden said.

'For now,' Kinimaka replied. 'We do not know their agenda. But I'm betting they have one.'

'We've taken down our fair share of secret organisations,' Mai said. 'I dare say, if required, we'll take down this one too.'

Drake nodded along with most of the team. Looking back into the store, across the assembled men and women who'd stood by them and fought silently with them, who'd stood still alongside them as Armageddon counted down, who'd risked it all to save London, he felt a wide sense of comradeship, of belief, of trust in humanity. They could still come together when needed. They could still stand side by side.

When your back was to the wall, when all seemed lost, when the darkness was darker than the deepest night, that was when your best colleagues, your worthiest friends, and your closest, most valuable family stood up for you the most.

What more could you ask for?

THE END

I hope you enjoyed reading the latest Matt Drake adventure as much as I did writing it. The next release will be on the 13th April, with the publication of the 3rd book in the Joe Mason series – *The Midnight Conspiracy* – (no relation to this book), to be followed in May by a brand new Alicia Myles *Gold* adventure. I hope you love them all!

If you enjoyed this book, please leave a rating or a review.

DAVID LEADBEATER

Other Books by David Leadbeater:

The Matt Drake Series
A constantly evolving, action-packed romp based in the escapist action-adventure genre:

The Bones of Odin (Matt Drake #1)
The Blood King Conspiracy (Matt Drake #2)
The Gates of Hell (Matt Drake 3)
The Tomb of the Gods (Matt Drake #4)
Brothers in Arms (Matt Drake #5)
The Swords of Babylon (Matt Drake #6)
Blood Vengeance (Matt Drake #7)
Last Man Standing (Matt Drake #8)
The Plagues of Pandora (Matt Drake #9)
The Lost Kingdom (Matt Drake #10)
The Ghost Ships of Arizona (Matt Drake #11)
The Last Bazaar (Matt Drake #12)
The Edge of Armageddon (Matt Drake #13)
The Treasures of Saint Germain (Matt Drake #14)
Inca Kings (Matt Drake #15)
The Four Corners of the Earth (Matt Drake #16)
The Seven Seals of Egypt (Matt Drake #17)
Weapons of the Gods (Matt Drake #18)
The Blood King Legacy (Matt Drake #19)
Devil's Island (Matt Drake #20)
The Fabergé Heist (Matt Drake #21)
Four Sacred Treasures (Matt Drake #22)
The Sea Rats (Matt Drake #23)
Blood King Takedown (Matt Drake #24)
Devil's Junction (Matt Drake #25)

Voodoo soldiers (Matt Drake #26)
The Carnival of Curiosities (Matt Drake #27)
Theatre of War (Matt Drake #28)
Shattered Spear (Matt Drake #29)
Ghost Squadron (Matt Drake #30)
A Cold Day in Hell (Matt Drake #31)
The Winged Dagger (Matt Drake #32)

The Alicia Myles Series
Aztec Gold (Alicia Myles #1)
Crusader's Gold (Alicia Myles #2)
Caribbean Gold (Alicia Myles #3)
Chasing Gold (Alicia Myles #4)
Galleon's Gold (Alicia Myles #5)

The Torsten Dahl Thriller Series
Stand Your Ground (Dahl Thriller #1)

The Relic Hunters Series
The Relic Hunters (Relic Hunters #1)
The Atlantis Cipher (Relic Hunters #2)
The Amber Secret (Relic Hunters #3)
The Hostage Diamond (Relic Hunters #4)
The Rocks of Albion (Relic Hunters #5)
The Illuminati Sanctum (Relic Hunters #6)
The Illuminati Endgame (Relic Hunters #7)
The Atlantis Heist (Relic Hunters #8)
The City of a Thousand Ghosts (Relic Hunters #9)

The Joe Mason Series
The Vatican Secret (Joe Mason #1)
The Demon Code (Joe Mason #2)
The Midnight Conspiracy (Joe Mason #3)

The Rogue Series
Rogue (Book One)

The Disavowed Series:
The Razor's Edge (Disavowed #1)
In Harm's Way (Disavowed #2)
Threat Level: Red (Disavowed #3)

The Chosen Few Series
Chosen (The Chosen Trilogy #1)
Guardians (The Chosen Trilogy #2)
Heroes (The Chosen Trilogy #3)

Short Stories
Walking with Ghosts (A short story)
A Whispering of Ghosts (A short story)

All genuine comments are very welcome at:

davidleadbeater2011@hotmail.co.uk

Twitter: @dleadbeater2011

Visit David's website for the latest news and information:
davidleadbeater.com

Printed in Great Britain
by Amazon